iPhone Open Application Development

Jonathan Zdziarski

O'REILLY®

Beijing · Cambridge · Farnham · Köln · Sebastopol · Taipei · Tokyo

iPhone Open Application Development
by Jonathan Zdziarski

Copyright © 2008 Jonathan Zdziarski. All rights reserved.
Printed in the United States of America.

Published by O'Reilly Media, Inc., 1005 Gravenstein Highway North, Sebastopol, CA 95472.

O'Reilly books may be purchased for educational, business, or sales promotional use. Online editions are also available for most titles (*safari.oreilly.com*). For more information, contact our corporate/institutional sales department: (800) 998-9938 or *corporate@oreilly.com*.

Editor: Andy Oram	**Cover Designer:** Karen Montgomery
Production Editor: Sumita Mukherji	**Interior Designer:** David Futato
Proofreader: Sumita Mukherji	**Illustrator:** Robert Romano
Indexer: John Bickelhaupt	

Printing History:

March 2008:   First Edition.

 This book uses RepKover™, a durable and flexible lay-flat binding.

ISBN: 978-0-596-51855-4
[M]   [7/08]

Table of Contents

Preface

So, you want to write applications for the iPhone. The first thing you should know is that the iPhone is by and large a closed device, and Apple has taken steps to lock users out of the operating system. This hasn't stopped people. In October 2007, Apple announced in an earnings statement that over 250,000 units had been sold with the intent of unlocking them for use on other networks. Within the first month of v1.1's software release, Nicholas Penree's *jailbreakme.com* site logged over one million units that were freed to run third-party applications. Sites hosting iPhone cracking tools have reported record traffic, and even Apple's own employees traipse around the Genius Bar touting their hacked devices. Well-respected hackers joined the effort to crack the iPhone, and once in, realized it's just as elegant on the inside—a well-planned mobile platform well worth developing applications on. Within a few months, a free, open source (*http://open-source.org*) compiler for building iPhone applications was released—not by Apple, but by the open source community. Today, full-featured iPhone applications are ubiquitous. And all of this was accomplished on a device that was intended to be closed.

Apple finally woke up to the fact that developers were not satisfied with Safari-based applications. In late 2007, they announced an SDK for the iPhone to be released the first quarter of 2008, but as of the time of this writing, we don't know what the availability will be, or what restrictions will be placed on it. What we do have today, however, is almost as good and in some ways better. The free SDK, affectionately called "the tool chain," isn't tied down with licensing, nor is it exclusive to running only on Apple's operating system. In fact, a Linux user (and soon Windows users) can build and install applications on their iPhone without ever touching a Mac.

The interfaces used by the free tool chain are in every way identical to what Apple must release with their own SDK. The frameworks available on the iPhone employ a standard set of interfaces used by Apple's preloaded iPhone applications. All major tasks are performed by these frameworks, including the entire user interface, playing sounds and music, working with graphics and animation, and even displaying web pages.

Within the first few months of the iPhone's high-profile life in the public market, the iPhone hacking community extracted these interfaces and built their own software development kit.

So this book, which was written based on the free tool chain, uses the same code that Apple's XCode or any other compiler would need to use to compile iPhone applications. Should Apple follow through with the release of a native SDK, the classes, methods, and examples presented in this book are very likely to work with both SDKs. In fact, Apple would have to rewrite every framework—and every single application on the iPhone—to make this book obsolete.

With tool chain in hand, and many sleepless nights of tomhackery, the community has been able to learn how to use the frameworks and interfaces available to design spectacular third-party applications. This book walks through the frameworks that are key to designing this full-featured software on the iPhone, with pointers to tools that are available to take advantage of the other frameworks not documented here.

The iPhone is a superb device, and in spite of the politics surrounding its availability to developers, the community is growing fast. With or without Apple's help, the iPhone is likely to give birth to many commercial markets for itself, and possibly grow beyond the success of its predecessors, the PocketPCs and the Symbians that formerly owned the mobile market space.

As you read this book, you probably won't realize just how good you've got it. The simplicity you'll see in this book reflects thousands of hours of work by the active development community chipping away at the nearly impossible challenges that were involved in this task. The old school methods for getting anything done on the iPhone were laborious if not exhausting, and could have filled up volumes of books alone. Even after we figured out how to jailbreak the very first iPhone, we couldn't do anything with it until we came up with a grand scheme to fool it into running SSH. It took another month beyond that before the first GUI application was even written.

Work continues today to figure out many of the proprietary interfaces on the iPhone, and we welcome anyone into the community with the know-how and perseverance to join us in this endeavor.

Audience for This Book

You'll need some prior knowledge of coding to find this book useful. The iPhone framework uses Objective-C, which we'll introduce you to in Chapter 2. The good news is that you can also use C and C++ in your applications, so anyone with pre-existing knowledge should be able to pick it up pretty quickly. If you don't understand C or C++, there are many books available on the subject. This book isn't a primer for any of these languages, but rather is designed to explain the proprietary classes and methods needed to write iPhone-specific applications.

Organization of the Material

Chapter 1, *Breaking Into and Setting Up the iPhone*, explains how to break into your iPhone.

Chapter 2, *Getting Started with Applications*, illustrates the makeup of an iPhone application and how to get the tool chain running on your desktop.

Chapter 3, *Introduction to UIKit*, introduces you to UIKit, which is at the core of developing iPhone applications and user interfaces.

Chapter 4, *Event Handling and Graphics Services*, covers basic geometric concepts as used in the Core Graphics framework and event notifications.

Chapter 5, *Advanced Graphics Programming with Core Surface and Layer Kit*, goes deeper into iPhone development by exploring raw video surfaces and 3-D transformations.

Chapter 6, *Making Some Noise*, covers the many different ways to record and play sounds and output a digital audio stream.

Chapter 7, *Advanced UIKit Design*, illustrates many of the advanced user interface components of UIKit.

The Appendix highlights many miscellaneous hacks and open source classes to do cool things in your iPhone application.

Conventions Used in This Book

The following typographical conventions are used in this book:

Plain text
> Used for menu titles, menu options, menu buttons, and keyboard accelerators.

Italic
> Indicates new terms, URLs, filenames, Unix utilities, and command-line options.

`Constant width`
> Indicates the contents of files, the output from commands, variables, types, classes, namespaces, methods, values, objects, and generally anything found in programs.

`Constant width bold`
> Shows commands or other text that should be typed literally by the user, and parts of code or files highlighted to stand out for discussion.

`Constant width italic`
> Shows text that should be replaced with user-supplied values.

This icon signifies a tip, suggestion, or general note.

 This icon indicates a warning or caution.

Using Code Examples

This book is here to help you get your job done. In general, you may use the code in this book in your programs and documentation. You do not need to contact us for permission unless you're reproducing a significant portion of the code. For example, writing a program that uses several chunks of code from this book does not require permission. Selling or distributing a CD-ROM of examples from O'Reilly books *does* require permission. Answering a question by citing this book and quoting example code does not require permission. Incorporating a significant amount of example code from this book into your product's documentation *does* require permission.

We appreciate, but do not require, attribution. An attribution usually includes the title, author, publisher, and ISBN. For example: "*iPhone Open Application Development* by Jonathan Zdziarski. Copyright 2008 Jonathan Zdziarski, 978-0-596-51855-4."

If you feel your use of code examples falls outside fair use or the permission given above, feel free to contact us at *permissions@oreilly.com*.

Safari® Books Online

 When you see a Safari® Books Online icon on the cover of your favorite technology book, that means the book is available online through the O'Reilly Network Safari Bookshelf.

Safari offers a solution that's better than e-books. It's a virtual library that lets you easily search thousands of top tech books, cut and paste code samples, download chapters, and find quick answers when you need the most accurate, current information. Try it for free at *http://safari.oreilly.com*.

Legal Disclaimer

The technologies discussed in this publication, the limitations on these technologies that the technology and content owners seek to impose, and the laws actually limiting the use of these technologies are constantly changing. Thus, some of the projects described in this publication may not work, may cause unintended harm to equipment or systems on which they are used, or may be inconsistent with applicable law or user agreements. Your use of these projects is at your own risk, and O'Reilly Media, Inc. disclaims responsibility for any damage or expense resulting from their use. In any event, you should take care that your use of these projects does not violate any applicable laws, including copyright laws.

We'd Like to Hear from You

Please address comments and questions concerning this book to the publisher:

O'Reilly Media, Inc.
1005 Gravenstein Highway North
Sebastopol, CA 95472
800-998-9938 (in the United States or Canada)
707-829-0515 (international or local)
707-829-0104 (fax)

We have a web page for this book, where we list errata, examples, and any additional information. You can access this page at:

http://www.oreilly.com/catalog/9780596518554/

To comment or ask technical questions about this book, send email to:

bookquestions@oreilly.com

For more information about our books, conferences, Resource Centers, and the O'Reilly Network, see our web site at:

http://www.oreilly.com

Acknowledgments

Special thanks to Patrick Walton, Brian Whitman, John Bafford, Nicholas Penree, Elliot Kroo, Dino Pastos, Nate True, Steve Dunham, Nicolas Bacca, Daniel Peebles, Alexander Pick, Piergiorgio Zambrini, Aaron Alexander, Richard Thally, Justin Lazarow, Chris Zimman, Eric McDonald, and many others wishing to remain anonymous in the iPhone development community who have contributed sleepless nights, great humor, and cash from their own pockets to open the iPhone and build a solid foundation for application development.

## CHAPTER 1

Breaking Into and Setting Up the iPhone

The iPhone is a closed device. We can't say this enough. Up to and including version 1.1.x of the iPhone software, users have been locked out of the operating system. This doesn't seem to stop a majority of iPhone users, but does make it more difficult to get started. Before hacking of any kind can take place, however, the iPhone must be broken free from its jail—literally.

The iPhone runs in a chrooted environment, where no user or desktop application—even iTunes—can see into the operating system; this is commonly known in the Unix world as a *chroot jail*. This jail (and the fact that you can't simply yank out the hard drive) is the only thing standing in the way of the iPhone functioning as a complete, portable Mac OS X computer. Fortunately, many free tools have been written to make the jailbreaking process simple.

In this chapter, you'll stage your iPhone for software development. This includes breaking free from the chroot jail (called *jailbreaking*) so you can access the filesystem. You'll also install a BSD Unix world, which is a set of common Unix binaries such as ls and cp. This allows you to navigate and manage the iPhone's operating system, which is believed to be a version of Mac OS X 10.5 (Leopard) for the arm processor. Finally, you'll get a secure login command environment, SSH, up and running. This is useful for copying files to and from your iPhone, and we'll use it to install applications and run examples.

Jailbreak Procedures

How you jailbreak your iPhone depends largely on what version of the software you are running. There is a lag time of a few weeks between new iPhone software releases and public hacks to jailbreak them. Small changes are generally introduced in new versions to make breaking into it a little bit harder each time. The good news is that once a new jailbreak has been written, all of the free tools available are updated to make it possible for just about anyone to go through the process.

Third-Party Jailbreak Software

There are many free tools available to jailbreak the iPhone, some more reliable than others. The best tools are full-service utilities that also allow you to set up a shell and install third party software with little effort. The best of breed tools include:

iNdependence, http://code.google.com/p/independence/ (v1.0.0–1.1.3)
> iNdependence is a utility for Mac OS X that performs jailbreak, activation, SSH installation, and even installation of ringtones, wallpaper, and third-party applications on the iPhone. iNdependence is under the GPL, and the author has made a library available called libPhoneInteraction, allowing developers to write other tools to communicate with the iPhone.

AppSnapp, http://www.jailbreakme.com (v1.1.1 only)
> Users running version 1.1.1 of the iPhone firmware can navigate to this web site using their iPhone and have the entire jailbreak process performed remotely. AppSnapp takes advantage of a vulnerability in one of the iPhone's image libraries to break into the phone. What's cool about this site is that it not only jailbreaks your phone, but it also fixes the vulnerability so that nobody else can maliciously take advantage of the phone. Version 1.1.1 and later of AppSnapp also patch the iPhone software to allow third-party applications, and installs AppTapp, the NullRiver installer, which can then be used to stage your iPhone for development.

AppTapp, http://iphone.nullriver.com (v1.0.0–1.0.2)
> Nullriver is a software manufacturer out of Ontario, Canada, and the designer of a package installer for the iPhone. Installer allows you to install any application on your iPhone that is included in their repository using a few easy taps. The installer software itself works with most versions of the iPhone software, but the installer's installer (if that makes sense) is capable only of jailbreaking iPhone firmware v1.0.x. The previous tool in this list, AppSnapp, automatically installs AppTapp on v1.1.1 devices. AppTapp is also useful for the software downgrade procedure, explained next.

ZiPhone, http://www.ziphone.org (v1.0.0–v1.1.3)
> ZiPhone is a jailbreak technique developed by the iPhone Dev Team. It was kept under a heavy shroud of secrecy in anticipation of the Apple SDK, but it was eventually leaked by one of the dev team's former members. ZiPhone has since been developed beyond a simple jailbreak technique and many other utilities have been added to it, including a full unlock for all iPhones up to OTB (Out-of-the-Box) v1.1.3.

Downgrading iPhone Software

The latest version of iPhone software as of the time of this writing is v1.1.3. If you have a newer version, check the web sites for the tools listed in the previous section to see whether they have been updated to support your version. If no jailbreak exists for your firmware version, you'll need to downgrade to an older version to gain access to your iPhone.

iTunes sports a feature that allows users to downgrade their software, so if you wind up with an iPhone running software that hasn't had a jailbreak written for it yet, you can usually downgrade to the latest breakable version. The instructions here have been tested with iTunes up to version 7.5. It's possible that newer versions of iTunes may remove or change this feature, but so far, there have been no signs from Apple that this will happen. In the event that it does, running an older version of iTunes might work.

Preparing for downgrade

To downgrade the iPhone's software, you'll first need a copy of the older version. Ideally, you'll want to get a copy of whatever the newest, breakable version of the software is, based on the versions supported by the applications in the previous section "Third-Party Jailbreak Software." These can be downloaded directly from Apple's distribution servers, but you'll have to know the URL. The web site *http://iphone.unlock.no* maintains a list of up-to-date download links for all versions of the iPhone firmware.

You'll also need a copy of the latest iPhone Utility Client (iPHUC) available in the "downloads" section of the iPhone-Elite site at *http://code.google.com/p/iphone-elite/*. The iPhone Utility Client is a tool for performing low-level functions on the iPhone, such as booting out of recovery mode and sending device firmware updates, used in the instructions to follow.

 The downgrade process restores your iPhone to a factory state, so any saved messages, recent calls, or other data will be completely erased. Be sure you've synced and backed up your contacts and calendar. Be sure to use the Image Capture utility to import any photos you've taken.

Downgrading the software

Perform these steps to downgrade to the older version you've downloaded:

1. Connect your iPhone to the dock and start iTunes. If it syncs on connect, wait until it has finished syncing.

2. Extract the contents of the iPhone firmware file you downloaded earlier. The file will have an *.ipsw* extension, but it is actually a *.zip* archive. You can use unzip from the command line, or your favorite graphical archival utility.

3. Locate the file in the archive beginning with WTF, for example, *WTF. s5l8900xall.RELEASE.dfu*. This is the file needed to place the iPhone into a device firmware update mode. Copy it into the same directory as your iPHUC tool.

4. Launch iPHUC from a command line. Type enterrecovery and press Enter. This will put the iPhone into recovery mode.

5. Quit iPHUC and then re-launch it. The available commands will have now changed. Use the filecopytophone command to send the WTF file to the iPhone. For example, filecopytophone WTF.s5l8900xall.RELEASE.dfu. Press Enter. Now type cmd go and press Enter again. This will place the iPhone into "device firmware update" mode.

6. Launch iTunes. You will be given the message that an iPhone was discovered in recovery mode. If you're on a mac, hold the Option key and click Restore. If you're on a PC, hold the Shift key and click Restore. You will be presented with a file selection window. Locate and select the *.ipsw* file you downloaded.

7. Your iPhone will restore back to the version of the firmware you've chosen.

8. After the iPhone has finished restoring, you may receive an error 1015. If this happens, the iPhone will boot into recovery mode. To fix this, use the iPHUC client once more and issue the following commands (be sure to escape the spaces as shown below):

```
cmd setenv\ auto-boot\ true
cmd saveenv
cmd fsboot
cmd bootx
```

Installing SSH

Once you have jailbroken your iPhone, installing a Secure Shell will allow you to access your iPhone's Unix environment and easily copy files to and from the phone over a WiFi connection.

Using SSH requires that your iPhone be connected to the same WiFi network as your desktop machine. If you don't have access to a WiFi network, you'll need to use a tool such as iNdependence to install applications on your iPhone instead, so you can skip this section. You might, however, consider installing MobileTerminal, a free terminal program for the iPhone. This will at least allow you to work in the iPhone's Unix environment, which is necessary to run a small number of examples. Mobile-Terminal can be downloaded from *http://code.google.com/p/mobileterminal/*.

If you used iNdependence to perform a jailbreak, OpenSSH can be installed at the touch of a button—namely, the SSH button. Click it and follow the installation procedure. If you used AppSnap or AppTapp, install SSH as follows:

1. AppSnapp and AppTapp load a software installer as part of their routine. Once you've completed their jailbreak and setup process, you should have a new icon on your iPhone called Installer. Press the icon to run the installer application. The installer may initially prompt you to update itself. If this is the case, continue through the update procedure and restart the installer.

2. You will be presented with a category list. Choose the Sources category and select the Community Sources package. Press the Install button at the upper right of the screen and the package will be downloaded and installed.

3. Restart the installer. You should now see a System category. Choose this and install the OpenSSH package. After installing, restart your iPhone.

SSH should now be running on the iPhone, but before you can connect to it, you'll need to know your iPhone's IP address on the local WiFi network. To find this, do the following:

1. Tap the Settings application on your iPhone.

2. Select the General tab, then Network, then Wi-Fi.

3. Your WiFi network should appear in the list with a blue disclosure arrow to the right.

4. Press the blue arrow. You'll be presented with a screen containing your IP address.

Set up your IP address in the hosts file on your desktop to simplify connectivity. If you're using Mac OS X or Unix, you can edit your */etc/hosts* file. If you're using Windows XP, edit or create the file *C:\WINDOWS\system32\drivers\etc\hosts*. Add the following line to your file:

```
x.x.x.x iphone
```

where *x.x.x.x* represents the IP address of the iPhone.

You're now ready to connect to your iPhone using an SSH client. If you're using Mac OS X or Linux with SSH preinstalled, you can do this from a terminal window.

```
$ ssh -l root iphone
```

If you're using Windows XP, you'll need to download an SSH client. One of the most popular free clients is PuTTY, available at *http://www.chiark.greenend.org.uk/ ~sgtatham/putty/*.

Depending on which version of the iPhone software you're running, the default root password is either `dottie` or `alpine`. Once logged in, you should be dropped to a shell prompt.

Installing BSD Subsystem

Being able to access a shell on your iPhone is of little use without a Unix world to provide the basic commands. The installer application has a package called BSD Subsystem in the System category. This is a collection of Unix commands that will allow you the same basic Unix functionality as a desktop Unix system such as Mac OS X or Linux. Choose and install this package through the installer.

Congratulations, you're now ready to enter the world of iPhone applications development!

Additional Resources

iPhone software is updated periodically by Apple, and so we can't document how every version of the software will act—especially newer versions that will be released after this book's publish date. To get the latest information about jailbreaking your iPhone or installing the tools listed in this chapter, the following development teams' web sites are invaluable resources:

iPhone Dev Team (http://www.iphone-dev.org)
> The official site for the iPhone dev team, responsible for all known v1.1.x jailbreaks to date.

iPhone Elite Team (http://code.google.com/p/iphone-elite/)
> The iPhone Elite Team is another group of developers working primarily on unlocking and other hacks. They service the iPhone Utility Client and other tools.

## CHAPTER 2

Getting Started with Applications

If you're new to Mac, you might be surprised to find that applications don't come in the form of *.EXE* files. The excellent design for which Apple is known in its hardware and graphics extends into its software architecture as well, and includes the way applications are laid out in the file system. The same strategy used in Apple desktop systems carries over into the iPhone.

Apple has adopted the practice of creating modular, self-contained applications with their own internal file resources. As a result, installing most applications is as easy as simply dragging them into your applications folder; deleting them as easy as dragging them into the trash. In this chapter, the structure of applications on the iPhone will be explained. You'll also get up and running with the free open source tool chain used to build executables, and you'll learn how to install applications on your iPhone. Finally, you'll be introduced to the Objective-C language and enough of its idiosyncrasies to make an easy transition from C or C++.

Anatomy of an Application

Apple came up with an elegant way to contain applications in their operating system. As OS X is a Unix-based platform, Apple wanted to make it adhere to basic Unix file conventions, and so the resource forks of olde were no longer sufficient (or efficient for that matter). The challenge was to design a structure that would allow an application to remain self-contained while surviving on a file system that didn't believe in cheapening its architecture with proprietary workarounds. The result was to treat an application as a *bundle* inside a *directory* and use standard APIs to access resources, execute binaries, and read information about the application.

If you look inside any Mac application, you'll find that the *.app* extension denotes not a file, but a directory. This is the application's *program directory*. Inside it is an organized structure containing resources the application needs to run, information about the application, and the application's executable binaries. A compiler doesn't generate this program directory structure, but only builds the executable binaries. So to build a complete application, it's up to the developer to create a skeleton structure that will eventually host the binary and all of its resources.

The program directory for an iPhone application is much less structured than desktop Mac applications. In fact, all of the files used by the application are in the root of the *.app* program folder.

```
drwxr-xr-x    root    admin    Terminal.app/
  -rw-r--r--    root    admin    Default.png
  -rw-r--r--    root    admin    Info.plist
  -rwxr-xr-x    root    admin    Terminal
  -rw-r--r--    root    admin    icon.png
  -rw-r--r--    root    admin    pie.png
```

The above reflects a very basic iPhone application called MobileTerminal. MobileTerminal is an open source terminal client for the iPhone, allowing the user to pull up a shell and work in a Unix environment (which also must be installed as third-party software). MobileTerminal illustrates all of the major components of an iPhone application:

Terminal.app
   The directory that all of the application's resources reside in.

Default.png
   A *PNG* image (Portable Network Graphics file). When the user starts the application, the iPhone animates it to give the appearance that it's zooming to the front of the screen. This is done by loading *Default.png* and scaling it up until it fills the screen. This 320×480 image zooms to the front and remains on the screen until the application finishes launching, at which point it serves as the background for whatever user interface elements are drawn on the screen. Applications generally use a solid black or white background.

Info.plist
   A property list containing information about the application. This includes the name of its binary executable and a bundle identifier, which is used by the SpringBoard application to launch it. You'll see an example property list later on in this section.

Terminal
   The actual binary executable that is called when the application is launched. This is what your compiler outputs when it builds your application. Your makefile can copy your binary into the application folder when doing a production build. This chapter will provide an example of this process.

icon.png
   An image forming the application's icon on the SpringBoard (the iPhone's desktop application). SpringBoard isn't concerned with the size of the file, and will attempt to draw the image outside of its icon space if it is large enough. Most icons are generally 60×60 pixels.

pie.png

An image resource used by the MobileTerminal application. There are many methods provided by the iPhone framework to fetch resources, and most of them accept only a filename instead of a path. The file supplied to these methods must therefore be stored directly in the program directory. This is consistent with Apple's effort to keep applications self-contained.

Creating an Application Skeleton

The first thing you'll need to do before building any applications is to put together a skeleton *.app* directory to contain it.* The skeleton will provide all of the information necessary for the iPhone to acknowledge the existence of your application so it can be run from the SpringBoard.

This book presents many fully functional code examples, and in order to properly run them, you'll need to build an example skeleton called *MyExample.app*. Creating the directory is easy enough:

```
$ mkdir MyExample.app
```

Next, write a property list to describe the application and how to launch it. The *Info. plist* file expresses the property list in XML, and should look like this:

```
<?xml version="1.0" encoding="UTF-8"?>
<!DOCTYPE plist PUBLIC "-//Apple Computer//DTD PLIST 1.0//EN"
  "http://www.apple.com/DTDs/PropertyList-1.0.dtd">
<plist version="1.0">
<dict>
    <key>CFBundleDevelopmentRegion</key>
    <string>English</string>
    <key>CFBundleExecutable</key>
    <string>MyExample</string>
    <key>CFBundleIdentifier</key>
    <string>com.oreilly.www.iphone.examples</string>
    <key>CFBundleInfoDictionaryVersion</key>
    <string>6.0</string>
    <key>CFBundlePackageType</key>
    <string>APPL</string>
    <key>CFBundleSignature</key>
    <string>????</string>
    <key>CFBundleVersion</key>
    <string>1.0</string>
</dict>
</plist>
```

---

* Technically, it's possible to run an application directly from the iPhone's command line, but this breaks many application-level functions. SpringBoard itself is heavily integrated with the user interface framework, and your applications will need to be assembled and invoked appropriately to make them entirely usable.

The most important options above have been bolded. These are the values for `CFBundleExecutable` and `CFBundleIdentifier`. The `CFBundleExecutable` property specifies the filename of the binary executable within the folder. This is the file that gets executed when your application is launched—the output from your compiler. In this example, the filename is the same as the application's name, but this isn't absolutely necessary.

The `CFBundleIdentifier` property specifies a unique identifier by which your application is known. The application layer of the iPhone is more concerned about addressing your application as a whole rather than the binary itself. Whenever SpringBoard (or another application) launches *MyExample*, it will be referenced using this identifier. The name must be unique among all other applications on the iPhone. It's common practice to incorporate the URL of your web site to ensure it's unique.

The application's *icon.png* and *Default.png* files are also copied in. If these are left out, the iPhone will use the worst looking images possible to serve as default images for both. We'll leave the files out of our example to show you what we mean. Make sure to create and include images with these names when you publish your own applications to make them look professional.

Our skeleton is now good enough to run examples. In the next section, you'll install the tool chain on your desktop, after which you can get started compiling example applications. In the coming chapters, you'll build many examples. After each has been built, the binary executable *MyExample* will need to be copied into your program folder. Your completed application will look like this:

```
drwxr-xr-x    root    admin    MyExample.app/
   -rw-r--r--    root    admin    Info.plist
   -rwxr-xr-x    root    admin    MyExample
```

The examples provided in this book generally do not need any additional resources, so images and sounds will be necessary only when the example calls for them. When they do, however, you'll copy the files required into the *MyExample.app* directory. Most examples make use of existing files on the iPhone to avoid filling up the book with binary code.

Building the Free Tool Chain

As we discussed in Chapter 1, the iPhone began life as a closed platform. This originally meant that no developer tools were publicly available to build iPhone-native applications. There has been much speculation about whether Apple secretly hoped the community would break into the phone, thus bolstering its status among the geek community. Over the first few months of the iPhone's life, this is exactly what happened. The open source community successfully cracked the phone and began writing a tool chain to build applications. It has since been released as free software.

The tool chain consists of a cross-compiler, a linker, an assembler, a C hook into the assembler called *Csu*, and class headers for Objective-C frameworks generated by a tool called *class-dump*.

The tool chain uses a cross-compiler, which is a compiler that runs on one machine (namely, your desktop) but builds executables that can run on a different machine (the arm processor in an iPhone). The commands and path names provided throughout this book presume that you've used the procedures from this chapter to build and install the tool chain. The tool chain is updated periodically as new versions of it are released, so its setup can sometimes change. The instructions here will guide you through the steps to install version 0.30 of the tool chain, which is the latest available at the time of this writing. Newer versions are documented on the official tool chain project page at *http://code.google.com/p/iphone-dev*.

The tool chain builds and installs into */usr/local* by default. All of the examples provided in this book will presume that this is where you've installed it. If you've built the tool chain before, or are just concerned about modifying files there, you'll want to move your current */usr/local* out of the way and start with a fresh directory.

 If you have a previous version of the tool chain, newer versions may not build correctly. To ensure that you start with a clean installation, move your old copy out of the way.

What You'll Need

While there are some unofficial binary distributions of the tool chain floating around the Internet, you'll be building it from sources in this section. The following are requirements for building from sources.

Supported desktop platform

The first thing you'll need is a desktop platform that is supported. Platforms currently supported by the tool chain are:

- Mac OS X 10.4 Intel or PPC
- Mac OS X 10.5 Intel
- Ubuntu Feisty Fawn, Intel
- Ubuntu Gusty Gibbon, Intel
- Fedora Core, Intel
- Gentoo Linux 2007.0, x86_64
- Debian 2.6.18
- CentOS 4

Nicholas Penree of Conceited Software (*http://www.conceitedsoftware.com*) took time to adapt the tool chain's installation to run on Leopard, which is what we'll use in our example. Other platforms follow the same basic steps as these. Official tool chain instructions can be found at *http://code.google.com/p/iphone-dev/wiki/Building*.

High speed Internet connection

The tool chain is several hundred megabytes in size—and that's just the sources. Unless you want to be sitting around for a few days, you'll likely want to download the sources over a high-speed connection. If you don't have one, it might be a good idea to perform the installation from a library or local coffee shop.

Open source tools

The next things you'll need are the necessary open source tools installed on your desktop:

- *bison* (v1.28 or later)
- *flex* (v2.5.4 or later)
- *gcc* (the GNU compiler that handles C, C++, and Objective-C)
- *svn* (the Subversion source control utility)

If you're missing any of these tools, download and install them before proceeding. On the Mac, these are included with XCode tools, and you'll want to install or upgrade to the latest version of XCode before proceeding. Most other operating systems provide them as optional components in their distribution.

> XCode tools can be downloaded from Apple's web site at *http://developer.apple.com/tools/xcode/*.

iPhone filesystem

Finally, the last thing you'll need is a copy of your iPhone's filesystem; specifically, the libraries and frameworks. For dramatic effect, and because our lawyers make us, we'll display this general disclaimer:

> Installing the tool chain requires that you copy libraries from your iPhone to your desktop. Check with your local, state, and federal laws to ensure this is legal where you reside.

Having installed SSH onto the iPhone in Chapter 1, use the following commands to download the files you need into a folder called */usr/local/share/iphone-filesystem*.

```
# mkdir -p /usr/local/share/iphone-filesystem
# cd /usr/local/share/iphone-filesystem
# mkdir -p ./System/Library ./usr
```

```
# scp -r root@iphone:/System/Library/Frameworks/ .
# mv Frameworks ./System/Library
# scp -r root@iphone:/usr/lib .
# mv lib ./usr
```

Compiling the Tool Chain

The source code for the tool chain is split into two repositories: one for the LLVM compiler framework and one for the rest of the tool chain. Create a build directory for yourself and *cd* into it. Now, use Subversion to check both projects out from their repositories.

```
$ svn co http://llvm.org/svn/llvm-project/llvm/trunk llvm-svn -r 42498
$ svn co http://iphone-dev.googlecode.com/svn/trunk/ iphone-dev
```

The download may take an hour or longer, depending on the speed of your connection. Once both repositories have been checked out, it's time to start building.

The instructions in the next sections presume you know how to use a terminal window. On the Mac, this can be found in your *Utilities* folder inside *Applications*. It is also assumed that you have some level of knowledge of Unix.

One convention that may be unfamiliar to you is the use of the built-in shell commands *pushd* and *popd*. These are similar to the cd command, but they push and pop directories on a stack. This makes it easy to do some work in a new directory and then return to a previous one without having to remember where you were.

You'll also see references to the *sudo* command. This is a Unix tool providing limited access to run privileged (root) commands. When you want to run a command that requires privileged access (because it accesses sensitive data on the operating system or could have dangerous effects hurting the operating system), type sudo on the command line followed by the command you wish to run. Mac OS X will then prompt you for the root password to your desktop before allowing the command to run. If you don't have *sudo*, you can safely leave it off of your commands, but you'll first need to invoke *su* to become root.

Step 1: Build and install the LLVM framework

The LLVM (Low Level Virtual Machine) framework provides a standard infrastructure for building compilers. It provides the necessary hooks and APIs to build a standardized compiler without having to rewrite all of the basic components of a compiler. Issue the following statements to compile and install a release build of the llvm compiler.

```
$ pushd llvm-svn
$ ./configure --enable-optimized
$ make ENABLE_OPTIMIZED=1
$ sudo make install
$ LLVMOBJDIR=`pwd`
$ popd
```

Step 2: Build and install cross-compiler tools

The following commands build and install the cross-compiler components of the tool chain. These are specific to Mac OS X, so be sure to read the official documentation if you're using a different platform.

```
$ pushd iphone-dev
$ sudo mkdir /usr/local/arm-apple-darwin
$ mkdir -p build/odcctools
$ pushd build/odcctools
$ ../../odcctools/configure --target=arm-apple-darwin --disable-ld64
$ export INCPRIVEXT="-isysroot /Developer/SDKs/MacOSX10.4u.sdk"
$ make
$ sudo make install
$ popd
$ HEAVENLY=/usr/local/share/iphone-filesystem
```

Step 3: Patch the system headers

The system headers found in your XCode SDK are shared by your desktop and the iPhone platform, but some pre-compiler macros are architecture-specific. Because the iPhone's architecture is different from the desktop's, these headers need to be patched to work for the iPhone. Issue the following commands to patch the headers (don't worry, the originals are automatically backed up).

```
$ pushd include
$ ./configure --with-macosx-sdk=/Developer/SDKs/MacOSX10.4u.sdk
$ sudo bash install-headers.sh
$ popd
```

Step 4: Install the Csu

The Csu provides C hooks into assembly's "start" entry point, and sets up the stack so that your program's main( ) function can be called. It's essentially glue code.

```
$ mkdir -p build/csu
$ pushd build/csu
$ ../../csu/configure --host=arm-apple-darwin
$ sudo make install
$ popd
```

Step 5: Build and install llvm-gcc

Now that the LLVM framework, cross-compiler tools, and Csu have been built, the compiler itself can now be built and installed. If you're doing this in stages or have since closed your terminal window, make sure that you've still got the environment variables $LLVMOBJDIR and $HEAVENLY set to the proper directories. The LLVMOBJDIR variable points to the location of LLVM object files, which were compiled when you built LLVM. These are used to build llvm-gcc. The HEAVENLY variable points to the location where you copied the iPhone's libraries onto your desktop. This directory is used by llvm-gcc to link to the iPhone's framework and library files when you compile applications. The name "heavenly" was the code name given by Apple to the 1.0 code base of the iPhone software. The 1.1 code base is code-named "snowbird," but the original name is still used in the tool chain.

```
$ set | grep -e LLVMOBJDIR -e HEAVENLY
```

If you don't see output from the previous command, you need to set the environment variables again. Get back into your build directory and run:

```
$ pushd llvm-svn && LLVMOBJDIR=`pwd` && popd
$ HEAVENLY=/usr/local/share/iphone-filesystem
```

Once you've ensured that these are set, issue the following commands to build and install the compiler:

```
$ mv llvm-gcc-4.0-iphone/configure llvm-gcc-4.0-iphone/configure.old
$ sed \
  's/^FLAGS_FOR_TARGET=$/FLAGS_FOR_TARGET=${FLAGS_FOR_TARGET-}/g' \
  llvm-gcc-4.0-iphone/configure.old > llvm-gcc-4.0-iphone/configure
$ sudo ln -s /usr/local/arm-apple-darwin/lib/crt1.o \
  /usr/local/arm-apple-darwin/lib/crt1.10.5.o
$ mkdir -p build/llvm-gcc-4.0-iphone
$ pushd build/llvm-gcc-4.0-iphone
$ export FLAGS_FOR_TARGET="-mmacosx-version-min=10.1"
$ sh ../../llvm-gcc-4.0-iphone/configure \
  --enable-llvm=`llvm-config --obj-root` \
  --enable-languages=c,c++,objc,obj-c++ \
  --target=arm-apple-darwin --enable-sjlj-exceptions \
  --with-heavenly=$HEAVENLY \
  --with-as=/usr/local/bin/arm-apple-darwin-as \
  --with-ld=/usr/local/bin/arm-apple-darwin-ld
$ make LLVM_VERSION_INFO=2.0-svn-iphone-dev-0.3-svn
$ sudo make install
$ popd
$ popd
```

Congratulations! You've built the free tool chain for iPhone. You're now ready to start compiling iPhone applications. The compiler itself can be invoked directly by calling */usr/local/bin/arm-apple-darwin-gcc*. We'll explain how to use it in the next section.

Building and Installing Applications

Now that the tool chain has been installed, the next step is to learn how to use it. There are two essential ways to build an executable: the command line or a makefile.

The examples in this book are simple enough that they can be built using the command line. The tool chain is compliant to standard compiler arguments, and should be familiar if you've ever used gcc in the past. You'll want to make sure */usr/local/bin* is in your path before you try to use the cross-compiler.

```
$ export PATH=$PATH:/usr/local/bin
```

The anatomy of a typical command line compile is:

```
$ arm-apple-darwin-gcc -o MyExample MyExample.m -lobjc \
-framework CoreFoundation -framework Foundation
```

arm-apple-darwin-gcc

> The name of the cross-compiler itself. This is located in *usr/local/bin*, so be sure you've added it to your path.

-o MyExample

> Tells the compiler to output the compiled executable to a file named *MyExample*.

MyExample.m

> The name of the source file(s) being included in the program, separated by spaces. The *.m* extension tells the compiler that the sources are written in Objective-C.

-lobjc

> Tells the compiler to link in the tool chain's Objective-C messaging library, which is needed by all iPhone applications. This library glues C-style function calls to Objective-C messages, among other things.

-framework CoreFoundation -framework Foundation

> Two of the base frameworks to be linked into the application. Depending on what components of the operating system are being used in the code, different frameworks provide different layers of functionality. You'll be introduced to many different frameworks throughout this book.

The command line will suffice for most small applications and examples, but for larger applications, it makes sense to write a *makefile*. A makefile is a simple text file that acts as a manifest for building applications. It is used by a program called *make*, which is a portable build utility included with most development kits. The *make* program is responsible for calling the compiler (and linker) and passing them whatever flags and parameters are needed. Makefiles are logical ways to lay out the composition of an application. They also allow the developer to easily clean up the object files in a directory, create application packages, and perform a number of other tasks useful to building applications.

The previous command line example could be rewritten as a makefile like the one below, named *Makefile*, and placed into the source directory.

```
CC = /usr/local/bin/arm-apple-darwin-gcc
LD = $(CC)
LDFLAGS = -lobjc \
          -framework CoreFoundation
CFLAGS =

all:    MyExample

MyExample: MyExample.o
          $(LD) $(LDFLAGS) -o $@ $^
```

```
%.o:        %.m
            $(CC) -c $(CFLAGS) $(CPPFLAGS) $< -o $@

%.o:        %.c
            $(CC) -c $(CFLAGS) $(CPPFLAGS) $< -o $@

%.o:        %.cpp
            $(CC) -c $(CFLAGS) $(CPPFLAGS) $< -o $@
```

 All indentations are actually tabs. Tabs must be used in order for the makefile to work properly.

Once the makefile file is in place, the application's executable can be built with one simple command:

```
$ make
```

In addition to building an application, functionality can be added to copy the application's executable into the program folder skeleton you made:

```
package:
            cp -p MyExample ./MyExample.app/
```

With this added to the makefile, you can run **make package** to automatically set up your *.app* directory.

Another popular use for makefiles is to clean the directory so that it can be sent to someone else. You can even tell the makefile to delete the executable that was copied into the program folder.

```
clean:
            rm -f *.o *.gch
            rm -f ./MyExample.app/MyExample
```

Installing an Application

Once an application has been built, it can be installed by copying the entire program directory into the */Applications* folder on the iPhone. Using the SSH server you set up in Chapter 1, you can do this over WiFi:

```
$ scp -r MyExample.app root@iphone:/Applications
```

Before the iPhone will recognize the application, either the iPhone must be powered down and rebooted, or the SpringBoard application must be restarted on the iPhone itself. Log in to the iPhone using SSH and execute the following command to restart SpringBoard:

```
$ killall SpringBoard
```

Once restarted, you should see the application on the SpringBoard. Pressing the icon will launch it.

Integrating with XCode

While most developers use the command line or a makefile to build iPhone applications, the tool chain can be partially integrated with XCode to take advantage of the feature-rich editor and one-click build process. XCode treats the tool chain as an external resource and calls it to perform the actual build.

To integrate with XCode, a template is required to glue the necessary pieces to the tool chain. John Robinson from Monster and Friends has designed an XCode template based on one written by tool chain developer Lucas Newman. We've made some changes to tailor it to this book. Our version can be found in the download section for this book at *http://www.oreilly.com/catalog/9780596518554/*. John's original version can be found at *http://www.monsterandfriends.com/?q=node/62*.

To integrate the cool chain with XCode, perform the following steps:

1. Download and install XCode version 3.0 or later from Apple's developer web site.
2. Download our version of the template from the O'Reilly web site and extract the archive's contents.
3. A folder named *iPhone UIKit Application* will be created. Copy this directory into */Developer/Library/Xcode/Project Templates/Application* on your Mac.

Once you've installed the template, you can now create a new iPhone project by performing these steps:

1. Launch XCode and select New Project from the File menu. A list of templates will be presented to you to choose from.
2. In the Application section of the list, scroll to the iPhone UIKit Application template and create a new project using it as the template.

A new project will now be created, and the project name will be reflected in the filenames used. To build the application, just click the Build button on the toolbar. XCode will call the tool chain's compiler and place a binary in the project's *build* folder.

Because XCode treats the tool chain as an external resource, it's not completely integrated with it. What happens under the hood is this: XCode kicks off a build process using a makefile present in the project template. This makefile calls the tool chain's compiler with the appropriate options. To add new files or frameworks to your project, you'll need to manually edit the file named *Makefile* shown in your project's file list. This will bear a resemblance to the one discussed in the last section.

Transitioning to Objective-C

Objective-C was written in the early 1980s by scientist and software engineer Brad Cox. It was designed as a way of introducing the capabilities of the Smalltalk language into a C programming environment. A majority of the iPhone's framework libraries are written in Objective-C, but because the language was designed to accommodate the C language, you can use C and C++ in your application as well. Objective-C is used primarily on Mac OS X and GNUstep (a free OpenStep environment). Many languages, such as Java and C#, have borrowed from the Objective-C language. The Cocoa framework makes heavy use of Objective-C on the Mac desktop, which carried over onto the iPhone.

If you've developed on the Mac OS X desktop before, you're already familiar with Objective-C, but if the iPhone is your first Apple platform, then you're likely transitioning from C or C++. This section will cover some of the more significant differences between these languages. If you have a prior background in C or C++, this should be enough to get you up and writing code using the examples in this book as a guide.

Messaging

The first thing you'll notice in Objective-C is the heavy use of brackets. In Objective-C, methods are not *called* in a traditional sense; instead, they are sent *messages*. Likewise, a method doesn't *return*, but rather *responds* to the message. Unlike C, where function calls must be predefined, Objective-C's messaging style allows the developer to dynamically create new methods and messages at runtime. The downside to this is that it's entirely possible to send an object a message to which it can't respond, causing an exception and likely program termination.

Given an object named myWidget, a message can be sent to its powerOn method this way:

```
returnValue = [ myWidget powerOn ];
```

The C++ equivalent of this might look like:

```
returnValue = myWidget->powerOn( );
```

The C equivalent might declare a function inside of its flat namespace:

```
returnValue = widget_powerOn(myWidget);
```

Arguments can also be passed with messages, provided that an object can receive them. The following example invokes a method named setSpeed and passes two arguments:

```
returnValue = [ myWidget setSpeed: 10.0 withMass: 33.0 ];
```

Notice the second argument is explicitly named in the message. This allows multiple methods with the same name *and* data types to be declared—polymorphism on steroids.

```
returnValue = [ myWidget setSpeed: 10.0 withMass: 33.0 ];
returnValue = [ myWidget setSpeed: 10.0 withGyroscope: 10.0 ];
```

Class and Method Declarations

While C++ classes can be defined in Objective-C, the whole point of using the language is to take advantage of Objective-C's own objects and features. This extends to its use of interfaces. In standard C++, classes are structures, and their variables and methods are contained inside the structure. Objective-C, on the other hand, keeps its variables in one part of the class and methods in another. The language also requires that the interface declaration be specifically declared in its own code block (called @interface) separate from the block containing the implementation (called @implementation). The methods themselves are also constructed in a Smalltalk-esque fashion, and look very little like regular C functions.

The interface for our widget example might look like Example 2-1, which is a file named *MyWidget.h.*

Example 2-1. Sample interface (MyWidget.h)

```
#import <Foundation/Foundation.h>

@interface MyWidget : BaseWidget
{
    BOOL isPoweredOn;
    @private float speed;
    @protected float mass;
    @protected float gyroscope;
}
+ (id)alloc;
+ (BOOL)needsBatteries;
- (BOOL)powerOn;
- (void)setSpeed:(float)_speed;
- (void)setSpeed:(float)_speed withMass:(float)_mass;
- (void)setSpeed:(float)_speed withGyroscope:(float)_gyroscope;
@end
```

Each of the important semantic elements in this file are explained in the following sections.

Imports

The preprocessor directive #import replaces the traditional #include directive (although #include may still be used). One advantage to using #import is that it has built-in logic to ensure that the same resource is never included more than once. This replaces the round-about use of macro flags found routinely in C code:

```
#ifndef _MYWIDGET_H
#define _MYWIDGET_H
...
#endif
```

Interface declaration

The interface is declared with the `@interface` statement followed by the interface's name and the base class (if any) it is derived from. The block is ended with the `@end` statement.

Methods

Methods are declared outside of the braces structure. A plus sign (+) identifies the method as a static method, while a minus sign (–) declares the method as an instance method. Thus, the `alloc` method (to allocate a new object) will be called using a reference directly to the `MyWidget` class, whereas methods that are specific to an instance of the `MyWidget` class, such as `needsBatteries` and `powerOn`, will be invoked on the instance returned by `alloc`.

Every declared argument for a method is represented by a data type, local variable name, and an optional external variable name. Examples of external variable names in Example 2-1 are `withMass` and `withGyroscope`. The notifier (calling function) that invokes the method refers to external variable names, but inside the method the arguments are referenced using their local variable name. Thus, the `setSpeed` method uses the local `_mass` variable to retrieve the value passed as `withMass`.

If no external variable name name is supplied in the declaration, the variable is referenced only with a colon, for example, `:10.0`.

Implementation

The code suffix for Objective-C source is `.m`. A skeleton implementation of the widget class from the last section might look like Example 2-2, which is named *MyWidget.m*.

Example 2-2. Sample implementation (MyWidget.m)

```
#import "MyWidget.h"

@implementation MyWidget

+ (id)alloc {
}

+ (BOOL)needsBatteries {
```

Example 2-2. Sample implementation (MyWidget.m) (continued)

```
    return YES;
}

- (BOOL)powerOn {
    isPoweredOn = YES;
    return YES;
}

- (void)setSpeed:(float)_speed {
    speed = _speed;
}

- (void)setSpeed:(float)_speed withMass:(float)_mass {
    speed = _speed;
    mass = _mass;
}

- (void)setSpeed:(float)_speed withGyroscope:(float)_gyroscope {
    speed = _speed;
    gyroscope = _gyroscope;
}
@end
```

Just as the interface was contained within its own code block, the implementation begins with an @implementation statement and ends with @end. In C++, it is common practice to prefix member variables with m_ so that public methods can accept the name of the variable. This makes it easy to reuse someone else's code because they can deduce a variable's purpose by its name. Since Objective-C allows for an external variable name to be used, the method is able to provide a sensible name for the developer to use while internally using some proprietary name. The true name can then be used inside the object, while the method's local variable name is prefixed with an underscore, e.g., _speed.

Categories

Objective-C adds a new element to object-oriented programming called *categories*. Categories were designed to solve the problem where base classes are treated as fragile to prevent seemingly innocuous changes from breaking the more complex derived classes. When a program grows to a certain size, the developer can often become afraid to touch the smaller base classes because it's too difficult by then to determine what changes are safe without auditing the entire application. Categories provide a mechanism to add functionality to smaller classes without affecting other objects.

A category class can be placed "on top" of a smaller class, adding to or replacing methods within the base class. This can be done without recompiling or even having access to the base classes' source code. Categories allows for base classes to be expanded within a limited scope, so that any objects using the base class (and not the category) will continue to see the original version. From a development perspective, this makes it much easier to improve on a class written by a different developer. At runtime, portions of code using the category will see the new version of the class, and code using the base class directly will see only the original version.

The difference between categories and inheritance is the difference between tricking out your car versus dressing it up as a parade float. When you soup up your sports car, new components are added to the internals of the vehicle that cause it to perform differently. Sometimes components are even pulled out and replaced with new ones. The act of adding a new component to the engine, such as a turbo, affects the function of the entire vehicle. This is how inheritance works.

Categories, on the other hand, are more like a parade float in that the vehicle remains completely intact, but cardboard cutouts and papier-mâché are affixed to the outside of the vehicle so that it appears different. In the context of a parade, the vehicle is a completely different animal, but when you take it to the mechanic, it's the same old stock car you've been driving around.

The widget factory is coming out with a new type of widget that can fly through space, but is concerned that making changes to their base class might break existing applications. By building a category, applications using the MyWidget base class will continue to see the original class, while the newer space applications will use a category instead. The following example builds a new category named MySpaceWidget on top of the existing MyWidget base class. Because we need the ability to blow things up in space, a method named selfDestruct is added. This category also replaces the existing powerOn method with its own. Contrast the use of parentheses here to hold the MySpaceWidget contained class with the use of a colon in Example 2-1 to carry out inheritance.

```
#import "MyWidget.h"

@interface MyWidget (MySpaceWidget)
- (void)selfDestruct;
- (BOOL)powerOn;
@end
```

Example 2-3 shows a complete source file implementing the category.

Example 2-3. Sample category (MySpaceWidget.m)

```
#import "MySpaceWidget.h"

@implementation MyWidget (MySpaceWidget)

- (void)selfDestruct {
    isPoweredOn = 0;
    speed = 1000.0;
    mass = 0;
}
```

Example 2-3. Sample category (MySpaceWidget.m) (continued)

```
- (BOOL)powerOn {
    if (speed == 0) {
        isPoweredOn = YES;
        return YES;
    }

    /* Don't power on if the spaceship is moving */
    return NO;
}
@end
```

Posing

In Objective-C, a subclass class can *pose* as one of its superclasses, virtually replacing it as the recipient of all messages. This is similar to overriding, only an entire class is being overridden instead of a single method. A posing class is not permitted to declare any new variables, although it may override or replace existing methods. Posing is similar to categories in that it allows a developer to augment an existing class at runtime.

In past examples, mechanical widget classes were created. Well, at some point after designing all of these widgets, perpetual energy was discovered. This allowed many of the newer widgets to be autonomous, while some legacy widgets still required batteries. Because autonomous widgets have such a significant amount of different code, a new object called MyAutonomousWidget was derived to override all of the functionality that has changed, such as the static needsBatteries method. See Examples 2-4 and 2-5.

Example 2-4. Sample interface for posing (MyAutonomousWidget.h)

```
#import <Foundation/Foundation.h>
#import "MyWidget.h"

@interface MyAutonomousWidget : MyWidget
{

}

+ (BOOL)needsBatteries;
@end
```

Example 2-5. Sample implementation for posing (MyAutonomousWidget.m)

```
#import "MyAutonomousWidget.h"

@implementation MyAutonomousWidget

+ (BOOL)needsBatteries {
    return NO;
```

Example 2-5. Sample implementation for posing (MyAutonomousWidget.m) (continued)

```
}
@end
```

Instead of changing all of the existing code to use this class, the autonomous class can simply pose as the widget class. The class_poseAs method is called from the main program or another high-level method to invoke this behavior:

```
MyAutonomousWidget *myAutoWidget = [ MyAutonomousWidget alloc ];
MyWidget *myWidget = [ MyWidget alloc ];
class_poseAs(myAutoWidget, myWidget);
```

At this point, any other methods we've replaced in the posing class (to change how we talk to autonomous devices) would pose as the original base class.

Further Study

To learn more about Objective-C programming, check out the following great resources from O'Reilly:

Learning Cocoa with Objective-C, Second Edition, by James Duncan Davidson (Apple Computers, Inc.)

> *http://www.oreilly.com/catalog/learncocoa2/*

Objective-C Pocket Reference by Andrew M. Duncan (O'Reilly)

> *http://www.oreilly.com/catalog/objectcpr/*

CHAPTER 3
Introduction to UIKit

UIKit is the largest iPhone framework in terms of file size, and rightly so—it's responsible for all user interface functions from creating windows and text boxes to reading multitouch gestures and hardware sensors. All of the graphical pleasantries that make the iPhone seem easy-to-use rely on the UIKit framework to deliver a polished and unified interface. The same UIKit APIs are available to all iPhone applications, and understanding how to use this framework will allow you to take advantage of the same tools that make Apple's own stock apps spectacular.

UIKit is more than a mere user interface kit; it is also the runtime foundation for iPhone GUI applications. When an application is launched, its main( ) function instantiates a UIApplication object within UIKit. This class is the base class for all applications having a user interface on the iPhone, and it provides the application access to the iPhone's higher-level functions. In addition to this, common application-level services such as suspend, resume, and termination are functions of the UIApplication object.

To tap into the UIKit, your application must be linked to the UIKit framework. As a framework, UIKit is a type of shared library. So, using the compiler tool chain, UIKit can be linked to your application by adding the following arguments to the compiler arguments we described in Chapter 2:

```
$ arm-apple-darwin-gcc -o MyApp MyApp.m -lobjc \
    -framework CoreFoundation \
    -framework Foundation \
    -framework UIKit
```

To add this option to the sample makefile from the previous chapter, add the UIKit framework to the linker flags section so that the library is linked in:

```
LDFLAGS =    -lobjc \
        -framework CoreFoundation \
        -framework Foundation \
        -framework UIKit
```

Basic User Interface Elements

This chapter is designed to get you up and running with a basic user interface. UIKit supports the following basic user interface elements. The more advanced features of UIKit are covered in Chapter 7.

Windows and views

Windows and views are the base classes for creating any type of user interface. A window represents a geometric space on a screen, while a view acts like a container for other objects. Smaller user interface components, such as navigation bars, buttons, and text boxes are all attached to a view, and that view is anchored to a window. Think of a window as the frame of a painting and the view as the actual canvas. A window can only frame up one view, but views can contain smaller subviews, including other views.

A *controlling view* is a view that controls how other views are displayed on the screen. The controlling view performs transitions to other views and responds to events occurring on the screen.

Text views

Text views are specialized view classes for presenting editor windows to view or edit text or HTML. The Notepad application is a good example of a simple text view. They are considered humble and are rarely used in light of UIKit's repertoire of more spectacular user interface tools.

Navigation bars

The iPhone user interface treats different screens as if they are "pages" in a book. Navigation bars are frequently used to provide a visual prompt to allow the user to return "back" to a previous view, supply them with buttons to modify elements on the current screen page, and provide formatted titles to the screen page they are viewing. Navigation bars are found in nearly all preloaded iPhone applications.

Transitions

A single screen page is rarely enough for any application to function, especially on a mobile device. Consistent with the spirit of Apple's user-friendly interfaces, window transitions were introduced with the iPhone to allow the user to perceive navigation through their application like pages in a book. Window transitions are used to make this visual transition from one window to another, and provide various types of different transitions from the familiar page flipping effect to fades and twists.

Alert sheets

The equivalent to a pop-up alert window on the iPhone is an alert sheet. Alert sheets appear as modal windows that slide up from the bottom when an operation requires the user's attention. They are frequently seen on preloaded iPhone applications when a user attempts to delete a number of items or clear important data, such as voicemail. Alert sheets can be programmed to ask the user any question, and present them with any number of different options. They prove useful in parts of an application needing immediate attention.

Tables

Tables are really lists that can be used to display files, messages, or other types of collections. They are used for selection of one or more items in a list-like fashion. The table objects are very flexible and allow the developer to define how a table cell should look and behave.

Status bar manipulation

The status bar is the small bar appearing at the top of the iPhone screen, and displays the time, battery life, and signal strength. The status bar's color, opacity, and orientation can be customized, and the status bar can be made to display icon images to notify the user of a particular application state.

Application badges

Applications needing to notify the user of time-sensitive information have the ability to display badges on the main applications screen. This alerts the user that the application needs attention, or that the user has messages or other information waiting to be viewed. These are used heavily by applications using the EDGE network to deliver messages.

Status bar icons

The status bar is the small bar appearing at the top of the iPhone screen, and displays the time, battery life, and signal strength. Changes can be made to the status bar depending on the application's needs for style, opacity, and orientation. Images can also be added to the status bar to notify the user of an ongoing operation (such as an alarm or background process).

Windows and Views

The most basic user interface component is a window. A window is a region of screen space: a picture frame. UIWindow is the iPhone's base window class and is derived from lower level functions that respond to mouse events, gestures, and other types of events that would be relevant to a window. The UIWindow class is ultimately responsible for holding the contents of a UIView object (the picture that fits in the window's frame). UIView is a base class from which many other types of display classes are derived. The window itself can only hold one object, whereas the UIView object is designed to accommodate many different types of subobjects, including other views. The two classes go hand-in-hand with each other, and both are required to display anything on the iPhone screen.

Creating a Window and View

Before you can display anything on the iPhone screen, you must create a window to hold content, and to build a window, you need a display region. A display region is a fancy term for rectangle and represents the portion of the screen where the window should be displayed. The underlying structure itself is a rectangle structure named CGRect that contains two pieces: the coordinates for the upper-left corner of the window and the window's size (its width and height). Every object displayed on the screen has a display region defining its display area. Most are set when the object is initialized, via an initWithFrame method. Others must be set after the fact using a ubiquitous method named setFrame. In the case of the main window, the region's coordinates are offset to the screen itself; however, all subsequent objects (including the window's view) are offset to the object that contains it. As other objects are nested inside the view, those objects' regions will be offset to the view, and so on.

An application uses the entire iPhone screen when it is displayed, and so the window should be assigned a set of coordinates reflecting the view region of the entire screen. This region can be obtained from a static method found inside a class named UIHardware.

```
CGRect windowRect = [ UIHardware fullScreenApplicationContentRect ];
```

This region, named windowRect above, is then used to create and initialize a new UIWindow object:

```
UIWindow *window = [ UIWindow alloc ];
[ window initWithContentRect: windowRect ];
```

The window frame has now been created, but contains nothing. An object that can render content is needed to place inside of it. A UIView object must be created to fill the window. Because a window can only hold one view object, the display region for it should likewise use the entire screen so that it will fill up the entire window.

```
CGRect viewRect = [ UIHardware fullScreenApplicationContentRect ];
viewRect.origin.x = viewRect.origin.y = 0.0;

UIView *mainView = [ [ MainView alloc ] initWithFrame: viewRect ];
```

Displaying the View

The window and view pair has been created, but the view has not been displayed on the screen. To do this, assign the window and instruct the window to display:

```
[ window setContentView: mainView ];
[ window orderFront: self ];
[ window makeKey: self ];
[ window _setHidden: NO ];
```

The Most Useless Application Ever

Before we even get to "Hello, World!", we need an even more useless application, "Hello, Window!". This application does nothing more than to create a window and view pair. In fact, because the base UIView class is just a container class, it can't even display any text for you. All you'll see is a black screen. What this application does do is serve as the first few lines of code any GUI application on the iPhone will use.

This application, shown in Examples 3-1 and 3-2, can be compiled from the tool chain using the following command line:

```
$ arm-apple-darwin-gcc -o MyExample MyExample.m -lobjc \
    -framework CoreFoundation -framework Foundation -framework UIKit
```

Example 3-1. Example window and view (MyExample.h)

```
#import <CoreFoundation/CoreFoundation.h>
#import <UIKit/UIKit.h>

@interface MyApp : UIApplication
{
    UIWindow *window;
    UIView *mainView;
}
- (void)applicationDidFinishLaunching:
    (NSNotification *)aNotification;
@end
```

Example 3-2. Example window and view (MyExample.m)

```
#import "MyExample.h"

int main(int argc, char **argv)
{
    NSAutoreleasePool *autoreleasePool = [
        [ NSAutoreleasePool alloc ] init
    ];
    int returnCode = UIApplicationMain(argc, argv, [ MyApp class ]);
    [ autoreleasePool release ];
    return returnCode;
}

@implementation MyApp

- (void)applicationDidFinishLaunching:(NSNotification *)aNotification {
    window = [ [ UIWindow alloc ] initWithContentRect:
        [ UIHardware fullScreenApplicationContentRect ]
    ];

    CGRect windowRect =
        [ UIHardware fullScreenApplicationContentRect ];
    windowRect.origin.x = windowRect.origin.y = 0.0f;
```

Example 3-2. Example window and view (MyExample.m) (continued)

```
    mainView = [ [ UIView alloc ] initWithFrame: windowRect ];

    [ window setContentView: mainView ];
    [ window orderFront: self ];
    [ window makeKey: self ];
    [ window _setHidden: NO ];
}
@end
```

What's Going On

The "Hello, Window!" application flows like this:

1. When the application starts, its main( ) function is called, just as in a regular C program. This hooks into Objective-C land and instantiates an application class named MyApp, which is derived from UIKit's UIApplication class. The main( ) function is also responsible for initializing an auto-release pool. Auto-release pools are used extensively throughout Apple's Cocoa framework to dispose of objects that have been designated as autorelease when they are created. This tells the application to simply throw them away when it's done with them, and they are deallocated later on.

2. The UIApplication class's applicationDidFinishLaunching method is called by the underlying application object's framework once the object has initialized. This is where the Objective-C application begins its life.

3. A call to UIHardware's fullScreenApplicationContentRect method is called to return the coordinates and size of the physical screen. This is then used to create a new window where the application's main view resides.

4. The main view is then created, using a display region beginning at 0×0 (the upper-left corner of the window). The view is set as the window's content.

5. The window is then instructed to bring itself to the front and show itself. This displays the view, which presently has no content.

Deriving from UIView

The "Hello, Window!" example showed the very minimal code needed to construct and display a window/view pair. Because the UIView class itself is merely a base class, it didn't actually display anything. To create a useful application, a new class can be derived from UIView, allowing its methods to be overridden to add functionality. This controlling view can then display other objects, such as text boxes, images, etc.

To derive a subclass from UIView, write a new interface and implementation declaring the subclass. The following snippet creates a subclass named MainView:

```
@interface MainView : UIView
{
```

```
    }

- (id)initWithFrame:(CGRect)rect;
- (void)dealloc;
@end
```

At the very least, two UIView class methods should be overridden. The initWithFrame method is called when the view is first instantiated and is used to initialize the view class. A display region is passed in to define its coordinates (offset to its parent) and size it should display as. Any code that initializes variables or other objects can go into this method. The second method, dealloc, is called when the UIView object is disposed of. Any resources previously allocated within your class should be released here.

These two methods are the basis for all other activity within the view class. Here are the templates for them:

```
@implementation MainView
- (id)initWithFrame:(CGRect)rect {

    if ((self == [ super initWithFrame: rect ]) != nil) {

        /* Initialize member variables here */

        /* Allocate initial resources here */
    }

    return self;
}

- (void)dealloc
{
    /* Deallocate any resources here */

    [ self dealloc ];
    [ super dealloc ];
}
@end
```

The Second Most Useless Application Ever

Now that you know how to derive a UIView class, you've got everything you need to write an application that does something—albeit a mostly useless something. In the tradition of our ancestors, we now present the official useless "Hello, World!" application.

This application, shown in Examples 3-3 and 3-4, can be built using the same command-line arguments as the previous example:

```
$ arm-apple-darwin-gcc -o MyExample MyExample.m -lobjc \
    -framework CoreFoundation -framework Foundation -framework UIKit
```

Example 3-3. "Hello World!" example (MyExample.h)

```
#import <CoreFoundation/CoreFoundation.h>
#import <UIKit/UIKit.h>
#import <UIKit/UITextView.h>

@interface MainView : UIView
{
        UITextView          *textView;
}
- (id)initWithFrame:(CGRect)frame;
- (void)dealloc;
@end

@interface MyApp : UIApplication
{
    UIWindow *window;
    MainView *mainView;
}
- (void)applicationDidFinishLaunching:
    (NSNotification *)aNotification;
@end
```

Example 3-4. "Hello World!" example (MyExample.m)

```
#import "MyExample.h"

int main(int argc, char **argv)
{
    NSAutoreleasePool *autoreleasePool = [
        [ NSAutoreleasePool alloc ] init
    ];
    int returnCode = UIApplicationMain(argc, argv, [ MyApp class ]);
    [ autoreleasePool release ];
    return returnCode;
}

@implementation MyApp

- (void)applicationDidFinishLaunching:(NSNotification *)aNotification {
    window = [ [ UIWindow alloc ] initWithContentRect:
        [ UIHardware fullScreenApplicationContentRect ]
    ];

    CGRect rect = [ UIHardware fullScreenApplicationContentRect ];
    rect.origin.x = rect.origin.y = 0.0f;

    mainView = [ [ MainView alloc ] initWithFrame: rect ];
```

Example 3-4. "Hello World!" example (MyExample.m) (continued)

```
    [ window setContentView: mainView ];
    [ window orderFront: self ];
    [ window makeKey: self ];
    [ window _setHidden: NO ];
}
@end

@implementation MainView
- (id)initWithFrame:(CGRect)rect {

    if ((self == [ super initWithFrame: rect ]) != nil) {

        textView = [ [ UITextView alloc ] initWithFrame: rect ];
        [ textView setTextSize: 18 ];
        [ textView setText: @"Hello, World!" ];
        [ self addSubview: textView ];
    }

    return self;
}

- (void)dealloc
{
    [ self dealloc ];
    [ super dealloc ];
}

@end
```

What's Going On

The "Hello, World!" example contains everything you've seen so far, with the addition of a new view designed to display text:

1. The application instantiates in the same way as before, by calling the program's main( ) function, which creates an instance of MyApp.

2. Instead of creating a generic UIView class, the application instantiates its own class called MainView, which is derived from UIView.

3. MainView's initWithFrame method is called, which in turn calls its super class (UIView) and its own initWithFrame method to let UIView do the work of creating the view itself.

4. A UITextView, which you'll learn more about in the upcoming "Text Views" section, is created and attached to the MainView object. This text view is given the text, "Hello, World!".

5. The window is instructed to display, displaying the MainView object and the UITextView object attached to it.

Further Study

Now that you have something to look at in your application, play around with it for a little while before proceeding.

- Try changing the origins and size of the frame passed to `mainView`. What happens to the window and its child? How about when changing the display origin of `textView`?
- Check out the *UIWindow.h* and *UIView.h* prototypes in your tool chain's include directory. You'll find them in */usr/local/arm-apple-darwin/include/UIKit/*.

Text Views

The `UITextView` class is based on a `UIView`, however, its functionality has been extended to present and allow editing of text, provide scrolling, and handle various fonts and colors. Text views can be easily abused, and are only recommended for text-based portions of an application, such as an electronic book, notes section of a program, or informational page to present unstructured information.

A `UITextView` object inherits from `UIScroller`, which is a generic scrollable class. This means that the text view itself comes pre-equipped with all scrolling functionality, so the developer can focus on presenting content rather than programming scroll bars. The `UIScroller` class inherits from `UIView`, which, as discussed in the last section, is the base class for all view classes.

Creating a Text View

Because `UITextView` is ultimately derived from `UIView`, it is created in the same fashion as the main view objects created in the last section—using an `initWithFrame` method.

```
UITextView *textView = [ [ UITextView alloc ]
    initWithFrame: viewRect ];
```

Once the view is created, a number of different properties can then be set.

Editing

If the text view is being used to collect user input, it will need to be made editable:

```
[ textView setEditable: YES ];
```

If the view is simply presenting data that should not be edited, this feature should be disabled.

Margins

The size of the top margin is the only margin that can be set in the text view. The value represents the number of pixels from the top of the text view that the text should be offset.

```
[ textView setMarginTop: 20 ];
```

Text properties

The text size, font and color can be set by passing point sizes and font and color objects into the class. These settings work for text and HTML uses, although they serve only as a default for HTML.

The text size is the simplest property, and is passed as an integer measuring point size.

```
[ textView setTextSize: 12 ];
```

The font is passed in as a CSS compliant string identifying the font properties.

```
[ textView setTextFont:
    @"font-family: Helvetica; font-style: italic; font-weight: bold" ];
```

The text color is a bit trickier and requires the use of another framework on the iPhone named Core Graphics. To create a simple RGB color, a set of four floating-point values for red, green, blue, and alpha (opacity) are specified with values between 0.0 and 1.0. These represent values ranging from 0% (0.0) to 100% (1.0). The values are used to create a color reference, which is then assigned in the text view as a CGColorRef ("Core Graphics color reference").

```
CGColorSpaceRef colorSpace =
    CGColorSpaceCreateWithName(kCGColorSpaceGenericRGB);
float opaqueRed[4] = { 1.0, 0.0, 0.0, 1.0 };
CGColorRef red = CGColorCreate(colorSpace, opaqueRed);
[ textView setTextColor: red ];
```

The Core Graphics framework will be explored more in Chapter 4.

Assigning Content

Two different methods can set the content of a text view: setText and setHTML. As the name suggests, invoking the setText method causes the content to be displayed as text, while the setHTML treats the content like a web page. If you try to call setText using HTML input, it will appear as HTML source code.

An example of the text display is:

```
[ textView setText: @"Hello, world!" ];
```

while HTML can be displayed like this:

```
[ textView setHTML: @"<b><center>Hello, World!</center></b>" ];
```

Displaying the Text View

Text views are generally attached to the main view of a window. This allows other subviews, such as navigation bars and controls, to be added to the same parent view later on.

```
[ mainView addSubview: textView ];
```

Example: Displaying iPhone Disclaimers

Every iPhone shipped by Apple contains a rather lengthy HTML file containing all of Apple's legal disclaimers. This is displayed in the legal section of Apple's Settings application. This example will take this file and display it in a text box.

To compile this application, you'll need to include the Core Graphics framework, which contains the routines needed to mix colors.

This application, shown in Examples 3-5 and 3-6, can be built using the tool chain on the following command line:

```
$ arm-apple-darwin-gcc -o MyExample MyExample.m -lobjc \
 -framework CoreFoundation -framework Foundation -framework UIKit \
 -framework CoreGraphics
```

Example 3-5. UITextView example (MyExample.h)

```
#import <CoreFoundation/CoreFoundation.h>
#import <Foundation/Foundation.h>
#import <UIKit/UIKit.h>
#import <UIKit/UITextView.h>

@interface MainView : UIView
{
        UITextView          *textView;
}

- (id)initWithFrame:(CGRect)frame;
- (void)dealloc;

@end

@interface MyApp : UIApplication
{
    UIWindow *window;
    MainView *mainView;
}

- (void)applicationDidFinishLaunching:(NSNotification *)aNotification;
@end
```

Example 3-6. UITextView example (MyExample.m)

```
#include <stdio.h>
#import "MyExample.h"

int main(int argc, char **argv)
{
    NSAutoreleasePool *autoreleasePool = [
        [ NSAutoreleasePool alloc ] init
    ];
    int returnCode = UIApplicationMain(argc, argv, [ MyApp class ]);
    [ autoreleasePool release ];
    return returnCode;
}

@implementation MyApp

- (void)applicationDidFinishLaunching:(NSNotification *)aNotification {
    window = [ [ UIWindow alloc ] initWithContentRect:
        [ UIHardware fullScreenApplicationContentRect ]
    ];

    CGRect rect = [ UIHardware fullScreenApplicationContentRect ];
    rect.origin.x = rect.origin.y = 0.0f;

    mainView = [ [ MainView alloc ] initWithFrame: rect ];

    [ window setContentView: mainView ];
    [ window orderFront: self ];
    [ window makeKey: self ];
    [ window _setHidden: NO ];
}
@end

@implementation MainView
- (id)initWithFrame:(CGRect)rect {
    if ((self == [ super initWithFrame: rect ]) != nil) {
        FILE *file;
        char buffer[262144], buf[1024];

        textView = [ [ UITextView alloc ] initWithFrame: rect ];
        [ textView setTextSize: 12 ];

        file = fopen("/Applications/Preferences.app/English.lproj/legal-disclaimer-iphone.
html", "r");

        if (!file) {
            CGColorSpaceRef colorSpace =
                CGColorSpaceCreateWithName(kCGColorSpaceGenericRGB);
            float opaqueRed[4] = { 1.0, 0.0, 0.0, 1 };
            CGColorRef red = CGColorCreate(colorSpace, opaqueRed);
            [ textView setTextColor: red ];

            [ textView setText: @"ERROR: File not found" ];
```

Example 3-6. UITextView example (MyExample.m) (continued)

```
        } else {
            buffer[0] = 0;
            while((fgets(buf, sizeof(buf), file))!=NULL) {
                strlcat(buffer, buf, sizeof(buffer));
            }
            fclose(file);

            [ textView setHTML:
                [ [ NSString alloc ] initWithCString: buffer ]];
        }

        [ self addSubview: textView ];
    }

    return self;
}

- (void)dealloc
{
    [ self dealloc ];
    [ super dealloc ];
}

@end
```

What's Going On

The example reads in and displays the contents of a file as follows:

1. When the application initializes, the main view is created and its `initWithFrame` method is called.

2. The `initWithFrame` method instantiates a new `UITextView` object and assigns a text size.

3. The file *legal-disclaimer-iphone.html* is opened using POSIX C's fopen method.

4. If the file cannot be found, a red color is created and an error message is set as the text of the window.

5. If the file is found, it is read into a text buffer and then set as the HTML content of the window.

6. The text view itself is added as a subview to the controlling view where it is displayed to the user.

Further Study

Here are some productive ways to play with this example:

- Copy your favorite web site's HTML over to the iPhone using SCP. Modify this example to display your file instead. What limitations does the `UITextView` appear to have when displaying HTML?

- What other font styling information can you pass to the text view's `setTextFont` method? See W3's CSS specification at *http://www.w3.org*.
- Check out the *UITextView.h* prototypes in the tool chain's include directory. You'll find it in */usr/local/arm-apple-darwin/include/UIKit/*.

Navigation Bars

The iPhone doesn't support toolbars in the traditional desktop sense. Because each screen of an application is considered a page in a book, Apple has made their version of the toolbar for iPhone to appear more book-like as well. In contrast to toolbars, which can display a clutter of different icons, navigation bars are limited to include a page title (e.g., "Saved Messages"), directional buttons to parent pages, and text buttons for context-sensitive functions such as turning on the speakerphone or clearing a list of items. Navigation bars can also support controls to add tabbed buttons such as the "All" and "Missed" call buttons when viewing recent calls.

Creating a Navigation Bar

To create a navigation bar, instantiate it as an object and call its `initWithFrame` method—just like a `UIView`.

```
UINavigationBar *navBar = [ [UINavigationBar alloc]
    initWithFrame: CGRectMake(0, 0, 320, 48)
];
```

The above creates a navigation bar 48 pixels high (the default) at position 0x0 (the upper-left corner of its parent view). This is the general convention, but a navigation bar can be created anywhere within the window. By using a different vertical offset, you can place the navigation bar at the bottom of the window or underneath another navigation bar.

To know when something happens on the navigation bar, such as a button press, use the navigation bar's *delegate*. A delegate is an object that acts on behalf of another object. By setting the navigation bar's delegate to `self`, you can have it send events such as button presses to the object that created the navigation bar.

```
[ navBar setDelegate: self ];
```

Animations are simple fade transitions that occur when transitioning from an old set of buttons to a new set—for example, if a button is changed after it is pressed. Calling `enableAnimation` uses these smoother transitions instead of an instantaneous change.

```
[ navBar enableAnimation ];
```

Once the navigation bar has been created and initialized, its title and buttons can then be configured. These can be changed even after the navigation bar is displayed; the bar will change to accommodate its new settings.

Setting the title

The navigation title appears as large white text centered in the middle of the bar. The title is frequently used to convey to the end user what sort of information is being displayed, for example, "Saved Messages."

The title is created as a UINavigationItem object. This is the base class for anything that natively attaches to a navigation bar, including buttons and other objects. When the title is added to the navigation bar, its UINavigationItem object is pushed onto it like an object on a stack. Because of this, you'll want to store a pointer to the title inside the program somewhere. This will let you go back and change the title without having to pull it off the stack first, which would reconfigure the entire navigation bar.

```
UINavigationItem *navItem = [ [ UINavigationItem alloc ]
    initWithTitle:@"My Example" ];
[ navBar pushNavigationItem: navItem ];
```

Here, navItem points to a newly created UINavigationItem object and is assigned the title "My Example." When the user does something that would cause the title to change, navItem can be changed to something else.

```
[ navItem setTitle: @"Another Example" ]
```

Buttons and button styles

Buttons can be added to the left and/or right sides of the navigation bar. Because space is limited, the only buttons that should be added are those for functions specific to the page being displayed. At any time, the navigation bar's buttons can be changed. With animations enabled, the user will see a smooth, animated transition to the new set of buttons.

Using the example navBar object created earlier, add two buttons to the navigation bar, one labeled "Good" and one "Evil."

```
[ navBar showLeftButton:@"Good" withStyle: 0
        rightButton:@"Evil" withStyle: 0 ];
```

If you need only one button, you can replace the other button's string with nil. For example, if you wanted to only provide the user with "Evil" as an option:

```
[ navBar showLeftButton:nil withStyle: 0
        rightButton:@"Evil" withStyle: 0 ];
```

In addition to setting button titles, UIKit also allows for different styles. For instance, notice that when you push the Speaker button in the iPhone's phone application, the button turns blue. Some buttons also appear to have an arrow shape, conveying the concept of "go back" to the user. By changing the value for the withStyle parameter in the method call previously shown, you can choose from one of four different button styles. Pay special attention to the style numbers, which are zero-indexed.

Style	Description
0	Default style, just a plain gray button
1	Colors the button red, useful for warning toggles such as Delete
2	Creates the button in the shape of a left (back) arrow
3	Colors the button blue, useful for emphasis or general toggles such as Speaker

Apple may add additional styles in future releases of iPhone software, but for now, any other value defers back to the default style.

If you don't plan on using styles at all, there's a shortcut method to creating navigation bar buttons that gets rid of some of the work involved:

```
[ navBar showButtonsWithLeftTitle:@"Back"
                        rightTitle: nil
                          leftBack: YES ];
```

This method can be used to create a quick set of buttons with no custom styles except for the back arrow button; it is specified by passing YES for the leftBack parameter.

Navigation bar style

The navigation bar itself can be displayed in one of a few different styles. The default style is the standard gray appearance. Three different styles are presently supported.

Style	Description
0	Default style, gray gradient background with white text
1	Solid black background with white text
2	Transparent black background with white text

The style is set using the call setBarStyle:

```
[ navBar setBarStyle: 0 ];
```

Displaying the Navigation Bar

Once you've laid out the initial look for your navigation bar, it's time to display it within your application. Navigation bars are attached to a view object, such as the main view you created in the last example.

```
[ self addSubview: navBar ];
```

If you would like to hide the navigation bar, just pull it off the view:

```
[ navBar removeFromSuperview ];
```

When you're finished with the navigation bar entirely, it can be disposed of by releasing it. This can be done in the view class's dealloc method:

```
[ navBar release ];
```

Intercepting Button Presses

At this point, your navigation bar is displayed on the screen, but the buttons do nothing. Earlier, the navigation bar's delegate was set to self, the calling view. Because the calling view is acting on the navigation bar's events, it will need the ability to intercept button presses.

To do this, a method named buttonClicked must be overridden. As you'll see in the coming chapters, many different types of objects have a buttonClicked method, but take different arguments. Objective-C supports *polymorphism*, which allows the developer to support multiple methods sharing the same name, but with different argument types. The runtime will choose the most appropriate version of the method to call.

As the view class has already been set as the delegate for the navigation bar, it will be receiving all button click events that occur on it. This requires that the view class have a method named buttonClicked accepting the same arguments as if it were the navigation bar itself.

```
- (void)navigationBar:(UINavigationBar *)navbar
    buttonClicked:(int)button;
```

The buttonClicked method in the view class gets notified as if it belonged to the navigation bar. It is called with the same arguments that the navigation bar's buttonClicked method would be called; a pointer to the navigation bar and an integer identifying the button number that was pressed. When using left and right navigation buttons, the value for button is either a 1 or a 0, signifying the left or right button, respectively.

```
- (void)navigationBar:(UINavigationBar *)navbar buttonClicked:(int)button
{
    switch(button) {
        case 1:
            /* Left button handled here */
            break;
        case 0:
            /* Right button handled here */
            break;
    }
}
```

Disabling Buttons

If at any point you would like to disable an existing navigation bar button, you have two options. You can make another call to one of the show-button methods (showLeftButton or showButtonsWithLeftTitle) using nil to make the button disappear. Alternatively, if you would like the button to remain visible, but be disabled so that the user can't press it, use the setButton method:

```
[ navBar setButton: 0 enabled: NO ];
```

Just as in the buttonClicked method, the button number used here corresponds with either the left (1) or the right (0) button.

Adding a Segmented Control

Controls are small, self-contained user interface components that can be used by various UIKit classes. They can be glued to many different types of objects, allowing the developer to add additional interaction to a window. One common control found in the navigation bars of Apple's preloaded applications is the segmented control.

You'll notice in many preloaded applications that Apple has added buttons to further separate the display of information. For example, the navigation bar in the iTunes WiFi Store application sports "New Releases," "What's Hot," and "Genres" buttons at the top. These further separate the user's music selection choice. Segmented controls are useful for any such situation where an overabundance of data would best be organized into separate tabs.

An example of setting up such a control with two segments follows:

```
UISegmentedControl *segCtl = [ [ UISegmentedControl alloc ]
    initWithFrame:CGRectMake(70.0, 8.0, 180.0, 30.0)
    withStyle: 2
    withItems: NULL ];
[ segCtl insertSegment:0 withTitle:@"All" animated: TRUE ];
[ segCtl insertSegment:1 withTitle:@"Missed" animated: TRUE ];
[ segCtl setDelegate:self ];
```

The control is then added to the navigation bar in the same way the navigation bar was added to the main view, by adding it as a subview. Only this time, the segmented control is added to the navigation bar. This means the offset of the display region is in relation to the navigation bar, not the enclosing view or the window.

```
[ navBar addSubview: segCtl ];
```

Each button in a segmented control is referred to as a segment. The selected segment can be accessed with a call to the selectedSegment method of the control itself.

```
int selectedSegment = [ segCtl selectedSegment ];
```

Chapter 7 offers more on controls.

Example: Mute Button for the Spouse

Someone is designing a mute button to mute their spouse during arguments. In this example application, a navigation bar will be created in an application's view and assigned a Mute button. When the button is selected, the button will be changed to red and will also change the title to reflect that the spouse is muted.

Examples 3-7 and 3-8 can be built using the tool chain on the following command line:

```
$ arm-apple-darwin-gcc -o MyExample MyExample.m -lobjc \
    -framework CoreFoundation -framework Foundation -framework UIKit
```

Example 3-7. Navigation bar example (MyExample.h)

```
#import <CoreFoundation/CoreFoundation.h>
#import <UIKit/UIKit.h>
#import <UIKit/UINavigationBar.h>
#import <UIKit/UINavigationItem.h>

@interface MainView : UIView
{
        UINavigationBar  *navBar;     /* Our navigation bar */
        UINavigationItem *navItem;    /* Navigation bar title */
        BOOL              isMuted;    /* Is mute turned on? */
}

- (id)initWithFrame:(CGRect)frame;
- (void)dealloc;
- (UINavigationBar *)createNavBar:(CGRect)rect;
- (void)setNavBar;
- (void)navigationBar:(UINavigationBar *)navbar buttonClicked:(int)button;
@end

@interface MyApp : UIApplication
{
    UIWindow *window;
    MainView *mainView;
}

- (void)applicationDidFinishLaunching:(NSNotification *)aNotification;
@end
```

Example 3-8. Navigation bar example (MyExample.m)

```
#import "MyExample.h"

int main(int argc, char **argv)
{
    NSAutoreleasePool *autoreleasePool = [
        [ NSAutoreleasePool alloc ] init
    ];
    int returnCode = UIApplicationMain(argc, argv, [ MyApp class ]);
    [ autoreleasePool release ];
    return returnCode;
}

@implementation MyApp

- (void)applicationDidFinishLaunching:(NSNotification *)aNotification {
    window = [ [ UIWindow alloc ] initWithContentRect:
        [ UIHardware fullScreenApplicationContentRect ]
    ];
```

Example 3-8. Navigation bar example (MyExample.m) (continued)

```
    CGRect rect = [ UIHardware fullScreenApplicationContentRect ];
    rect.origin.x = rect.origin.y = 0.0f;

    mainView = [ [ MainView alloc ] initWithFrame: rect ];

    [ window setContentView: mainView ];
    [ window orderFront: self ];
    [ window makeKey: self ];
    [ window _setHidden: NO ];
}
@end

@implementation MainView
- (id)initWithFrame:(CGRect)rect {
    if ((self == [ super initWithFrame: rect ]) != nil) {
        isMuted = NO;

        navBar = [ self createNavBar: rect ];

        /* Update the navBar for the first time */
        [ self setNavBar ];

        [ self addSubview: navBar ];
    }

    return self;
}

- (void)dealloc
{
    [ navBar release ];
    [ navItem release ];
    [ self dealloc ];
    [ super dealloc ];
}

- (UINavigationBar *)createNavBar:(CGRect)rect {
    UINavigationBar *newNav = [ [UINavigationBar alloc]
      initWithFrame:
      CGRectMake(rect.origin.x, rect.origin.y, rect.size.width, 48.0)
    ];

    [ newNav setDelegate: self ];
    [ newNav enableAnimation ];

    /* Add our title */
    navItem = [ [UINavigationItem alloc]
        initWithTitle:@"My Example" ];
    [ newNav pushNavigationItem: navItem ];
```

Example 3-8. Navigation bar example (MyExample.m) (continued)

```objc
    return newNav;
}

- (void)setNavBar
{
    if (isMuted == YES) {
        [ navItem setTitle: @"Spouse (Muted)" ];
        [ navBar showLeftButton:nil withStyle: 0
                   rightButton:@"Mute" withStyle: 1 ];
    } else {
        [ navItem setTitle: @"Spouse" ];
        [ navBar showLeftButton:nil withStyle: 0
                   rightButton:@"Mute" withStyle: 0 ];
    }
}

- (void)navigationBar:(UINavigationBar *)navbar buttonClicked:(int)button
{
    if (button == 0) /* Right button */
    {
        if (isMuted == YES) /* Toggle isMuted */
            isMuted = NO;
        else
            isMuted = YES;

        [ self setNavBar ]; /* Update navbar buttons */
    }
}

@end
```

What's Going On

This example shows you how to accomplish the user-interface portion of this application. You'll have to write the source code to do the actual spouse muting yourself. Here's how the example works:

1. The application instantiates through the main( ) function and returns an instance of the application, just as in previous examples.

2. A window is created with mainView as the content. The statement creating the MainView object also calls its initWithFrame method. This creates the view and navigation bar, and sets the value for isMuted to NO so that the application starts out in an unmuted state.

3. The initWithFrame method proceeds to call the setNavBar method to set up the navigation bar in whatever configuration is presently reflected by the state of isMuted. The first call sets up the buttons and title for the NO value.

4. When the user taps on mute, the `buttonClicked` method gets called in the view (the bar's delegate). This toggles the `isMuted` variable and then calls `setNavBar` again, which resets the navigation bar's configuration. This transitions the button to red (button style 1) and sets the title to include `Muted` in the text.

5. If the user taps on the mute button again, the `buttonClicked` method is called again, resetting `isMuted` back to `NO`. It then updates the navigation bar once more with a call to `setNavBar`.

Further Study

With the example snippets from this section and the previous examples, try having a little fun with this example:

- Try changing this code to support the Good and Evil buttons example, so that pressing the Good button will cause it to turn blue, and pressing the Evil button will cause it to turn red.

- Take the `UITextView` code in Example 3-2 and add two buttons, one for HTML and one for Text. Tapping each button should change the text view to display the file in the corresponding format.

- Check out the *UINavigationBar.h* and *UINavigationItem.h* prototypes in the tool chain's include directory. These can be found in */usr/local/arm-apple-darwin/ include/UIKit/*. Experiment with some of the different methods available.

Transition Views

If there's one thing Apple is well known for, it's their devotion to aesthetics in their user interfaces. The effect of sliding pages left and right gives the user a sense of the flow of data through an application, or a sense of "forward" and "back." Even applications lacking a book type of structure can appreciate the smooth slide and fade transitions offered by UIKit. Transition views are objects that allow the current view on the screen to be swapped out smoothly and replaced by another view, with very little programming on the developer's part.

Creating a Transition

Transition views inherit from `UIView`, so they have most of the properties of a regular view, including a frame. To create a transition, the display region belonging to the view is passed to the transition's `initWithFrame` method.

```
UITransitionView *transitionView = [ [ UITransitionView alloc ]
    initWithFrame: viewRect ];
```

The same transition view can be used for multiple transition calls and even multiple transition types, so generally only one transition view is needed for a particular display region. If a navigation bar is being used, you must account for its presence by subtracting its height and coordinates from the transition view's display region:

```
UITransitionView *transitionView = [ [ UITransitionView alloc ]
    initWithFrame:
    CGRectMake(viewRect.origin.x, viewRect.origin.y + 48.0,
        viewRect.size.width, viewRect.size.height - 48.0)
];
```

Once the transition has been created, it is added to the view in the same way as other view objects, as a sublayer.

```
[ self addSubview: transitionView ];
```

Calling a Transition

To effect a transition, call the class's `transition` method. You'll supply the transition style and pointers to the two views between which you are transitioning.

```
[ transitionView transition: 0
    fromView: myOldView
    toView: myNewView
];
```

Alternatively, a transition can be called supplying only the new view, not the old one. But be forewarned that this appears to work with only some transitions. Those that do not support this behavior automatically default to using no transition.

```
[ transitionView transition: 0 toView: myNewView ];
```

UIKit presently supports 10 distinct transitions. A single transition view can be called repeatedly with different styles, listed in the following table. This allows developers to choose the best transition depending on the particular action at hand, without having to worry about creating a new object for every possible transition they might want to perform.

Style	Description
0	No transition/instant transition
1	Pages scroll left
2	Pages scroll right
3	Pages scroll up
4	Old page peels up, new page peels down
5	Old page peels down, new page peels up
6	New page fades over old page
7	Pages scroll down
8	New page peels up over old page
9	New page peels down over old page

Example: Page Flipping

The best example of using page transitions is to illustrate reading a book. In this example, 10 pages of text are created using the UITextView object covered earlier in this chapter. Using a navigation bar, the user is presented with two buttons to navigate to the previous or next page. Depending on which direction the user has chosen, a different transition is used. When the user reached either end of the book, the corresponding navigation button is disabled to keep them from going any further.

Examples 3-9 and 3-10 can be compiled using the tool chain on the following command line:

```
$ arm-apple-darwin-gcc -o MyExample MyExample.m -lobjc \
    -framework CoreFoundation -framework Foundation -framework UIKit
```

Example 3-9. Page-flipping example (MyExample.h)

```
#import <CoreFoundation/CoreFoundation.h>
#import <UIKit/UIKit.h>
#import <UIKit/UINavigationBar.h>
#import <UIKit/UINavigationItem.h>
#import <UIKit/UITransitionView.h>
#import <UIKit/UITextView.h>

#define MAX_PAGES 10

@interface MainView : UIView
{
    UINavigationBar     *navBar;     /* Our navigation bar */
    UINavigationItem    *navItem;    /* Navigation bar title */
    UITransitionView    *transView;  /* Our transition */
    int                 pageNum;     /* Current page number */

    /* Some pages to scroll through */
    UITextView          *textPage[MAX_PAGES];
}

- (id)initWithFrame:(CGRect)frame;
- (void)dealloc;
- (UINavigationBar *)createNavBar:(CGRect)rect;
- (void)setNavBar;
- (void)navigationBar:(UINavigationBar *)navbar buttonClicked:(int)button;
- (void)flipTo:(int)page;

@end

@interface MyApp : UIApplication
{
    UIWindow *window;
    MainView *mainView;
}
```

Example 3-9. Page-flipping example (MyExample.h) (continued)

```
- (void)applicationDidFinishLaunching:(NSNotification *)aNotification;
@end
```

Example 3-10. Page-flipping example (MyExample.m)

```
#import "MyExample.h"

int main(int argc, char **argv)
{
    NSAutoreleasePool *autoreleasePool = [
        [ NSAutoreleasePool alloc ] init
    ];
    int returnCode = UIApplicationMain(argc, argv, [ MyApp class ]);
    [ autoreleasePool release ];
    return returnCode;
}

@implementation MyApp

- (void)applicationDidFinishLaunching:(NSNotification *)aNotification {
    window = [ [ UIWindow alloc ] initWithContentRect:
        [ UIHardware fullScreenApplicationContentRect ]
    ];

    CGRect rect = [ UIHardware fullScreenApplicationContentRect ];
    rect.origin.x = rect.origin.y = 0.0f;

    mainView = [ [ MainView alloc ] initWithFrame: rect ];

    [ window setContentView: mainView ];
    [ window orderFront: self ];
    [ window makeKey: self ];
    [ window _setHidden: NO ];
}
@end

@implementation MainView
- (id)initWithFrame:(CGRect)rect {
    if ((self == [ super initWithFrame: rect ]) != nil) {
        CGRect viewRect;
        int i;

        /* Create a new view port below the navigation bar */
        viewRect = CGRectMake(rect.origin.x, rect.origin.y + 48.0,
            rect.size.width, rect.size.height - 48.0);

        /* Set our start page */
        pageNum = MAX_PAGES / 2;

        /* Create ten UITextView objects as pages in our book */

        for(i=0;i<MAX_PAGES;i++) {
```

Example 3-10. Page-flipping example (MyExample.m) (continued)

```
              textPage[i] = [ [ UITextView alloc ]
                  initWithFrame: rect ];
              [ textPage[i] setText: [ [ NSString alloc ]
                  initWithFormat: @"Some text for page %d", i+1 ] ];
          }

          /* Create a navigation bar with 'Prev' and 'Next' buttons */
          navBar = [ self createNavBar: rect ];
          [ self setNavBar ];
          [ self addSubview: navBar ];

          /* Create our transition view */
          transView = [ [ UITransitionView alloc ]
                  initWithFrame: viewRect ];
          [ self addSubview: transView ];

          /* Transition to the first page */
          [ self flipTo: pageNum ];
      }

    return self;
}

- (void)dealloc
{
    [ navBar release ];
    [ navItem release ];
    [ self dealloc ];
    [ super dealloc ];
}

- (UINavigationBar *)createNavBar:(CGRect)rect {
    UINavigationBar *newNav = [ [UINavigationBar alloc]
      initWithFrame:
      CGRectMake(rect.origin.x, rect.origin.y, rect.size.width, 48.0)
    ];

    [ newNav setDelegate: self ];
    [ newNav enableAnimation ];

    /* Add our title */
    navItem = [ [UINavigationItem alloc]
        initWithTitle:@"My Example" ];
    [ newNav pushNavigationItem: navItem ];

    [ newNav showLeftButton:@"Prev"  withStyle: 0
            rightButton:@"Next" withStyle: 0 ];

    return newNav;
}

- (void)setNavBar
```

Example 3-10. Page-flipping example (MyExample.m) (continued)

```
{

    /* Enable or disable our page buttons */

    if (pageNum == 1)
        [ navBar setButton: 1 enabled: NO ];
    else
        [ navBar setButton: 1 enabled: YES ];

    if (pageNum == MAX_PAGES)
        [ navBar setButton: 0 enabled: NO ];
    else
        [ navBar setButton: 0 enabled: YES ];
}

- (void)navigationBar:(UINavigationBar *)navbar buttonClicked:(int)button
{
    /* Next Page */
    if (button == 0)
    {
        [ self flipTo: pageNum+1 ];
    }

    /* Prev Page */
    else {
        [ self flipTo: pageNum-1 ];
    }

}

- (void)flipTo:(int)page {
    int transitionNum; /* What transition number should be used? */

    if (page < pageNum)
        transitionNum = 2;
    else if (page > pageNum)
        transitionNum = 1;
    else
        transitionNum = 0;

    [ transView transition: transitionNum
      fromView: textPage[pageNum-1] toView: textPage[page-1] ];

    pageNum = page;

    [ self setNavBar ];
}

@end
```

What's Going On

Here's how the page-flipping example works:

1. When the application instantiates, a `MainView` object is created and its `initWithFrame` method is called. This creates ten `UITextView` objects to serve as reading page examples, and then creates the navigation bar and one transition object. Finally, an example method named `flipTo` is called, which is responsible for flipping to the page number specified.

2. The `flipTo` method decides on a transition style, based on whether the page being flipped to is the next page or the previous one.

3. After deciding which transition to use, the `flipTo` method calls the transition view to do the work of moving to the desired page. It then sets the active page number, which is a variable in the class.

4. When the user presses the `Prev` or `Next` navigation buttons, the `buttonClicked` method gets called with a pointer to the navigation bar and the button number. From here, the `flipTo` method is called again to transition to the new page and disable either navigation button if it has reached one end of the book.

Further Study

Here are some productive things you can do with the page-flipping example:

- Experiment with the different transition styles available and think of actions where you would want to use each transition.

- Use the page-flip example and fill in each box with a frame from an ASCII doodle. Now, write a rapid transition across all 10 pages to create an ASCII animation that acts like an old style movie projector.

- Check out the *UITransitionView.h* prototypes in your tool chain's include directory. You'll find it in */usr/local/arm-apple-darwin/include/UIKit/*.

Alert Sheets

The iPhone is a relatively small device with limited screen space and no stylus. This means users are going to fumble with their fingers and tap buttons on accident. When this happens, a well-written application prompts the user for confirmation before just blowing away important data. On a desktop computer, applications pop up windows when they need attention. On the iPhone, an alert sheet is slid up from the bottom, graying out the rest of the screen until the user chooses an option. The term "sheet" continues the page metaphor that Apple uses for the iPhone.

Creating an Alert Sheet

The alert sheet is an object that can be instantiated on top of any view, and a single view can host a number of different alert sheets. A basic alert sheet consists of a title, body text, and whatever choices the user should be presented with. It is instantiated in the same way as other UIView objects, using an initWithFrame method. Because alert sheets appear at the bottom, the window's origin can begin halfway down the screen (Y = 240).

```
UIAlertSheet *alertSheet = [ [ UIAlertSheet alloc ]
    initWithFrame: CGRectMake(0, 240, 320, 240) ];
[ alertSheet setTitle:@"Computer doesn't like people" ];
[ alertSheet setBodyText: [ NSString stringWithFormat:
    @"I did not complete your request because I don't like humans." ]
];
[ alertSheet setDelegate: self ];
```

Alert sheets can stretch their frame to accommodate whatever elements it's required to hold, so a static 320×240 rectangle should be sufficient for standard alert sheets.

Like navigation bars, alert sheets can be set to support one of three different styles.

Style	Description
0	Default style, gray gradient background with white text
1	Solid black background with white text
2	Transparent black background with white text

The style can be set with a call to setAlertSheetStyle.

```
[ alertSheet setAlertSheetStyle: 0 ];
```

Alert Sheet Buttons

On rare occasion, it makes sense to display an alert sheet without buttons—for example, to display a progress bar (explained in Chapter 7). In most cases, however, alert sheets are displayed for the purpose of prompting the user. An alert sheet can accommodate as many buttons as can fit on the screen. To add a button, call the alert sheet's addButtonWithTitle method:

```
[ alertSheet addButtonWithTitle:@"OK" ];
```

Destructive buttons

Buttons that confirm permanent deletion or some other action that could result in data being destroyed should use what the API refers to as a *destructive button*. Destructive buttons appear in bright red to alert the user that they are about to perform a significant action that cannot be undone.

The setDestructiveButton method is used to mark a button as destructive. It accepts a button object as its input, and because addButtonWithTitle returns a pointer to the new button, the setDestructiveButton method can be wrapped around it.

```
[ alertSheet setDestructiveButton: [ alertSheet
              addButtonWithTitle:@"Confirm Delete" ] ];
```

Displaying the Alert Sheet

Once you've set up the text and buttons to be displayed, you can then display the sheet to the user. Five different methods can be called depending on the behavior desired. Each of these methods accepts a class derived as a UIView, which should be a pointer to whatever view class affected by the alert sheet.

```
[ alertSheet presentSheetFromAboveView: myView ];
[ alertSheet presentSheetFromBehindView: myView ];
[ alertSheet presentSheetFromButtonBar: buttonBar ];
[ alertSheet presentSheetInView: myView ];
[ alertSheet presentSheetToAboveView: myView ];
```

The most common way to call an alert sheet is with presentSheetInView, which can be called from within a view using self as an argument.

Intercepting Button Presses

When the alert sheet has been displayed, control returns to the program. As seen earlier in the chapter, many objects use a callback method named buttonClicked whenever the user taps a button. This allows the application to continue running in the background, to be interrupted only when something actually happens.

The prototype for the alert sheet callback method is below. If the alert sheet's delegate has been set to the calling view, it is the calling view that will be expected to respond to a button click.

```
- (void)alertSheet:(UIAlertSheet *)sheet buttonClicked:(int)button;
```

The buttonClicked method is called with a pointer to the selected sheet and the index of the button. Buttons are numbered from topmost position to bottom, beginning with 1 (they are not zero-indexed like other values).

```
- (void)alertSheet:(UIAlertSheet *)sheet buttonClicked:(int)button {
    if (sheet == alertSheet) {
        switch(button) {
            case 1:
                /* Top-most button was clicked */
                break;
            case 2:
                /* Second-to-top button was clicked */
                break;
        }
    }
}
```

Dismissing an Alert Sheet

Finally, after processing a button press, the alert sheet should vanish—unless, of course, the application has a reason for the user to press more than one button. Use the dismiss method to make the sheet go away:

```
[ sheet dismiss ];
```

Example: End-of-the-World Button

The government thought it would be more convenient for the President to carry an iPhone around instead of a suitcase with a big red button. One of their chief programmers conveniently wrote *End-of-the-World.app*, which the President can press at any time to launch nukes and end the world (or at least start a pie fight). The problem, however, is that he's almost pressed it accidentally many times. You've been contracted to add a confirmation sheet to it—just in case the President didn't really mean to end the world.

Our example application displays a navigation bar with an End World button. When pressed, it will first confirm before ending the world as we know it. Polymorphism will be illustrated with the presence of two buttonClicked methods. When the navigation bar's button is pressed, the correct buttonClicked method will be automatically called.

Examples 3-11 and 3-12 can be built using the tool chain on the following command line:

```
$ arm-apple-darwin-gcc -o MyExample MyExample.m -lobjc \
    -framework CoreFoundation -framework Foundation -framework UIKit
```

Example 3-11. Alert sheet example (MyExample.h)

```
#import <CoreFoundation/CoreFoundation.h>
#import <UIKit/UIKit.h>
#import <UIKit/UIAlertSheet.h>
#import <UIKit/UINavigationBar.h>

@interface MainView : UIView
{
    UIAlertSheet    *endWorldSheet;
    UIAlertSheet    *deniedSheet;
    UINavigationBar *navBar;
}

- (id)initWithFrame:(CGRect)frame;
- (void)dealloc;
@end

@interface MyApp : UIApplication
{
    UIWindow *window;
```

Example 3-11. Alert sheet example (MyExample.h) (continued)

```
    MainView *mainView;
}

- (void)applicationDidFinishLaunching:(NSNotification *)aNotification;
@end
```

Example 3-12. Alert sheet example (MyExample.m)

```
#import "MyExample.h"

int main(int argc, char **argv)
{
    NSAutoreleasePool *autoreleasePool = [
        [ NSAutoreleasePool alloc ] init
    ];
    int returnCode = UIApplicationMain(argc, argv, [ MyApp class ]);
    [ autoreleasePool release ];
    return returnCode;
}

@implementation MyApp

- (void)applicationDidFinishLaunching:(NSNotification *)aNotification {
    window = [ [ UIWindow alloc ] initWithContentRect:
        [ UIHardware fullScreenApplicationContentRect ]
    ];

    CGRect rect = [ UIHardware fullScreenApplicationContentRect ];
    rect.origin.x = rect.origin.y = 0.0f;

    mainView = [ [ MainView alloc ] initWithFrame: rect ];

    [ window setContentView: mainView ];
    [ window orderFront: self ];
    [ window makeKey: self ];
    [ window _setHidden: NO ];
}
@end

@implementation MainView
- (id)initWithFrame:(CGRect)rect {
    if ((self == [ super initWithFrame: rect ]) != nil) {

        /* Create a button to end the world */

        navBar = [ [UINavigationBar alloc] initWithFrame:
            CGRectMake(rect.origin.x, rect.origin.y, rect.size.width, 48.0f)
        ];
        [ navBar setDelegate: self ];
        [ navBar enableAnimation ];
        [ navBar showLeftButton:nil withStyle: 0
                    rightButton:@"End World" withStyle: 1 ];
```

Example 3-12. Alert sheet example (MyExample.m) (continued)

```
        [ self addSubview: navBar ];
    }

    return self;
}

- (void)alertSheet:(UIAlertSheet *)sheet buttonClicked:(int)button
{
    if (sheet == endWorldSheet) {
        if (button == 1) {

            /* Oops, Access Denied */
            deniedSheet = [ [ UIAlertSheet alloc ] initWithFrame:
                CGRectMake(0, 240, 320, 240)
            ];
            [ deniedSheet setTitle: @"Access Denied" ];
            [ deniedSheet setBodyText: @"Sorry, you must be super-user to end the world"
];
            [ deniedSheet addButtonWithTitle:@"OK" ];
            [ deniedSheet setDelegate: self ];
            [ deniedSheet presentSheetInView: self ];
        }
    }

    [ sheet dismiss ];
}

- (void)navigationBar:(UINavigationBar *)navbar buttonClicked:(int)button
{
    /* Ask about the end of the world */

    endWorldSheet = [ [ UIAlertSheet alloc ] initWithFrame:
        CGRectMake(0, 240, 320, 240)
    ];
    [ endWorldSheet setTitle: @"Please Confirm" ];
    [ endWorldSheet setBodyText:@"I noticed you are trying to end the world. Are you sure
you want to do this?" ];
    [ endWorldSheet setDestructiveButton:
        [ endWorldSheet addButtonWithTitle:@"End World" ]
    ];
    [ endWorldSheet addButtonWithTitle:@"Cancel" ];
    [ endWorldSheet setDelegate: self ];
    [ endWorldSheet presentSheetInView: self ];

}


- (void)dealloc
{
    [ self dealloc ];
    [ super dealloc ];
```

Example 3-12. Alert sheet example (MyExample.m) (continued)

```
}

@end
```

What's Going On

The process flow for this program works in the following fashion.

1. When the application is instantiates, a MainView object is created and its initWithFrame method is called. This creates the view and navigation bar and displays them to the user.

2. When the user presses the End World button, the object notifies its delegate's buttonClicked method. Because the navigation bar object is expecting to pass a pointer to itself, the buttonClicked method that accepts a UINavigationBar * parameter is the one that gets called (based on the rules of polymorphism).

3. The buttonClicked method creates an alert sheet called endWorldSheet and presents it to the user. It immediately returns control, but causes the contents of the view to be dimmed and inaccessible to the user.

4. When the user presses a button on the alert sheet, the alert sheet object notifies its delegate's buttonClicked method. Because the alert sheet class passes a UIAlertSheet * parameter, its corresponding version of buttonClicked is called.

5. The method compares the pointer passed to it with the pointer to endWorldSheet. If they are the same pointer, the method knows that a button in that sheet was pressed. It then looks at the index number of the button and takes the appropriate action.

6. If the user confirmed by pressing End World, the buttonClicked method itself creates and displays a new alert sheet informing the user that an error has occurred.

7. When the user presses the OK button, the same buttonClicked method is called again, only this time, the pointer of the alert sheet passed in will be that of deniedSheet. The method summarily ignores this and simply dismisses the sheet without taking any further action.

Further Study

Play around with alert sheets for a bit to get a feel for how they work:

- Experiment with adding different buttons to the alert sheet. How many buttons will fit on the screen? How much text can they hold?

- Create an alert sheet with no buttons—one that informs the user a file is loading. Use an NSTimer to wait 10 seconds and then dismiss the sheet without using the buttonClicked method at all.

- Check out the *UIAlertSheet.h* prototypes in your tool chain's include directory. You'll find it in */usr/local/arm-apple-darwin/include/UIKit/*. Experiment with some of the less-documented methods.

Tables

Tables are the foundation for most types of selectable lists on the iPhone. Voicemail, recent calls, and even email all use the feature-rich UITable class to display their lists of items. In addition to being a basic list selector, the UITable class includes built-in functionality to add disclosures, swipe-to-delete, animations, labels, and even images.

Creating the Table

A table has three primary components: the table itself, table columns, and table cells (the individual rows in a table). The table's data is queried from a table's *data binding*. A data binding is an interface used by the table to query information about what data to display, such as filenames, email messages, etc. The *data source* is an object that responds to this query. When the table is created, a data source must be attached to it in order for the table to display anything. It gets called whenever the table is reloaded or new cells are scrolled into view and tells the table which columns and rows to display, along with the data within them.

Subclassing UITable

For most specialized uses, the table can serve as its own data source. This allows the table class and the table's data to be wrapped cleanly into a single class. To do this, subclass the UITable object to create a new class for your data. In the following example, a subclass named MyTable is created. The base class methods used to initialize and destroy the object are overridden to provide the table portion of the class:

```
@interface MyTable : UITable
{

}
-(id)initWithFrame:(struct CGRect)rect;
-(void) dealloc;
```

To add the data source portion of the class, two methods are used to make the table's data binding load data: numberOfRowsInTable and cellForRow. Because the table is acting as its own data source, you must write these methods into your subclass, where the methods will be responsible for returning column and row data for the table.

```
- (int)numberOfRowsInTable:(UITable *)_table;
- (UITableCell *)table:(UITable *)table
    cellForRow:(int)row
    column:(UITableColumn *)col;
```

We'll look at these methods later in the section "Data binding."

Overriding UITable methods

When creating a subclass of UITable, the initialization and destructor methods should be overridden. This enables the subclass to define its own columns and style when it's created, and properly release any resources it creates for itself.

The initialization method for a UITable object is initWithFrame:

```
- (id)initWithFrame:(struct CGRect)rect {
    if ((self == [ super initWithFrame: rect ]) != nil) {

        /* Add additional initialization code here */
    }
}
```

Because the table is acting as its own data source, the initWithFrame method can be used to define the table's columns. A column is created as a UITableColumn class and has its own title, identifier, and width inside the table. The UITableColumn object is also used by many derivative classes such as pickers, discussed in Chapter 7.

```
UITableColumn *myColumn = [ [ UITableColumn alloc ]
    initWithTitle: @"Column 1"
    identifier:@"column1"
    width: rect.size.width
];
[ self addTableColumn: myColumn ];
```

To create a self-contained table class, the UITable object can be designated as its own data source. Issue setDataSource to bind self as the data source.

```
[ self setDataSource: self ];
```

Override the dealloc method so you can add code to free any resources that should be disposed of when the object is destroyed. When a MyTable object is disposed of, the dealloc method should release its columns and any other resource it has allocated. It will also need to call its superclass's dealloc method, to free any resources created internally by the UITable class.

```
- (void)dealloc {
    [ myColumn release ];
    [ super dealloc ];
}
```

Data binding

The data binding for a UITable consists of two methods to provide the row data for the table, as mentioned earlier in the section "Subclassing UITable." The numberOfRowsInTable method simply returns an integer reflecting the number of rows of data for the table. This value is used by the table object to set the number of rows.

```
- (int)numberOfRowsInTable:(UITable *)_table {
    return 3;
}
```

The second method, cellForRow, returns the individual rows of the table. It is called for every row whenever the row is brought into view. Individual rows are derived from the UITableCell class. The following example defines a cellForRow method that creates a cell from the UITableCell class, sets its title based simply on the row number, and returns the cell.

```
- (UITableCell *)table:(UITable *)table
  cellForRow:(int)row
  column:(UITableColumn *)col
{
    UISimpleTableCell *cell = [ [ UISimpleTableCell alloc ] init ];
    NSString *title;

    title = [ [ NSString alloc ] initWithFormat: @"Row %d", row ];
    [ cell setTitle: title ];
    return [ cell autorelease ];
}
```

This simple cell is a text-only cell containing a title, separator, and optional disclosure (described shortly). Because these properties are set for each row cell, any cell in a table can be specially formatted to meet the needs of the data.

Labels

Labels are miniature view classes that can be added to table cells to further augment the table cell with decorated text. Different classes of labels exist for different purposes. For instance, a web view label appears as a gray transparent oval containing text. In the following example, a UIWebViewLabel class is created with offsets that will cause it to appear in the upper-left corner of the cell.

```
UIWebViewLabel *label = [ [ UIWebViewLabel alloc ] initWithFrame:
    CGRectMake(0.0, 3.0f, 320.0, 20.0) ];
[ label setText: @"My UIWebView" ];
[ cell addSubview: label ];
```

The following label classes are available.

Class	Description
UITextLabel	Displays simple text in its view region
UITextLabelField	Provides a text entry window where users can enter text
UIDateLabel	Displays a date in its view region
UIWebViewLabel	Displays text within a gray transparent surface

Disclosures

Disclosures are icons appearing at the right side of a table cell to disclose that there is another level of information to be displayed when the cell is selected. These are commonly used on desktop in interfaces such as iTunes, where the user first selects a genre, then artist, and finally, a song.

To enable the disclosure for a particular table cell, use the cell's `setShowDisclosure` method:

```
[ cell setShowDisclosure: YES ];
```

The disclosure style can also be changed:

```
[ cell setDisclosureStyle: 0 ];
```

Two disclosure styles are available.

Style	Description
0	Black arrow
1	Blue circle with white arrow

Image and text cells

Tables can display images next to row text. This requires the use of a different type of table cell named `UIImageAndTextTableCell`. In the example `MyTable` class, this type of object would be returned instead of a `UISimpleTableCell` in the `cellForRow` method.

```
UIImageAndTextTableCell *cell =
    [ [ UIImageAndTextTableCell alloc ] init ];
UIImageView *image = [ [ UIImage alloc ]
    initWithContentsOfFile: @"/path/to/file.png" ];
[ cell setTitle: @"My row, now with image!" ];
[ cell setImage: image ];
 return [ cell autorelease ];
```

The `UIImage` class is used to load an image file. This class is further explained in Chapter 7.

This type of data cell also allows the image and text alignment to be changed using a method called `setAlignment`.

```
[ cell setAlignment: 2 ];
```

The following alignment styles are supported.

Style	Description
0	Image and text left-aligned with margin separator
1	Image and text left-aligned with no margin separator
2	Image left-aligned, text centered
3	Image left-aligned, text right-aligned

Depending on the size of the images that will be loaded, the row height may need to be changed to accommodate the images. The `setRowHeight` method is part of the `UITable` base class, and can be set when the table is initialized:

```
[ self setRowHeight: 64 ];
```

Because this is a table-level setting, the row height will affect all cells equally.

Swipe-to-delete

The UITable object has built-in logic to intercept swipe gestures and display delete confirmations. This allows the user to swipe his finger across a row he'd like to delete.

To intercept swipe gestures, override the swipe method in the subclass you derive fom UITable.

```
- (int)swipe:(int)type withEvent:(struct __GSEvent *)event;
{
    CGPoint point = GSEventGetLocationInWindow(event);
    CGPoint offset = _startOffset;

    point.x += offset.x;
    point.y += offset.y;
    int row = [ self rowAtPoint:point ];

    [ [ self visibleCellForRow: row column:0 ]
      _showDeleteOrInsertion: YES
      withDisclosure: NO
      animated: YES
      isDelete: YES
      andRemoveConfirmation: YES
    ];

    return [ super swipe:type withEvent:event ];
}
```

The swipe method is passed a gesture event, which is handled by a framework named Graphics Services (covered in Chapter 4). Calling this framework's GSEventGetLocationInWindow method will determine the point on the screen where the swipe occurred. Because the point on the screen (and not within the window) is returned, the offset of the window's position on the screen must be taken into account. For example, if the window appears below a 48-point navigation bar, then the vertical offset must take this into account. In this example, the _startOffset variable is used to offset screen coordinates to window coordinates.

Once the screen coordinates of the swipe been determined, the row number is then found by handing the coordinates to the rowAtPoint method belonging to the UITable class. This returns the row number as an integer.

Next, find the table cell itself using UITable's visibleCellForRow method. This will return a pointer to the selected table cell, whose _showDeleteOrInsertion method can be invoked to display the delete confirmation. This appears as a red delete button.

To disable the user's ability to delete rows from the table, this method can just return without taking any action.

When the user confirms that she wants to delete the row (by pressing the delete button), an internal method named _willDeleteRow is called. When a row is deleted, the row must be removed from the data source; otherwise, it will appear again should the user scroll it off the screen and back. There may also be additional operations the application will need to perform, such as deleting a file or message associated with the cell.

```
- (void)_willDeleteRow:(int)row
    forTableCell:(id)cell
    viaEdge:(int)edge
    animateOthers:(BOOL)animate
{
    /* Perform any additional deletion operations here */

    [ fileList removeObjectAtIndex: row ];
    [ super _willDeleteRow: row
        forTableCell: cell
        viaEdge: edge
        animateOthers: animate
    ];
}
```

Item selection

When the user selects a table cell, the table's `tableRowSelected` method is called. This method should be overridden to act on the selection, for example, when opening a file or launching an application. The row number can be accessed using the base class's `selectedRow` method.

```
- (void)tableRowSelected:(NSNotification *)notification
{
    int index = [ self selectedRow ];

    /* A file was selected. Do something here. */
}
```

Once the row's index is found, as shown above, you can use it to reference the actual row value from your own data and act on it appropriately. For example, if your table is an array of files, then you would use the index to reference the correct filename in your array. From there, you can load the file or perform whatever other operations your application is designed for.

Example: File Browser

In this example, we create a custom `UITable` class for general use as a file browser. The browser reads a directory supplied by caller, using its `setPath` method, and displays all of the files downwind of it matching a file extension also supplied by the caller, using its `setExtension` method. The swipe-to-delete functionality has been added for the sake of the example, but (in order to prevent you from trashing files by mistake while experimenting with the example) it deletes the item only from the list, not from the iPhone's filesystem.

This example can be easily added to any iPhone application to display lists of files by including the following code in an application's view class:

```
#import "FileTable.h"

FileTable *fileTable = [ [ FileTable alloc ] initWithFrame: rect ];
[ fileTable setPath: @"/Applications" ];
[ fileTable setExtension: @"app" ];
[ fileTable reloadData ];
[ self addSubview: fileTable ];
```

A complete application, shown in Examples 3-13 through 3-18, can be compiled from the tool chain using the following command line:

```
$ arm-apple-darwin-gcc -o MyExample MyExample.m FileTable.m DeletableCell.m \
    -lobjc -framework CoreFoundation -framework Foundation -framework UIKit
```

Example 3-13. Application class header (MyExample.h)

```
#import <CoreFoundation/CoreFoundation.h>
#import <UIKit/UIKit.h>
#import "FileTable.h"

@interface MainView : UIView
{
        FileTable *fileTable;
}
- (id)initWithFrame:(CGRect)frame;
- (void)dealloc;
@end

@interface MyApp : UIApplication
{
    UIWindow *window;
    MainView *mainView;
}
- (void)applicationDidFinishLaunching:(NSNotification *)aNotification;
@end
```

Example 3-14. Application class implementation (MyExample.m)

```
#import "MyExample.h"

int main(int argc, char **argv)
{
    NSAutoreleasePool *autoreleasePool = [ [ NSAutoreleasePool alloc ] init ];
    int returnCode = UIApplicationMain(argc, argv, [ MyApp class ]);
    [ autoreleasePool release ];
    return returnCode;
}

@implementation MyApp
```

Example 3-14. Application class implementation (MyExample.m) (continued)

```
- (void)applicationDidFinishLaunching:(NSNotification *)aNotification {
    window = [ [ UIWindow alloc ] initWithContentRect:
        [ UIHardware fullScreenApplicationContentRect ]
    ];

    CGRect rect = [ UIHardware fullScreenApplicationContentRect ];
    rect.origin.x = rect.origin.y = 0.0f;

    mainView = [ [ MainView alloc ] initWithFrame: rect ];

    [ window setContentView: mainView ];
    [ window orderFront: self ];
    [ window makeKey: self ];
    [ window _setHidden: NO ];
}
@end

@implementation MainView
- (id)initWithFrame:(CGRect)rect {

    if ((self == [ super initWithFrame: rect ]) != nil) {

        fileTable = [ [ FileTable alloc ] initWithFrame: rect ];
        [ fileTable setPath: @"/Applications" ];
        [ fileTable setExtension: @"app" ];
        [ fileTable reloadData ];
        [ self addSubview: fileTable ];
    }

    return self;
}

- (void)dealloc
{
    [ self dealloc ];
    [ super dealloc ];
}
@end
```

Example 3-15. File selector class headers (FileTable.h)

```
#import <UIKit/UIKit.h>
#import <UIKit/UISimpleTableCell.h>
#import <UIKit/UIImageAndTextTableCell.h>
#import <UIKit/UITableColumn.h>
#import <UIKit/UIImage.h>
#import <GraphicsServices/GraphicsServices.h>

@interface FileTable : UITable
{
    NSString *path;
    NSString *extension;
```

Example 3-15. File selector class headers (FileTable.h) (continued)

```
    NSMutableArray *fileList;
    UITableColumn *colFilename;
    UITableColumn *colType;
}
- (id)initWithFrame:(struct CGRect)rect;
- (void)setPath:(NSString *)_path;
- (void)setExtension:(NSString *)_extension;
- (void)reloadData;
- (int)swipe:(int)type withEvent:(struct __GSEvent *)event;
- (int)numberOfRowsInTable:(UITable *)_table;
- (UITableCell *)table:(UITable *)table
    cellForRow:(int)row
    column:(UITableColumn *)col;
- (void)_willDeleteRow:(int)row forTableCell:(id)cell viaEdge:(int)edge animateOthers:
(BOOL)animate;
- (void)dealloc;
@end
```

Example 3-16. File selector class implementation (FileTable.m)

```
#import "FileTable.h"
#import "DeletableCell.h"

@implementation FileTable

- (id)initWithFrame:(struct CGRect)rect {
    if ((self == [ super initWithFrame: rect ]) != nil) {

        colFilename = [ [ UITableColumn alloc ]
            initWithTitle: @"Filename"
            identifier:@"filename"
            width: rect.size.width - 75
        ];
        [ self addTableColumn: colFilename ];

        colType = [ [ UITableColumn alloc ]
            initWithTitle: @"Type"
            identifier:@"type"
            width: 75
        ];
        [ self addTableColumn: colType ];

        [ self setSeparatorStyle: 1 ];
        [ self setDelegate: self ];
        [ self setDataSource: self ];
        [ self setRowHeight: 64 ];

        fileList = [ [ NSMutableArray alloc] init ];
    }

    return self;
}
```

Example 3-16. File selector class implementation (FileTable.m) (continued)

```objc
- (void) setPath:(NSString *)_path {
    path = [ _path copy ];
}

- (void) setExtension:(NSString *)_extension {
    extension = [ _extension copy ];
}

- (void) reloadData {
    NSFileManager *fileManager = [ NSFileManager defaultManager ];
    NSDirectoryEnumerator *dirEnum;
    NSString *file;

    if ([ fileManager fileExistsAtPath: path ] == NO) {
        return;
    }

    [ fileList removeAllObjects ];

    dirEnum = [ [ NSFileManager defaultManager ] enumeratorAtPath: path ];
    while ((file = [ dirEnum nextObject ])) {
        if ([ file hasSuffix: extension ] == YES) {
            [ fileList addObject: file ];
        }
    }

    [ super reloadData ];
}

- (int)numberOfRowsInTable:(UITable *)_table {
    return [ fileList count ];
}

- (UITableCell *)table:(UITable *)table
  cellForRow:(int)row
  column:(UITableColumn *)col
{
    if (col == colFilename) {
        DeletableCell *cell = [ [ DeletableCell alloc ] init ];
        [ cell setTable: self ];

        UIImageView *image = [ [ UIImage alloc ]
            initWithContentsOfFile:
            [ [ NSString alloc ]
                initWithFormat: @"/Applications/%@/icon.png",
                    [ fileList objectAtIndex: row ] ] ];
        [ cell setTitle: [ [ fileList objectAtIndex: row ]
        stringByDeletingPathExtension ]];
        [ cell setImage: image ];
        [ cell setShowDisclosure: YES ];
        [ cell setDisclosureStyle: 3 ];
        return [ cell autorelease ];
```

Example 3-16. File selector class implementation (FileTable.m) (continued)

```
    } else if (col == colType) {
        DeletableCell *cell = [ [ DeletableCell alloc ] init ];
        [ cell setTable: self ];
        [ cell setTitle: extension ];
        return [ cell autorelease ];
    }
}

- (int)swipe:(int)type withEvent:(struct __GSEvent *)event;
{
    CGPoint point= GSEventGetLocationInWindow(event);
    CGPoint offset = _startOffset;

    if (point.x < 100 || point.x > 200) {
        point.x += offset.x;
        point.y += offset.y;
        int row = [ self rowAtPoint:point ];

        [ [ self visibleCellForRow: row column: 1 ]
            _showDeleteOrInsertion: YES
            withDisclosure: NO
            animated: YES
            isDelete: YES
            andRemoveConfirmation: YES
        ];

        return [ super swipe:type withEvent:event ];
    }
}

- (void)_willDeleteRow:(int)row
    forTableCell:(id)cell
    viaEdge:(int)edge
    animateOthers:(BOOL)animate
{
    [ fileList removeObjectAtIndex: row ];
    [ super _willDeleteRow: row forTableCell: cell viaEdge: edge
      animateOthers: animate ];
}

- (void)tableRowSelected:(NSNotification *)notification {
    NSString *fileName = [ fileList objectAtIndex: [ self selectedRow ] ];

    /* A file was selected. Do something here. */
}

- (void)dealloc {
    [ colFilename release ];
    [ colType release ];
    [ fileList release ];
    [ super dealloc ];
}
@end
```

Example 3-17. Deletable cell class header (DeletableCell.h)

```
#import "FileTable.h"

@interface DeletableCell : UIImageAndTextTableCell
{
    FileTable *table;
}
- (void)setTable:(FileTable *)_table;

@end
```

Example 3-18. Deletable cell class implementation (DeletableCell.m)

```
#import "DeletableCell.h"

@implementation DeletableCell

- (void)removeControlWillHideRemoveConfirmation:(id)fp8
{
    [ self _showDeleteOrInsertion:NO
         withDisclosure:NO
         animated:YES
         isDelete:YES
         andRemoveConfirmation:YES
    ];
}

- (void)_willBeDeleted
{
    int row = [ table _rowForTableCell: self ];

    /* Do something; this row is being deleted */
}

- (void)setTable:(FileTable *)_table {
    table = _table;
}
@end
```

What's Going On

The FileTable class works like this:

1. When the calling class allocates a new FileTable object, it calls its initWithFrame method.

2. This causes two UITableColumn objects to be created, which serve as the table's columns: Filename and Type. The class also sets itself as the data source and sets some aesthetic properties.

3. The file table's setPath and setExtension methods are used to set the desired path and extension for the files to display.

4. The calling class calls the object's reloadData method. This causes the file table to generate a list of files in the directory at the specified path with the extension specified. This list is stored in an array named fileList. The super class's reloadData method is then called, which queries the number of rows from the data source through the numberOfRowsInTable method.

5. As the file table is ready to display cells, it calls its data binding again to obtain data for each cell in view. The method's cellForRow method is called for each column and row in view. The method returns the appropriate row cells as requested.

6. If the user swipes across a row, the class's swipe method is called. This displays a delete confirmation button by calling the cell's visibleCellForRow method with the appropriate properties.

7. If the user confirms deletion, the table cell's _willDeleteRow method is called. This removes the row from the data source so that it will not be redisplayed should the cell be scrolled out of view, then back in.

Further Study

Try some of these exercises to test your knowledge of tables:

- Incorporate this table into the "Hello, World!" example from the beginning of the chapter. Instead of displaying a UITextView object, build a FileTable object from this example. Be sure to #import the class's header and include it in the source list when compiling.

- Modify this example to add a method to enable or disable deletions. This should change the behavior of the swipe method so that it returns prematurely when deletion is disabled.

- Use this example to display applications in the */Applications* folder. Modify the example to use the UIImageAndTextTableCell object to display the application's icon next to its name.

- Check out the *UITable.h*, *UISimpleTableCell.h*, *UIImageAndTextTableCell.h*, and *UITableColumn.h* prototypes in your tool chain's directory. These can be found in */usr/local/arm-apple-darwin/UIKit/*.

- Check out the various types of labels. *UITextLabel.h*, *UIDateLabel.h*, *UITextFieldLabel.h*, and *UIWebViewLabel.h* prototypes can be found in your tool chain's directory. These can be found in */usr/local/arm-apple-darwin/UIKit/*.

Status Bar Manipulation

The status bar's appearance can be customized to meet the look and feel of your application, and can also display notifications about your application. For instance, the iPod application uses the status bar to display a triangular play icon when music is playing in the background. The alarm clock application displays a small clock on the status bar when an alarm is active. Many properties of the status bar can be changed using the UIApplication and UIHardware classes.

Status Bar Mode

The status bar mode determines its color, opacity, and orientation. It can also be used to animate the status bar when transitioning between different modes. To set the mode, one of four different setStatusBarMode methods can be used from within the instance of your application, a UIApplication object.

```
- (void)setStatusBarMode:(int)mode duration:(float)duration
- (void)setStatusBarMode:(int)mode orientation:(int)orientation
    duration:(float)duration
- (void)setStatusBarMode:(int)mode orientation:(int)orientation
    duration:(float)duration fenceID:(int)fenceID
- (void)setStatusBarMode:(int)mode orientation:(int)orientation
    duration:(float)duration fenceID:(int)fenceID
    animation:(int)animation;
```

Mode

The status bar mode sets the overall appearance in color and opacity. The following modes are supported.

Mode	Description
0	Default, white status bar
1	Black transparent status bar
2	Removes status bar image entirely (be sure to also use _setStatusBarSize)
3	Solid black status bar
4	Entirely transparent status bar
5	Flashing green status bar with "Touch to return to call" text
6	Red transparent status bar

Orientation

The orientation determines where the status bar is displayed on the iPhone's screen. If the iPhone is being held in a landscape fashion, the application may choose to re-orient itself to accommodate the wider display. The value passed with the orientation argument represents the angle at which the iPhone's screen will be displayed.

Angle	Description
0	Status bar is displayed at the natural top of the iPhone
90	Status bar is displayed in landscape across the right portion of the screen
-90	Status bar is displayed in landscape across the left portion of the screen

Duration

This specifies the number in seconds that an animated transition should take between the previous status bar state and the new one. Use the value 0 for an instantaneous transition.

Fence ID

Used internally. We have no idea what it means.

Animation

Sets the animation for transitioning from the previous status bar state to the new one. The following animations are presently supported:

Animation	Description
0	Fade out/fade in
1	New status bar enters screen from bottom
2	Old status bar exits screen from bottom
3	Old status bar exits screen from top; new status bar enters from top
4	New status bar enters screen from bottom using a different animation
5	No animation

Status Bar Size

If you're planning on removing the status bar for a particular purpose, its size must be altered to release the screen space to other views. The status bar size can be set using the UIHardware class.

To remove the status bar entirely, set its height to zero:

```
[ UIHardware _setStatusBarHeight: 0.0 ];
[ self setStatusBarMode:2 duration: 0 ];
```

To restore it:

```
[ UIHardware _setStatusBarHeight: 20.0 ];
[ self setStatusBarMode:0 duration: 0 ];
```

Status Bar Images

Images can be placed on the status bar to notify the user that your application is in a particular state, such as playing music or being logged in to a chat room. Images remain on the status bar even when your application has exited, allowing the user to be notified of future events, such as an alarm. If your application exits prematurely, the image can be automatically removed.

Status bar images are controlled by the SpringBoard application. This makes for a slightly complicated setup in that your application will need to copy the images you use into SpringBoard's program folder (and restart SpringBoard) before they will work.

Two files are needed to correctly display a status bar image: one for the white status bar and one for the black. Depending on what application is running, the status bar used will automatically switch to the appropriate image.

Installation

The first time your application runs, it should copy two files into the SpringBoard folder located at */System/Library/CoreServices/SpringBoard.app*. Choose a one-word descriptor for your images and name them Default_*NAME*.png and FSO_*NAME*.png. The Default image will be displayed when the white status bar is used, and the FSO image will be shown on the black status bar.

After these files have been copied into the SpringBoard folder, the SpringBoard program will need to be restarted for them to be recognized. To do this, invoke launchctl in a shell on the iPhone:

```
# launchctl stop com.apple.SpringBoard
```

Alternatively, you can instruct the user to reboot his iPhone. If SpringBoard isn't restarted, your status bar images will be ignored until the user reboots his iPhone, which may be acceptable.

Displaying and removing the status bar image

Once you've gotten everything set up, use the addStatusBarImageNamed method to display the new status bar using the one-word descriptor you came up with before.

```
[ UIApp addStatusBarImageNamed: @"NAME" removeOnAbnormalExit: YES ];
```

The removeOnAbnormalExit argument instructs the iPhone whether to automatically remove the image if your application crashes.

When you're ready to remove the image by hand, use the removeStatusBarImageNamed method:

```
[ UIApp removeStatusBarImageNamed: @"NAME" ];
```

Application Badges

With the iPhone's numerous different connections—EDGE, WiFi, and Bluetooth (not to mention the cellular network)—lots of things can happen while you've got that little device stuck in your pocket. Without some notification to the user that there are pending notifications, they're likely to miss everything that's happened while they were busy having a real life. Application badges are small message bubbles that appear on the program's SpringBoard icon. Application badges are used heavily by Apple's preloaded applications to alert the user to missed calls, voicemail, text messages, and email.

One of the nice features about these types of badges is that the application doesn't necessarily need to be running for the badge to display on the SpringBoard. This is useful in serving as a reminder to the user even after they've exited the application. This also means you'll need to clean up any lingering badges when your program exits.

Displaying an Application Badge

Application badges are one of the easier features to take advantage of, requiring only one call to the UIApplication class.

```
[ UIApp setApplicationBadge: @"Hi!" ];
```

The setApplicationBadge method takes an NSString object, which can be built with standard string formatting.

```
NSString *badgeText = [ [ NSString alloc ]
    initWithFormat:@"%d", numNewMessages ];
[ UIApp setApplicationBadge: badgeText ];
```

Removing an Application Badge

An application badge should be removed when the user has clicked to the page with the important events they were being notified about. Removing the application badge is also an easy task. A good place to put such code is after transitioning to the view with the events. For example:

```
[ transitionView transition: 0 toView: missedCalls ];
[ UIApp removeApplicationBadge ];
```

An application badge will continue to hang around even after an application has terminated. This can be useful, but it's not always what you want. If an application badge should be removed when the program exits, you'll also need to make a call to removeApplicationBadge in the application's applicationWillTerminate method.

```
- (void)applicationWillTerminate {
    /* We are about to exit, so remove the application badge */
    [ UIApp removeApplicationBadge ];
}
```

You'll learn more about this kind of application state control in the next section.

Further Study

Before going on to learn some of the situations in which application badges can help improve your application's response to state changes, do a little exploration:

- Experiment and determine the maximum amount of text that can be added to an application badge. What happens when you exceed this limit?
- Check out *UIApplication.h* in your tool chain's include directory. You'll find it in */usr/local/arm-apple-darwin/include/UIKit/*. We'll cover some more UIApplication methods in Chapter 7.

Application Services

The state of an application is more important on the iPhone than it is on the desktop. This is because many events on the iPhone can cause an application to suspend, run in the background, or terminate. These different states occur when the user presses the home button, locks the screen, or receives a phone call. It's important for an application to know when its state is about to change to save any settings, halt threads, or perform other actions.

The UIApplication base class contains many functions for application state changes, which can be overridden by the application. While there's nothing the application can generally do about the state it's about to enter, it can at least take whatever actions are appropriate to prepare for it.

Suspending

When the home button is pressed, the default behavior for an application is to suspend. It's also told to suspend during a phone call or when the screen is locked. When this happens, the application's suspend methods are called.

Depending on the nature of the event, three different suspend methods might be called.

applicationWillSuspendUnderLock
> The iPhone screen is locked either by pressing the power button or during an idle screen lock.

applicationWillSuspendForEventsOnly
> Events that force the application into the background, such as receiving a phone call, cause this method to be called. Also, if the display is locked, but no applicationWillSuspendUnderLock method is overridden, this method gets called instead.

applicationSuspend

> This method is called when the user presses the home button. It's also the last chance for an application to perform any necessary actions. If neither of the other two methods have been overridden, this method gets called for all suspend events.

Because one method picks up the slack for others, most applications can service all suspend events by simply overriding applicationSuspend.

```
- (void)applicationSuspend:(struct __GSEvent *)event {
    /* We're about to suspend, so do something here */
}
```

Resources are always a concern with the iPhone, as memory and battery life are finite. If the application doesn't need to run in the background and there's no reason to keep the state of the application, it may make sense to just terminate instead of suspending. The iPhone is smart enough to restart the last application being used, so the user might not even know the difference.

```
- (void)applicationSuspend:(struct __GSEvent *)event {
    [ self terminate ];
}
```

It may also be appropriate to suspend or terminate depending on the state of the application. For example, if the application is an instant messaging client, it makes sense to suspend only if it's got a live connection to a server, so that it continue running in the background and maintain the connection. If the user is logged out, there's no reason to stay alive, and so terminating makes more sense.

```
- (void)applicationSuspend:(struct __GSEvent *)event {
    if (connected == NO) {
        [ self terminate ];
    }else {
        /* Set away in IM Client */
    }
}
```

When the application is suspended, it's simply moved to the background and can continue to run. If a separate thread is running to check for new events, such as new instant messages, it is still able to communicate with the process and even send sound events to alert the user (discussed in Chapter 6).

Resuming

When an application is brought back to a run state, another set of methods are called to prepare the application after it has been brought back to life. These can be overridden to check (and reestablish) connectivity or perform other tasks.

The same three methods used earlier to handle different types of suspends also have complementary resume methods.

applicationDidResumeFromUnderLock
> The application resumed from an iPhone whose screen was locked and powered off.

applicationDidResumeForEventsOnly
> The application resumed after the end of a phone call or other event that forced it into the background.

applicationDidResume
> Catch-all for all other resume events.

The resume methods are overridden in the same way as their suspend counterparts.

```
-   (void)applicationDidResume {

    /* We've resumed. Do something */
}
```

Program Termination

Unless an application terminates itself, it's generally not terminated unless the iPhone is being shut down. Because most good applications do terminate themselves (rather than suspend), it's a good idea to override the termination method just before an application terminates.

The applicationWillTerminate method is called whenever an application is about to be cleanly terminated. It is *not* called when an application is killed by holding down the home button. This method should perform any remaining cleanup of resources, make sure all connections are properly closed, and any other tasks necessary before the program exits.

```
- (void)applicationWillTerminate {
    /* We're about to exit, so do something */
}
```

Further Study

Here are some other ways you can play with the various application services:

- Use a pthread or NSThread to create a background thread that maintains an active connection to a server. What happens to the connection when the application suspends?

- Check out *UIApplication.h* in your tool chain's include directory. You'll find it in */usr/local/arm-apple-darwin/include/UIKit/*. We'll cover some more UIApplication methods in Chapter 7.

## CHAPTER 4

Event Handling and Graphics Services

In Chapter 3, you were introduced to some of the basic user interface elements of the iPhone. Many objects support high-level events such as buttonClicked and tableRowSelected to notify the application of certain actions taken by the user. These actions rely on lower-level mouse events provided by the UIView class and a base class underneath it: UIResponder. The UIResponder class provides methods to recognize and handle the basic mouse events that occur when the user taps or drags on the iPhone's screen. These methods are incorporated into other events created in UIView to detect two-fingered gestures. Higher-level objects, such as tables and alert sheets, take these low-level events and wrap them into even higher-level ones to handle button clicks, row selection, and other types of behavior. All such screen-oriented events are processed using the Graphics Services framework, which provides screen coordinates, fingering information, and other data related to the graphics of the event. These functions tell the application exactly what has occurred on the screen and provide the information needed to interact with the user.

Introduction to Geometric Structures

Before diving into events management, you'll need a basic understanding of some geometric structures commonly used on the iPhone. You've already seen some of these in Chapter 3. The Core Graphics framework provides many general structures to handle graphics-related functions. Among these structures are points, window sizes, and window regions. Core Graphics also provides many C-based functions for creating and comparing these structures.

CGPoint

A CGPoint is the simplest Core Graphics structure, and contains two floating-point values corresponding to horizontal (X) and vertical (Y) coordinates on a display. To create a CGPoint, use the CGPointMake method:

```
CGPoint point = CGPointMake (320.0, 480.0);
```

The first value represents X, the horizontal pixel value, and the second Y, the vertical pixel value. These values can also be accessed directly:

```
float x = point.x;
float y = point.y;
```

The iPhone's display resolution is 320×480 pixels. The upper-left corner of the screen is referenced at 0×0, and the lower right at 319×479 (pixel values are zero-indexed).

Being a general-purpose structure, a CGPoint can refer equally well to a coordinate on the screen or within a window. For example, if a window is drawn at 0×240 (halfway down the screen), a CGPoint with values (0, 0) could address either the upper-left corner of the screen or the upper-left corner of the window (0×240). Which one it means is determined by the context where the structure is being used in the program.

Two CGPoint structures can be compared using the CGPointEqualToPoint function:

```
BOOL isEqual = CGPointEqualToPoint(point1, point2);
```

CGSize

A CGSize structure represents the size of a rectangle. It encapsulates the width and height of an object, and is primarily found in the iPhone APIs to dictate the size of screen objects—namely windows. To create a CGSize object, use CGSizeMake:

```
CGSize size = CGSizeMake(320.0, 480.0);
```

The values provided to CGSizeMake indicate the width and height of the element being described. Values can be directly accessed using the structure's width and height variable names:

```
float width = size.width;
float height = size.height;
```

Two CGSize structures can be compared using the CGSizeEqualToSize function:

```
BOOL isEqual = CGSizeEqualToSize(size1, size2);
```

CGRect

The CGRect structure combines a CGPoint and CGSize structure to describe the frame of a window on the screen. The frame includes an origin, which represents the location of the upper-left corner of the window, and the size of the window. To create a CGRect, use the CGRectMake function:

```
CGRect rect = CGRectMake(0, 200, 320, 240);
```

This example describes a 320×240 window whose upper-left corner is located at coordinates 0×200. As with the CGPoint structure, these coordinates could reference a point on the screen itself or offsets within an existing window; it depends on where and how the CGRect structure is used.

The components of the CGRect structure can also be accessed directly:

```
CGPoint windowOrigin = rect.origin;
float x = rect.origin.x;
float y = rect.origin.y;

CGSize windowSize = rect.size;
float width = rect.size.width;
float height = rect.size.height;
```

Containment and intersection

Two CGRect structures can be compared using the CGRectEqualToRect function:

```
BOOL isEqual = CGRectEqualToRect(rect1, rect2);
```

To determine whether a given point is contained inside a CGRect, use the CGRectContainsPoint method. This is particularly useful when determining whether a user has tapped inside a particular region. The point is represented as a CGPoint structure:

```
BOOL containsPoint = CGRectContainsPoint(rect, point);
```

A similar function can be used to determine whether one CGRect structure contains another CGRect structure. This is useful when testing whether certain objects overlap:

```
BOOL containsRect = CGRectContainsRect(rect1, rect2);
```

To determine whether two CGRect structures intersect, use the CGRectIntersectsRect function:

```
BOOL doesIntersect = CGRectIntersectsRect(rect1, rect2);
```

Edge and center detection

The following functions can be used to determine the various edges of a rectangle and calculate the coordinates of the rectangle's center. All of these functions accept a CGRect structure as their only argument and return a float value:

CGRectGetMinX
> Returns the coordinate of the left edge of the rectangle.

CGRectGetMinY
> Returns the coordinate of the bottom edge of the rectangle.

CGRectGetMidX
> Returns the center X coordinate of the rectangle.

CGRectGetMidY
> Returns the center Y coordinate of the rectangle.

CGRectGetMaxX
> Returns the coordinate of the right edge of the rectangle.

CGRectGetMaxY
> Returns the coordinate of the upper edge of the rectangle.

Introduction to GSEvent

The GSEvent structure is the standard object that describes graphics-level events to a class's event handling methods. It can be used in conjunction with the Graphics Services framework to decode details about the event having occurred.

All event methods receive a pointer to a GSEvent structure when notified of an event. The prototype for an event typically follows this standard:

```
- (void)eventName: (struct __GSEvent *)event
{
    /* Event handling code */
}
```

Graphics Services

Whenever an event is received, the object communicates with Graphics Services to get the specifics of the event. The Graphics Services framework provides many different decoding functions to extract the event's details.

Event location

For one-fingered events, the GSEventGetLocationInWindow function returns a CGPoint structure containing the X, Y coordinates where the event occurred. These coordinates are generally offset to the position of the window that received the event. For example, if a window located at the bottom half of the screen, whose origin was 0×240, received an event at 0×0, this means the event actually took place at 0×240 on the screen, which is where the window's 0×0 origin is located.

The GSEventGetLocationInWindow method returns a CGPoint structure, which you can unpack as follows:

```
CGPoint point = GSEventGetLocationInWindow(event);
float x = point.x;
float y = point.y;
```

If a two-fingered gesture is being used, you must call two separate functions to obtain the window coordinates for each finger. The left-most finger is considered the inner finger, making the right-most finger the outer one. The GSEventGetInnerMostPathPosition and GSEventGetOuterMostPathPosition methods return CGPoint structures containing the X, Y window coordinates for each finger.

```
CGPoint leftFinger = GSEventGetInnerMostPathPosition(event);
CGPoint rightFinger = GSEventGetOuterMostPathPosition(event);
```

When the iPhone is oriented for landscape mode, these positions are reversed:

```
int orientation = [ UIHardware deviceOrientation: YES ];

if ( orientation == kOrientationHorizontalLeft
   || orientation == kOrientationHorizontalRight )
{
    leftFinger = GSEventGetOuterMostPathPosition(event);
    rightFinger = GSEventGetInnerMostPathPosition(Event);
}
```

Event type

The event type identifies whether a single finger or gesture was used, and whether the event involved a finger being placed down or raised from the screen.

Most events can be easily identified through the method that was notified. For example, if a finger is pressed down, this notifies the mouseDown method, whereas a two-finger gesture will result in the gestureStarted method being notified.

```
unsigned int eventType = GSEventGetType(event);
```

For a one-fingered event, the event type would begin as a single finger down, followed by all fingers up (when the user released). A two-fingered gesture is a little more complex. It begins life with a single finger down, and then changes to a two-finger gesture. If the user lifts one finger, the event type then changes to a one-finger up event, followed by an all-fingers up event when the user removes the second finger.

The following events are tied to event type values.

Type	Description
1	One finger down, including first finger of a gesture
2	All fingers up
5	One finger up in a two-fingered gesture
6	Two-finger gesture

Event chording (multiple-finger events)

When more than one note is played on a piano, it's considered a chord. The same philosophy is used in processing gestures. A single finger represents one note being played on the screen, whereas two are considered a chord.

The GSEventIsChordingHandEvent method can be used to determine how many fingers are down on the screen at the time of the event.

```
int eventChording = GSEventIsChordingHandEvent(event);
```

This function returns a value of 0 if the event is a single finger event, or a value of 1 if it is considered a chording event.

Mouse Events

Mouse events are considered to be any touch screen event where a single finger is used. All classes derived from the UIResponder class inherit mouse events, and some classes override these to form new types of events, such as row selection within a table or changing the position of switches and sliders in a control.

To receive notifications for any of the six supported mouse events, create a subclass of the object for which you want to receive events and override its methods. For example, the following class will receive events sent to a UITable object and define custom handling for single-finger actions by the user. This will cause the custom methods to be called whenever the user presses a finger within the table's window region.

```
@interface MyTable : UITable
{

}
- (void) mouseDown:(struct __GSEvent *)event;
- (void) mouseUp:(struct __GSEvent *)event;
@end
```

Because the base class might also take advantage of the mouse event, you'll want to call the superclass's version of the method either before or after you've processed the event:

```
- (void) mouseDown:(struct __GSEvent *)event {

    /* Handle mouse down */

    [ super mouseDown: event ];
}
```

mouseDown

The mouseDown method is called whenever a single finger is pressed on the screen. This includes the first finger of two-fingered gestures before a gesture is started. The event location represents the coordinates at which the screen press occurred within the object's window.

```
- (void) mouseDown:(struct __GSEvent *)event {
    CGPoint pointDown = GSEventGetLocationInWindow(event);

    /* Handle mouse down */

    [ super mouseDown: event ];
}
```

mouseUp

The mouseUp event method is notified whenever the user lifts a finger off of the screen. It is the most appropriate method for performing value checks of controls, such as a segmented control, or other classes that are not equipped with their own custom notifications for such events. The superclass's method should be called first, to allow values of controls to change before reading them. The event location represents the last coordinates of the user's finger before lifting off the screen.

```
- (void) mouseUp:(struct __GSEvent *)event {
    CGPoint pointUp = GSEventGetLocationInWindow(event);

    [ super mouseUp: event ];

    /* Check value of control, etc. */
}
```

mouseDragged

If the user continues to hold her finger down after a mouseDown event is sent, the mouseDragged method is notified if the finger is moved from its original position on the screen. This is the equivalent of a click-and-drag function on the desktop. The event location represents the coordinates to which the user dragged the finger before lifting it.

```
- (void) mouseDragged:(struct __GSEvent *)event {
    CGPoint movedTo = GSEventGetLocationInWindow(event);

    [ super mouseDragged: event ];

    /* Handle mouse drag */
}
```

This method tracks with the user's finger, so it is called at regular intervals as the finger moves.

mouseEntered, mouseExited, mouseMoved

On the desktop, these methods notify the application when the mouse is scrolled into, out of, and within an object's frame in the absence of any click event. The iPhone doesn't have a real mouse, so when you tap with your finger it's treated as a mouse down. These methods are relatively useless for the iPhone, but future mobile devices from Apple might make use of a real mouse or trackball.

Gesture Events

When the user switches from a one-finger tap to using two fingers, it's considered the beginning of a *gesture*. This causes gesture events to be created, which can be intercepted by overriding the appropriate methods. Gestures are provided in the UIView base class, and only objects that inherit from it support them.

The order of events is this: as a gesture is started, the gestureStarted method is invoked. Should the user change his finger position, the gestureChanged method gets called to notify the object of each new gesture position. When the user has ended their gesture, gestureEnded is finally called.

In order for gesture events to be sent, the class must override a method named canHandleGestures, which returns a Boolean value. By returning YES, you tell the iPhone to send events.

```
- (BOOL)canHandleGestures
{
    return YES;
}
```

gestureStarted

The gestureStarted method is notified when the user makes screen contact with two fingers or transitions from using one finger to two. This method is the two-fingered version of mouseDown. The inner and outer coordinates correspond to the first point of contact on the screen. The event locations in the CGPoint structures returned represent the coordinates at which each finger was pressed.

```
- (void)gestureStarted:(struct __GSEvent)event {
    CGPoint leftFinger = GSEventGetInnerMostPathPosition(event);
    CGPoint rightFinger = GSEventGetOuterMostPathPosition(event);

    [ super gestureStarted: event ];

    /* Handle gesture started event */
}
```

gestureEnded

The gestureEnded method is the two-fingered equivalent to mouseUp, and lets the application know that the user has removed at least one finger from the screen. If the user removes both fingers at the same time, the iPhone sends both events to the gestureEnded and mouseUp methods. If the user lifts fingers separately, the first finger to be removed causes a call to gestureEnded and the second causes a call to mouseUp.

The screen coordinates provided with the gestureEnded method identify the point, if any, that remains in a pressed-down state when just one finger was removed and the other finger is still down. When the second finger is removed, the mouseUp method will be notified, as the gesture will have been demoted to a mouse event when the first finger was removed.

```
- (void)gestureEnded:(struct __GSEvent)event {
    CGPoint leftFinger = GSEventGetInnerMostPathPosition(event);
    CGPoint rightFinger = GSEventGetOuterMostPathPosition(event);

    [ super gestureEnded: event ];

    /* Handle gesture ended event */
}
```

gestureChanged

Whenever the user moves his fingers while in a two-fingered gesture, the gestureChanged method is called. This is the two-fingered equivalent of mouseDragged. When it occurs, the application should reevaluate the finger positions of the gesture and make the appropriate response. The event locations represent the new coordinates to which the fingers have been dragged.

```
- (void)gestureChanged:(struct __GSEvent)event {
    CGPoint leftFinger = GSEventGetInnerMostPathPosition(event);
    CGPoint rightFinger = GSEventGetOuterMostPathPosition(event);

    [ super gestureChanged: event ];

    /* Handle gesture change event */
}
```

Status Bar Events

The iPhone's status bar is a window itself, capable of receiving mouse events. The Safari application sets a precedent for the type of behavior that should ensue on such events, which is to have the primary view scroll to the beginning. The UIApplication class contains three status bar notifications that can be overridden in your program.

The statusBarMouseDown event is notified whenever the user taps the status bar.

```
- (void)statusBarMouseDown:(struct __GSEvent *)event;
```

If the user leaves her finger down and drags it to a different position, the statusBarMouseDragged method is notified with an event containing the coordinates of the position it has been dragged to on the screen.

```
- (void)statusBarMouseDragged:(struct __GSEvent *)event;
```

Finally, when the user lifts her finger, the statusBarMouseUp method is notified with an event containing the coordinates of the last position held by the user's finger on the screen.

```
- (void)statusBarMouseUp:(struct __GSEvent *)event;
```

Example: The Icon Shuffle

This example creates four icons on the screen and allows the user to move them around freely, either individually or two at a time using a gesture. This illustrates the use of various geometry structures and functions, event notifications, and Graphics Services functions. To pick up an icon, tap and hold it, move it where it should go, then release your finger. If the status bar is tapped, the icons are reset to their original positions.

To compile this example from the command line, you'll need to use several different frameworks: Core Graphics, Graphics Services, and UIKit, in addition to the foundation frameworks:

```
$ arm-apple-darwin-gcc -o MyExample MyExample.m -lobjc \
    -framework CoreFoundation -framework Foundation \
    -framework UIKit -framework CoreGraphics \
    -framework GraphicsServices
```

Examples 4-1 and 4-2 contain the header file and executable methods for the example.

Example 4-1. Mouse and gesture example (MyExample.h)

```
#import <CoreFoundation/CoreFoundation.h>
#import <UIKit/UIKit.h>
#import <UIKit/UITextView.h>

@interface MainView : UIView
{
    UIImage *images[4];
    CGRect positions[4];
    CGPoint offsets[4];
    int dragLeft, dragRight;
}
- (id)initWithFrame:(struct CGRect)windowRect;
- (void)reInit;
- (void)mouseDown: (struct __GSEvent *)event;
- (void)mouseUp: (struct __GSEvent *)event;
- (void)mouseDragged: (struct __GSEvent *)event;
- (void)gestureStarted: (struct __GSEvent *)event;
- (void)gestureEnded: (struct __GSEvent *)event;
- (void)gestureChanged: (struct __GSEvent *)event;
- (void)drawRect:(CGRect)rect;
@end

@interface MyApp : UIApplication
{
    UIWindow *window;
    MainView *mainView;
}
- (void)applicationDidFinishLaunching:(NSNotification *)aNotification;
- (void)statusBarMouseDown:(struct __GSEvent *)event;
@end
```

Example 4-2. Mouse and gesture example (MyExample.m)

```
#import <Foundation/Foundation.h>
#import <CoreFoundation/CoreFoundation.h>
#import <GraphicsServices/GraphicsServices.h>
#import "MyExample.h"

int main(int argc, char **argv)
{
    NSAutoreleasePool *autoreleasePool = [
```

Example 4-2. Mouse and gesture example (MyExample.m) (continued)

```
        [ NSAutoreleasePool alloc ] init
    ];
    int returnCode = UIApplicationMain(argc, argv, [ MyApp class ]);
    [ autoreleasePool release ];
    return returnCode;
}

@implementation MyApp
- (void)applicationDidFinishLaunching:(NSNotification *)aNotification {
    window = [ [ UIWindow alloc ] initWithContentRect:
        [ UIHardware fullScreenApplicationContentRect ]
    ];

    CGRect rect = [ UIHardware fullScreenApplicationContentRect ];
    rect.origin.x = rect.origin.y = 0.0f;

    mainView = [ [ MainView alloc ] initWithFrame: rect ];
    [ window setContentView: mainView ];
    [ window orderFront: self ];
    [ window makeKey: self ];
    [ window _setHidden: NO ];

}

- (void)statusBarMouseDown:(struct __GSEvent *)event {
    [ mainView reInit ];
    [ mainView setNeedsDisplay ];
}

@end

@implementation MainView
- (id)initWithFrame:(struct CGRect)windowRect {
    if ((self == [ super initWithFrame: windowRect ]) != nil) {
        int i;

        images[0] = [ UIImage
          imageAtPath: @"/Applications/MobilePhone.app/icon.png" ];
        images[1] = [ UIImage
          imageAtPath: @"/Applications/MobileMail.app/icon.png" ];
        images[2] = [ UIImage
          imageAtPath: @"/Applications/MobileSafari.app/icon.png" ];
        images[3] = [ UIImage
            imageAtPath:
            @"/Applications/MobileMusicPlayer.app/icon.png" ];

        [ self reInit ];
    }
    return self;
}

- (void)reInit {
```

Example 4-2. Mouse and gesture example (MyExample.m) (continued)

```
        positions[0] = CGRectMake(98, 178, 60, 60);
        positions[1] = CGRectMake(162, 178, 60, 60);
        positions[2] = CGRectMake(98, 242, 60, 60);
        positions[3] = CGRectMake(162, 242, 60, 60);

        dragLeft = dragRight = -1;
}

- (void)drawRect:(CGRect)rect {
    float black[4] = { 0, 0, 0, 1 };
    CGContextRef ctx = UICurrentContext();
    int i;

    CGContextSetFillColor(ctx, black);
    CGContextFillRect(ctx, rect);

    for(i=0;i<4;i++) {
        [ images[i] draw1PartImageInRect: positions[i] ];
    }
}

- (void)mouseDown: (struct __GSEvent *)event {
    CGPoint point = GSEventGetLocationInWindow(event);
    int i;

    for(i=0;i<4;i++) {
        if (CGRectContainsPoint(positions[i], point)) {
            dragLeft = i;
            offsets[i] = CGPointMake
              ( point.x - positions[i].origin.x,
                point.y - positions[i].origin.y );
        }
    }
}

- (void)mouseUp: (struct __GSEvent *)event {
    CGPoint point = GSEventGetLocationInWindow(event);
    int i;

    dragLeft = -1;
}

- (void)mouseDragged: (struct __GSEvent *)event {
    CGPoint point = GSEventGetLocationInWindow(event);
    CGRect old;
    int i;

    if (dragLeft != -1) {
        old = positions[dragLeft];
        positions[dragLeft].origin.x = point.x - offsets[dragLeft].x;
        positions[dragLeft].origin.y = point.y - offsets[dragLeft].y;
        [ self setNeedsDisplayInRect: old ];
```

Example 4-2. Mouse and gesture example (MyExample.m) (continued)

```
        [ self setNeedsDisplayInRect: positions[dragLeft] ];
    }
}

- (void)gestureStarted: (struct __GSEvent *)event {
    CGPoint leftFinger = GSEventGetInnerMostPathPosition(event);
    CGPoint rightFinger = GSEventGetOuterMostPathPosition(event);
    int i;

    for(i=0;i<4;i++) {
        if (CGRectContainsPoint(positions[i], leftFinger)) {
            dragLeft = i;
            offsets[i] = CGPointMake
              ( leftFinger.x - positions[i].origin.x,
                leftFinger.y - positions[i].origin.y );
        }
        else if (CGRectContainsPoint(positions[i], rightFinger)) {
            dragRight = i;
            offsets[i] = CGPointMake
              ( rightFinger.x - positions[i].origin.x,
                rightFinger.y - positions[i].origin.y );
        }
    }
}

- (void)gestureEnded: (struct __GSEvent *)event {
    CGPoint leftFinger = GSEventGetInnerMostPathPosition(event);
    CGPoint rightFinger = GSEventGetOuterMostPathPosition(event);
    int i;

    dragLeft = dragRight = -1;

    for(i=0;i<4;i++) {
        if (CGRectContainsPoint(positions[i], leftFinger))
            dragLeft = i;
        else if (CGRectContainsPoint(positions[i], rightFinger))
            dragRight = i;
    }
}

- (void)gestureChanged: (struct __GSEvent *)event {
    CGPoint leftFinger = GSEventGetInnerMostPathPosition(event);
    CGPoint rightFinger = GSEventGetOuterMostPathPosition(event);
    CGRect old;
    int i;

    if (dragLeft != -1) {
        old = positions[dragLeft];
        positions[dragLeft].origin.x
            = leftFinger.x - offsets[dragLeft].x;
        positions[dragLeft].origin.y
            = leftFinger.y - offsets[dragLeft].y;
```

Example 4-2. Mouse and gesture example (MyExample.m) (continued)

```
        [ self setNeedsDisplayInRect: old ];
        [ self setNeedsDisplayInRect: positions[dragLeft] ];
    }

    if (dragRight != -1) {
        old = positions[dragRight];
        positions[dragRight].origin.x
            = rightFinger.x - offsets[dragRight].x;
        positions[dragRight].origin.y
            = rightFinger.y - offsets[dragRight].y;
        [ self setNeedsDisplayInRect: old ];
        [ self setNeedsDisplayInRect: positions[dragRight] ];
    }
}

- (BOOL)canHandleGestures {

    return YES;
}

@end
```

What's Going On

Here's how the icon shuffle works:

1. When the application instantiates, a `MainView` object is created, which is derived from `UIView`, and its `initWithFrame` method is called. This initializes the images and positions of four icons on the screen: Phone, Mail, Safari, and iPod. The view class is then told to display itself.

2. As the view class is drawn, the class's `drawRect` method is called. This causes a black rectangle to first be rendered to blank the screen's background. Next, each icon is individually rendered on the screen using methods from the `UIImage` class (discussed more in Chapter 7).

3. When a single finger is used to move an icon, the `mouseDown` method is first called. This checks to see which icon the user has pressed and sets it in the object's `dragLeft` variable as the actively moving icon. The delta between where the user pressed inside the icon and the upper-left corner (origin) of the icon is stored so that the example can track the exact part of the icon that was pressed with the user's finger.

4. When the user's finger moves, the `mouseDragged` method is called, which sets the icon position to the current finger position, adjusting for where the user actually pressed inside the icon. This way, if the user pressed the center of the icon, the icon is moved so that its center will track with the user's finger. The `setNeedsDisplayInRect` method is called to invoke the view class's `drawRect` method again.

5. When the user's finger lifts up, the mouseUp method is called, which resets the active icon.

6. If two fingers are used, the gesture methods perform the same tasks, but process both finger positions, allowing two icons to track with the user's fingers. Because you don't know whether the fingers will be put down and raised in the same order, separate information must be stored on the left and right fingers. Note that putting down a second finger causes the information saved by the mouseDown method to be thrown away and replaced by the information returned by the the gestureStarted method. Similarly, raising the second finger causes the information saved by the gestureChanged method to be thrown away and replaced by the information returned by the mouseDraqgged method.

Further Study

It's a good idea to explore all of the different methods supported in these lower-level classes. Check out the following prototypes in your tool chain's *include* directory. These can be found in */usr/local/arm-apple-darwin/include*: *UIKit/UIResponder.h*, *UIKit/UIView.h*, *GraphicsServices/GraphicsServices.h*, and *CoreGraphics/CGGeometry.h*.

## CHAPTER 5

Advanced Graphics Programming with Core Surface and Layer Kit

Core Surface is a C-based framework used for building video buffers in which raw pixel data can be written directly to a screen layer. The framework is used when more advanced rendering is needed than basic graphics files, and is designed for applications that draw their own graphics, created while the program is running. Many different types of pixel formats are supported, and because surfaces have a direct interface to a screen layer, drawing is much faster than using higher-level image classes.

The Layer Kit framework is referred to as Core Animation on the Leopard desktop. Layer Kit provides the underlying classes for managing the content of UIView objects. It is also used to glue a Core Surface buffer to an object on the screen and to create 3-D transformations of 2-D objects for stunning animations and effects.

This chapter will introduce you to both frameworks and illustrate how the two can interoperate to manipulate screen surfaces and deliver different effects.

Understanding Layers

A layer is a low-level object found in many displayable classes. Layers act like a sheet of poster board to which an object's contents are affixed. It acts as a flexible backing for the object's display contents and can bend or contort the object in many ways on the screen. Every object that is capable of rendering itself—namely, those derived from the UIView class—has at least one layer to which its contents are glued.

For example, the UIImageView class contains all the basic information about an image—its display region, resolution, and various methods for working with the image. The image itself is glued to a layer, and the layer is used to display the image. The most basic layer behaves like a single clear sheet, and merely presents the image as is. More advanced classes, such as the UICompositeImageView (covered in Chapter 7), contain multiple layers that are treated like transparencies, each with different content, stacked on top of each other to produce one composite image.

Being flexible, layers can be used to manipulate the image. The layer's class, LKLayer, controls how this "flexible backing" is manipulated as it's displayed. If you bend the layer, the image will bend with it. If you rotate the layer, the image will come along for the ride. The layer's transparency (alpha) can be adjusted, an animation can be added, or the object can be rotated, skewed, and scaled as if it were sitting on top of silly putty. The object sitting on top of the layer is completely oblivious to how it is being manipulated, allowing your program to continue seeing the image (or other object) as if it were still a 2-D object. When the user sees the image, however, it's been contorted to whatever shape the layer has been twisted to.

A layer isn't limited to just holding image contents. The display output for a UITextView, or any other view class covered in Chapter 3, also sits on top of a layer. This means that navigation bars, tables, text boxes, and many other types of view classes can be transformed, scaled, rotated and even animated.

The important thing to remember about layers is that all UIView objects have one or more, and they control the way in which its contents are ultimately rendered on the screen.

Screen Surfaces

A screen surface is a Core Surface object used to access a raw pixel buffer that is rendered directly to a layer. This allows advanced games or applications to write pixel data directly to a surface on the screen. Core Surface supports many different color value configurations to host different types of pixel data.

Screen surfaces are attached to a layer, which is how the surface can eventually be displayed in a view. The surface is glued to the layer, and the layer is added to a view class, which renders it. This also means that the image rendered on a screen surface can be manipulated using the layer's methods.

Creating a Screen Surface

A screen surface is an object containing a raw video buffer. It supports a specific resolution, pitch, and pixel format. To create a new screen surface, a buffer is initialized using a dynamic dictionary class named CFMutableDictionary. This is used to provide information about the desired makeup and behavior of the surface. CFMutableDictionary is a class used on both the desktop and mobile platforms of Mac OS X and is part of the Core Foundation framework. Full documentation for this class can be found on the Apple Developer Connection web site.

The following example builds a dictionary object specifying a 320×480 video buffer. It uses RGBA, a four-byte pixel format containing one byte each for red, green, blue, and alpha blending channels. The last method called in the example allocates enough space in the dictionary for all the four-byte pixels in the $X \times Y$ rectangle.

```
CFMutableDictionaryRef dict;
int x = 320, y = 480, pitch = x*4, size = 4*x*y;
char *pixelFormat = "RGBA";

dict = CFDictionaryCreateMutable(kCFAllocatorDefault, 0,
  &kCFTypeDictionaryKeyCallBacks, &kCFTypeDictionaryValueCallBacks);

CFDictionarySetValue(dict, kCoreSurfaceBufferGlobal, kCFBooleanTrue);
CFDictionarySetValue(dict, kCoreSurfaceBufferPitch,
  CFNumberCreate(kCFAllocatorDefault, kCFNumberSInt32Type, &pitch));
CFDictionarySetValue(dict, kCoreSurfaceBufferWidth,
  CFNumberCreate(kCFAllocatorDefault, kCFNumberSInt32Type, &x));
CFDictionarySetValue(dict, kCoreSurfaceBufferHeight,
  CFNumberCreate(kCFAllocatorDefault, kCFNumberSInt32Type, &y));
CFDictionarySetValue(dict, kCoreSurfaceBufferPixelFormat,
  CFNumberCreate(kCFAllocatorDefault, kCFNumberSInt32Type,
  pixelFormat));
CFDictionarySetValue(dict, kCoreSurfaceBufferAllocSize,
  CFNumberCreate(kCFAllocatorDefault, kCFNumberSInt32Type, &size));
```

Once a dictionary has been built to define the type of buffer needed, the screen surface can be created using its properties.

```
CoreSurfaceBufferRef screenSurface = CoreSurfaceBufferCreate(dict);
```

Displaying the Screen Surface

Before a screen surface can be displayed, it needs to be attached to a layer. Create a new layer using the Layer Kit framework's LKLayer object.

```
LKLayer *screenLayer;

screenLayer = [ [ LKLayer layer ] retain ];
[ screenLayer setFrame: viewRect ];
[ screenLayer setOpaque: YES ];
```

Now, attach the contents of the screen surface to the newly created layer. Note that you always have to lock the screen surface while handling it.

```
CoreSurfaceBufferLock(screenSurface, 3);
[ screenLayer setContents: screenSurface ];
CoreSurfaceBufferUnlock(screenSurface);
```

The UIView objects you've been working with throughout this book contain their own base layer. To display the surface's contents, add the newly created layer to the existing UIView as a sublayer.

```
[ [ self _layer ] addSublayer: screenLayer ];
```

The screen surface is now glued to the layer, and the layer is added to the view. If there are other layers in the UIView object, the new layer will be placed on top of previous layers, meaning you'll need to adjust its transparency (alpha) in order to see the layers underneath.

Writing to the Screen Surface

Even after you add the surface's layer to a view, nothing is displayed yet because the video buffer itself is empty. The CoreSurfaceBuffer object contains a pointer to a raw video buffer. To access the base address of this raw video buffer, use the CoreSurfaceBufferGetBaseAddress function:

```
unsigned long *baseAddress = CoreSurfaceBufferGetBaseAddress(screenSurface);
```

The buffer is a single-dimensioned array, even though your application and the user think of it as two-dimensional. Pixels run from left to right and from top to bottom. For instance, baseAddress[0] addresses the upper-left pixel in the surface, baseAddress[319] addresses the upper-right pixel for the 320×480 resolution used in this surface, and baseAddress[320] addresses the leftmost pixel in the second row.

Because an RGBA pixel type is used in this example, each pixel is four bytes long. Using an unsigned long pointer (which is also four bytes long) allows entire pixels to be addressed as elements in an array.

You may also choose to use an unsigned char pointer, which would allow you to address the individual pixel values (one byte for each channel). Keep in mind, however, that you'll need to increment your pointer four bytes at a time to reach the next pixel (assuming a four-byte pixel type). For example, (unsigned char *) baseAddress[0] references the red channel of the first pixel, baseAddress[1] the green channel, baseAddress[2] the blue channel, baseAddress[3] the alpha channel, and finally baseAddress[4] the red channel of the next pixel.

16-Bit Pixel Formats

16-bit pixel formats are commonly used in lieu of the 32-bit RGBA pixel to deliver faster performance when color accuracy isn't critical—and because only expensive desktop displays can even support true 32-bit color, there's not much reason to use it on a cell phone. Because there's less memory to move around, a 16-bit frame can be copied in half the time as a 32-bit frame. To use this pixel format, make the following changes to the screen surface's dictionary properties before the surface is created.

```
int x = 320, y = 480, pitch = x*2, size = 2*x*y;
char *pixelFormat = "565L";
```

The 16-bit pixel format uses two bytes per pixel, and is identified by the pixel format 565L. Once the surface has been created, it can then be accessed using an unsigned short pointer, which is two bytes long instead of four.

```
unsigned short *baseAddress = CoreSurfaceBufferGetBaseAddress(screenSurface);
```

To convert RGB values to 16-bit values suitable for writing to such a buffer, you can define a macro, allowing your application to move smoothly between 16-bit and 32-bit RGBA.

```
#define RGB2565L(R, G, B) ((R >> 3) << 11) | (( G >> 2) << 5 ) \
    | (( B >> 3 ) << 0 )
```

Frame Buffer

A frame buffer is a secondary memory buffer used to construct a video frame before it is displayed on a screen surface. This can help prevent flickering by applications that render graphics one scan-line at a time (such as emulators) and can also be used to synchronize programs needing to display in frames per second. Using a frame buffer is also useful for aggregating multiple video layers together before displaying a finished frame. For example, if you are writing a game that draws several different video layers—a background, sprites, and a HUD—then each individual video layer can be drawn onto an internal frame buffer before the finished frame is rendered on the screen. The setup and copying of a frame buffer, if you choose to use one, is the job of the application. When the screen surface is created, its size is calculated as the pixel size multiplied by the width and height of the surface. To use a frame buffer, create a buffer of the same size:

```
workBuffer = malloc(2 * x * y);
```

Now, move all of your video processing so that it takes place in this work buffer until the program has finished rendering a frame. When the frame is complete, it is ready to be copied to the surface's video buffer. The period between the completed frame and the rendering of the next frame is called the v-blank period; this period is when the work buffer can safely be written out to the screen surface's buffer.

```
memcpy(baseAddress, workBuffer, 2 * x * y);
[ screenView setNeedsDisplay ];
```

Example: Random Snow

The first graphics program usually written by any geek is the display of random colors across the resolution of the screen. In keeping with this tradition, our example here creates and displays a screen surface, then applies a coat of rand( ) to each pixel every fifth of a second. When the example is run, the entire screen will be filled with colorful geek snow™.

To build this example, the Core Surface and Layer Kit frameworks must be linked in:

```
$ arm-apple-darwin-gcc -o MyExample MyExample.m -lobjc \
   -framework CoreFoundation -framework Foundation -framework UIKit \
   -framework CoreSurface -framework LayerKit
```

Examples 5-1 and 5-2 contain the code for the application.

Example 5-1. Core Surface example (MyExample.h)

```
#import <CoreFoundation/CoreFoundation.h>
#import <UIKit/UIKit.h>
#import <CoreSurface/CoreSurface.h>

@interface MainView : UIView
{
```

Example 5-1. Core Surface example (MyExample.h) (continued)

```
    CoreSurfaceBufferRef screenSurface;
    unsigned short *baseAddress;
    LKLayer *screenLayer;
}

- (id)initWithFrame:(CGRect)frame;
- (void)drawRect:(CGRect)rect;
- (CoreSurfaceBufferRef)screenSurface;
- (void)dealloc;

@end

@interface MyApp : UIApplication
{
    UIWindow *window;
    MainView *mainView;
}

- (void)applicationDidFinishLaunching:(NSNotification *)aNotification;
@end
```

Example 5-2. Core Surface example (MyExample.m)

```
#import "MyExample.h"

int main(int argc, char **argv)
{
    NSAutoreleasePool *autoreleasePool = [ [ NSAutoreleasePool alloc ] init ];
    int returnCode = UIApplicationMain(argc, argv, [ MyApp class ]);
    [ autoreleasePool release ];
    return returnCode;
}

@implementation MyApp
- (void)applicationDidFinishLaunching:(NSNotification *)aNotification {
    window = [ [ UIWindow alloc ] initWithContentRect:
        [ UIHardware fullScreenApplicationContentRect ]
    ];

    CGRect rect = [ UIHardware fullScreenApplicationContentRect ];
    rect.origin.x = rect.origin.y = 0.0f;

    mainView = [ [ MainView alloc ] initWithFrame: rect ];

    [ window setContentView: mainView ];
    [ window orderFront: self ];
    [ window makeKey: self ];
    [ window _setHidden: NO ];

    NSTimer *timer = [ NSTimer scheduledTimerWithTimeInterval: 0.05
            target: self
            selector: @selector(handleTimer:)
```

Example 5-2. Core Surface example (MyExample.m) (continued)

```
            userInfo: nil
            repeats: YES ];
}

- (void) handleTimer: (NSTimer *) timer
{
    CoreSurfaceBufferRef screenSurface;
    unsigned short *baseAddress;
    int i;
    screenSurface = [ mainView screenSurface ];
    baseAddress = CoreSurfaceBufferGetBaseAddress(screenSurface);

    for(i=0;i < 320 * 480;i++)
        baseAddress[i] = rand( ) % 0xFFFF;
    [ mainView setNeedsDisplay ];
}
@end

@implementation MainView
- (id)initWithFrame:(CGRect)rect {

    if ((self == [ super initWithFrame: rect ]) != nil) {
        CFMutableDictionaryRef dict;
        int x = 320, y = 480, pitch = x * 2, size = 2 * x * y, i;
        char *pixelFormat = "565L";

        /* Create a screen surface */
        dict = CFDictionaryCreateMutable(kCFAllocatorDefault, 0,
            &kCFTypeDictionaryKeyCallBacks, &kCFTypeDictionaryValueCallBacks);
        CFDictionarySetValue(dict, kCoreSurfaceBufferGlobal, kCFBooleanTrue);
        CFDictionarySetValue(dict, kCoreSurfaceBufferPitch,
            CFNumberCreate(kCFAllocatorDefault, kCFNumberSInt32Type, &pitch));
        CFDictionarySetValue(dict, kCoreSurfaceBufferWidth,
            CFNumberCreate(kCFAllocatorDefault, kCFNumberSInt32Type, &x));
        CFDictionarySetValue(dict, kCoreSurfaceBufferHeight,
            CFNumberCreate(kCFAllocatorDefault, kCFNumberSInt32Type, &y));
        CFDictionarySetValue(dict, kCoreSurfaceBufferPixelFormat,
            CFNumberCreate(kCFAllocatorDefault, kCFNumberSInt32Type,
            pixelFormat));
        CFDictionarySetValue(dict, kCoreSurfaceBufferAllocSize,
            CFNumberCreate(kCFAllocatorDefault, kCFNumberSInt32Type, &size));

        screenSurface = CoreSurfaceBufferCreate(dict);

        screenLayer = [ [ LKLayer layer ] retain ];
        [ screenLayer setFrame: rect ];
        [ screenLayer setContents: screenSurface ];
        [ screenLayer setOpaque: YES ];

        CoreSurfaceBufferLock(screenSurface, 3);

        [ [ self _layer ] addSublayer: screenLayer ];
```

Example 5-2. Core Surface example (MyExample.m) (continued)

```
        CoreSurfaceBufferUnlock(screenSurface);
    }

    return self;
}

- (void)drawRect:(CGRect)rect {

}

- (CoreSurfaceBufferRef)screenSurface {
    return screenSurface;
}

- (void)dealloc
{
    [ screenLayer release ];
    [ self dealloc ];
    [ super dealloc ];
}

@end
```

What's Going On

The geek snow example works like this:

1. When the application instantiates, a `MainView` object is created and its `initWithFrame` method is called.

2. `initWithFrame` creates a 16-bit 320×480 screen surface and glues it to its own `LKLayer` object. It then adds this layer to the main view.

3. An `NSTimer` object is created, causing a method named `handleTimer` to be called every 0.05 seconds. This steps through the entire surface and applies a random color value to each pixel. It also calls the object's `setNeedsDisplay` method, which instructs the object to repaint the screen.

Layer Animation

While Layer Kit proved useful in the previous section to glue a Core Surface buffer to the user interface, its capabilities extend far beyond a mere sticky layer. Layer Kit can be used to transform a 2-D object into a stunning 3-D texture that can be used to create beautiful transitions between views.

Chapter 3 introduced the `UITransitionView` class as a means of transitioning between different `UIView` objects. This class offered some basic animation, but was largely two-dimensional. The Layer Kit framework provides a more advanced set of tools for performing layer animation, allowing more spectacular transitions.

Creating a Layer Transition

Layer transitions augment the existing `UITransitionView` class by providing a way to override its transitions with new ones using Layer Kit's animation engine. This allows the developer to take advantage of the more advanced 3-D capabilities offered by Layer Kit without making significant changes to their code. When a layer transition, represented by an `LKTransition` object, is attached to a `UITransitionView`, the transition invokes Layer Kit to spawn a new thread that takes over all of the graphics processing for the transition. The developer needs only to add the desired transition to enhance an existing application. One such animation is added by the following code:

```
LKAnimation *animation = [ LKTransition animation ];
[ animation setType: @"pageCurl" ];
[ animation setSubtype: @"fromRight" ];
[ animation setTimingFunction:
    [ LKTimingFunction functionWithName: @"easeInEaseOut" ] ];
[ animation setFillMode: @"extended" ];
[ animation setTransitionFlags: 3 ];
[ animation setSpeed: 0.25 ];
```

Available animations

The previous example specifies the `pageCurl` animation using the `setType` method. The following animation types are available from Layer Kit.

Type	Description
pageCurl	The previous view curls off as if being peeled from a note pad, revealing the new view underneath.
pageUnCurl	The new view is curled over the old; reverse of `pageCurl`.
suckEffect	The old view is sucked through the bottom center of the window, revealing the new page underneath.
spewEffect	The new view is regurgitated up through the bottom center of the window; reverse of `suckEffect`.
genieEffect	The old view is sucked through the bottom left or right of the window, revealing the new page underneath.
unGenieEffect	The new view is regurgitated up through the bottom left or right of the window; reverse of `genieEffect`.
twist	The view is turned horizontally in a twisted cyclone fashion.
tubey	The view is turned vertically in an elastic fashion.
swirl	The old view fades to the new view, while the window itself swirls 360 degrees.
rippleEffect	The new view ripples into the window. This does not appear to work properly with full screen transitions.
cameraIris	A camera shutter closes on the old view, and opens to reveal the new view.

Type	Description
cameraIrisHollow	Same as cameraIris, only the old view is removed before the shudder is closed.
cameraIrisHollowOpen	A camera shutter opens into the new view only; animation begins with the shutter closed.
cameraIrisHollowClose	A camera shutter closes onto the old view; animation does not reopen the shutter.
charminUltra	The old view gently and comfortably fades into the new view, making you feel clean and refreshed.
zoomyIn	The new view zooms in from the back; the old view zooms out the front and vanishes.
zoomyOut	The new view zooms in from the front; the old view zooms out the back.
oglApplicationSuspend	The old view zooms out the back; the new view displays immediately. Resembles pressing the home button in an application.
oglFlip	The view flips horizontally, revealing the new page.

Available subtypes

The following subtypes can be used to define the direction in which the animation flows. These are set using the setSubtype method.

Type	Description
fromLeft	The animation flows from left to right.
fromRight	The animation flows from right to left.
fromTop	The animation flows from top to bottom.
fromBottom	The animation flows from bottom to top.

Animation speed and timing

The animation speed has a very small value range, from 0.0 (not moving) to about 5.0 (instantaneous). The fastest desirable speed will likely be 1.0.

The timing function defines the balance between the transition-out part of the animation and the transition-in part of the animation. The following different timings can be used.

Type	Description
easeInEaseOut	Both halves of the animation receive equal time.
easeIn	The second half of the animation is performed faster.
easeOut	The first half of the animation is performed faster.

Transition flags

The transition flags determine how edges are anti-aliased. The value is an OR'd set of values based on the following macros.

Macro	Meaning	Bit position
kLKLayerLeftEdge	Anti-alias left edges	1 << 0 (bit 0)
kLKLayerRightEdge	Anti-alias right edges	1 << 1
kLKLayerBottomEdge	Anti-alias bottom edges	1 << 2
kLKLayerTopEdge	Anti-alias top edges	1 << 3

Displaying the Layer Transition

Once a Layer Kit animation has been configured, it is executed through a UITransitionView object. Before the transition view's transition method is called, the animation must first attach to the view that will be animated. To animate all of the contents on the screen, the animation can be applied to the main view. This will cause all objects belonging to the view, such as navigation bars and buttons, to be included in the animation. If you're working with a smaller object, such as a UITextView or UIPushButton object, apply the animation to the transition view itself. This will cause only the smaller object to be affected.

```
[ [ transitionView _layer ] addAnimation: animation forKey: 0 ];
```

This line adds the animation to the layer so that when it is transitioned, the Layer Kit animation will be run in place of transition #0. Now, the only thing left is to call the transition:

```
[ transitionView transition: 0 toView: newView ];
```

Example: Page Flipping with Style

In Chapter 3, you built a page-flipping program to illustrate transitions. We'll use the same example here, but add Layer Kit animations to flip between pages.

This example can be compiled using the tool chain on the command line:

```
$ arm-apple-darwin-gcc -o MyExample MyExample.m -lobjc \
    -framework UIKit -framework CoreSurface \
    -framework CoreFoundation -framework LayerKit \
    -framework Foundation
```

Examples 5-3 and 5-4 contain the code for the new version of the page-flipping program.

Example 5-3. LayerKit animation example (MyExample.h)

```
#import <CoreFoundation/CoreFoundation.h>
#import <UIKit/UIKit.h>
#import <UIKit/UINavigationBar.h>
#import <UIKit/UINavigationItem.h>
#import <UIKit/UITransitionView.h>
#import <UIKit/UITextView.h>
#import <LayerKit/LKTransition.h>
#import <LayerKit/LKAnimation.h>
```

Example 5-3. LayerKit animation example (MyExample.h) (continued)

```
#define MAX_PAGES 10

@interface MainView : UIView
{
    UINavigationBar     *navBar;    /* Our navigation bar */
    UINavigationItem    *navItem;   /* Navigation bar title */
    UITransitionView    *transView; /* Our transition */
    int                 pageNum;    /* Current page number */

    /* Some pages to scroll through */
    UITextView          *textPage[MAX_PAGES];
}

- (id)initWithFrame:(CGRect)frame;
- (void)dealloc;
- (UINavigationBar *)createNavBar:(CGRect)rect;
- (void)setNavBar;
- (void)navigationBar:(UINavigationBar *)navbar buttonClicked:(int)button;
- (void)flipTo:(int)page;

@end

@interface MyApp : UIApplication
{
    UIWindow *window;
    MainView *mainView;
}

- (void)applicationDidFinishLaunching:(NSNotification *)aNotification;
@end
```

Example 5-4. LayerKit animation example (MyExample.m)

```
#import "MyExample.h"

int main(int argc, char **argv)
{
    NSAutoreleasePool *autoreleasePool = [
        [ NSAutoreleasePool alloc ] init
    ];
    int returnCode = UIApplicationMain(argc, argv, [ MyApp class ]);
    [ autoreleasePool release ];
    return returnCode;
}

@implementation MyApp

- (void)applicationDidFinishLaunching:(NSNotification *)aNotification {
    window = [ [ UIWindow alloc ] initWithContentRect:
        [ UIHardware fullScreenApplicationContentRect ]
    ];
```

Example 5-4. LayerKit animation example (MyExample.m) (continued)

```objc
    CGRect rect = [ UIHardware fullScreenApplicationContentRect ];
    rect.origin.x = rect.origin.y = 0.0f;

    mainView = [ [ MainView alloc ] initWithFrame: rect ];

    [ window setContentView: mainView ];
    [ window orderFront: self ];
    [ window makeKey: self ];
    [ window _setHidden: NO ];
}
@end

@implementation MainView
- (id)initWithFrame:(CGRect)rect {
    if ((self == [ super initWithFrame: rect ]) != nil) {
        CGRect viewRect;
        int i;

        /* Create a new view port below the navigation bar */
        viewRect = CGRectMake(rect.origin.x, rect.origin.y + 48.0,
            rect.size.width, rect.size.height - 48.0);

        /* Set our start page */
        pageNum = MAX_PAGES / 2;

        /* Create ten UITextView objects as pages in our book */

        for(i=0;i<MAX_PAGES;i++) {
            textPage[i] = [ [ UITextView alloc ] initWithFrame: rect ];
            [ textPage[i] setText: [ [ NSString alloc ] initWithFormat:
                @"This is some text for page %d", i+1 ] ];
        }

        /* Creat a navigation bar with 'Prev' and 'Next' buttons */
        navBar = [ self createNavBar: rect ];
        [ self setNavBar ];
        [ self addSubview: navBar ];

        /* Create our transition view */
        transView = [ [ UITransitionView alloc ] initWithFrame: viewRect ];
        [ self addSubview: transView ];

        /* Transition to the first page */
        [ self flipTo: pageNum ];
    }

    return self;
}

- (void)dealloc
{
    [ navBar release ];
```

Example 5-4. LayerKit animation example (MyExample.m) (continued)

```objc
    [ navItem release ];
    [ self dealloc ];
    [ super dealloc ];
}

- (UINavigationBar *)createNavBar:(CGRect)rect {
    UINavigationBar *newNav = [ [UINavigationBar alloc] initWithFrame:
        CGRectMake(rect.origin.x, rect.origin.y, rect.size.width, 48.0f)
    ];

    [ newNav setDelegate: self ];
    [ newNav enableAnimation ];

    /* Add our title */
    navItem = [ [UINavigationItem alloc] initWithTitle:@"My Example" ];
    [ newNav pushNavigationItem: navItem ];

    [ newNav showLeftButton:@"Prev"  withStyle: 0
                rightButton:@"Next" withStyle: 0 ];

    return newNav;
}
- (void)setNavBar
{

    /* Enable or disable our page buttons */

    if (pageNum == 1)
        [ navBar setButton: 1 enabled: NO ];
    else
        [ navBar setButton: 1 enabled: YES ];

    if (pageNum == MAX_PAGES)
        [ navBar setButton: 0 enabled: NO ];
    else
        [ navBar setButton: 0 enabled: YES ];
}

- (void)navigationBar:(UINavigationBar *)navbar buttonClicked:(int)button
{
    /* Next Page */
    if (button == 0)
    {
        [ self flipTo: pageNum+1 ];
    }

    /* Prev Page */
    else {
        [ self flipTo: pageNum-1 ];
    }

}
```

Example 5-4. LayerKit animation example (MyExample.m) (continued)

```objc
- (void)flipTo:(int)page {

    LKAnimation *animation = [ LKTransition animation ];
    [ animation setType: @"oglFlip" ];
    [ animation setSubtype: @"fromLeft" ];
    [ animation setTimingFunction:
        [ LKTimingFunction functionWithName: @"easeOut" ] ];
    [ animation setFillMode: @"extended" ];
    [ animation setTransitionFlags: 3 ];
    [ animation setSpeed: 0.50 ];
    [ [ self  _layer ] addAnimation: animation forKey: 0 ];

    [ transView transition: 0 toView: textPage[page-1] ];
    pageNum = page;
    [ self setNavBar ];
}

@end
```

What's Going On

This example works in an almost identical fashion to Examples 3-9 and 3-10 in Chapter 3.

1. When the application initializes, a MainView object is created and its initWithFrame method is called. This creates 10 UITextView objects to serve as our reading page examples. It then creates the navigation bar and one transition view. Finally, a method called flipTo is called, which is responsible for flipping to the page number specified.

2. The flipTo member function builds an LKAnimation object and adds it to the main view's layer. It then calls the transition view to do the work of triggering the animation while simultaneously moving to the desired page. The main view layer's animation is automatically used, which causes the contents of the entire main view to transition, instead of just the page being flipped.

3. When the user presses the Prev or Next navigation buttons, the buttonClicked method gets called with a pointer to the navigation bar and the button number. From here, the flipTo method is called again to transition to the new page and disable either navigation button if it has reached one end of the book.

Further Study

Check out the *LKLayer.h, LKAnimation.h*, and *LKTransition.h* prototypes in your tool chain's *include* directory. You'll find it in */usr/local/arm-apple-darwin/include/ LayerKit/*.

Layer Transformations

Layer Kit's rendering capabilities allow a 2-D image to be freely manipulated as if it were 3-D. An image can be rotated on an X-Y-Z axis to any angle, scaled, and skewed. The LKTransform object is the magic behind Apple's Cover Flow® technology. The Apple desktop uses the Core Animation framework to process 3-D transformations. The iPhone's Layer Kit framework uses many of the same functions, but has renamed them with the prefix LK (Layer Kit) instead of CA (Core Animation). The iPhone supports scale, rotation, affine, and translation transformations. More information about these various transformations can be found in Apple's Core Animation Programming Guide available on the Apple Developer Connection web site.

A transformation is carried out on the level of individual layers. The Layer Kit framework performs transformations using an LKTransform object. This object is applied to a view's layer to bend or otherwise manipulate its layer into the desired 3-D configuration. The application continues to treat the object as if it's a 2-D object, but when it is presented to the user, the object conforms to whatever transformation has been applied to the layer. The following example creates a transformation for the purpose of rotating a layer.

```
LKTransform myTransform;
myTransform = LKTransformMakeRotation(angle, x, y, z);
```

The LKTransformMakeRotation method creates a transformation that will rotate a layer by angle radians using an axis of X-Y-Z. The values for X-Y-Z define the axis and magnitude for each space (between -1 and +1). Assigning a value to an axis instructs the transformation to rotate using that axis. For example, if the X-axis is set to either -1 or +1, the object will be rotated on the X-axis in that direction, meaning it will be rotated vertically. Think of these values as inserting straws through the image for each axis. If a straw were inserted across the X-axis, the image would spin around the straw vertically. More complex rotations can be created using axis angle values. For most uses, however, values of -1 and +1 are sufficient.

To rotate a layer by 45 degrees on its horizontal axis (rotating vertically), the following might be used:

```
myTransform = LKTransformMakeRotation(0.78, 1.0, 0.0, 0.0);
```

To rotate the same amount horizontally, specify a value for the Y-axis instead:

```
myTransform = LKTransformMakeRotation(0.78, 0.0, 1.0, 0.0);
```

The value 0.78 used above represents the radian value of the angle. To calculate radians from degrees, use the simple formula $M\pi/180$. For example, $45\pi/180 = 45(3.1415)/180 = 0.7853$.

Once the transformation has been created, it's then applied to the layer being operated on. To access the layer, use the _layer method inside of any view object to return its LKLayer object. The LKLayer object has a setTransform method that you use to attach the transformation to it. This instructs the layer to perform the transformation as specified.

```
[ [ imageView _layer ] setTransform: myTransform ];
```

Example: Spinning Wallpaper Demo

This example makes use of Layer Kit's LKTransformMakeRotate transformation to spin the desktop wallpaper many different ways on the X, Y, and Z axes. The wallpaper is loaded into a UIAutocorrectImageView class, which is used to scale the image down to half its size (more specifics will be covered in Chapter 7). A timer is then used to adjust the image's rotation every 0.01 seconds, changing the axis at the end of every 360-degree spin.

To compile this example, use the tool chain on the command line:

```
$ arm-apple-darwin-gcc -o MyExample MyExample.m -lobjc \
-framework Foundation -framework CoreFoundation -framework UIKit \
-framework LayerKit
```

Examples 5-5 and 5-6 show the code.

Example 5-5. Layer transformation example (MyExample.h)

```
#import <CoreFoundation/CoreFoundation.h>
#import <UIKit/UIKit.h>
#import <LayerKit/LayerKit.h>
#import <LayerKit/LKTransform.h>

@interface MainView : UIView
{
    UIAutocorrectImageView *imageView;
    LKTransform transform;
    NSTimer *timer;

    float angle, x, y, z;
}

- (id)initWithFrame:(CGRect)frame;
- (void) handleTimer: (NSTimer *) timer;
- (void)dealloc;

@end

@interface MyApp : UIApplication
{
    UIWindow *window;
    MainView *mainView;
}
```

Example 5-5. Layer transformation example (MyExample.h) (continued)

```
- (void)applicationDidFinishLaunching:(NSNotification *)aNotification;
@end
```

Example 5-6. Layer transformation example (MyExample.m)

```
#import <UIKit/UIKit.h>
#import <UIKit/UIAutocorrectImageView.h>
#import "MyExample.h"

int main(int argc, char **argv)
{
    NSAutoreleasePool *autoreleasePool = [
        [ NSAutoreleasePool alloc ] init
    ];
    int returnCode = UIApplicationMain(argc, argv, [ MyApp class ]);
    [ autoreleasePool release ];
    return returnCode;

}

@implementation MyApp

- (void)applicationDidFinishLaunching:(NSNotification *)aNotification {
    window = [ [ UIWindow alloc ] initWithContentRect:
        [ UIHardware fullScreenApplicationContentRect ]
    ];

    CGRect rect = [ UIHardware fullScreenApplicationContentRect ];
    rect.origin.x = rect.origin.y = 0.0f;

    mainView = [ [ MainView alloc ] initWithFrame: rect ];

    [ window setContentView: mainView ];
    [ window orderFront: self ];
    [ window makeKey: self ];
    [ window _setHidden: NO ];
}

@end

@implementation MainView
- (id)initWithFrame:(CGRect)rect {

    if ((self == [ super initWithFrame: rect ]) != nil) {
        UIImage *tempImage;

        angle = y = z = 0;
        x = 1;

        tempImage = [ UIImage defaultDesktopImage ];
        imageView = [ [ UIAutocorrectImageView alloc ]
```

Example 5-6. Layer transformation example (MyExample.m) (continued)

```
            initWithFrame: CGRectMake(80, 120, 160, 240)
            image: tempImage ];
        [ [ self _layer ] addSublayer: [ imageView _layer ] ];

        transform = LKTransformMakeRotation(angle, x, y, z);
        [ imageView _layer ].transform = transform;

        [ self setNeedsDisplay ];

        timer = [ NSTimer scheduledTimerWithTimeInterval: 0.01
            target: self
            selector: @selector(handleTimer:)
            userInfo: nil
            repeats: YES ];
    }

    return self;
}

- (void) handleTimer: (NSTimer *) timer
{
    angle += 0.01;
    if (angle > 6.283) {
        angle = 0;
        if (z == 1) {
            x = 0;
        }
        else {
            if (y == 1) {
                z = 1;
            }
            y = 1;
        }
    }

    [ [ imageView _layer] setTransform:
        LKTransformRotate(transform, angle, x, y, z)
    ];
}

- (void)dealloc
{
    [ imageView release ];
    [ self dealloc ];
    [ super dealloc ];
}

@end
```

What's Going On

The transformation demo works like this:

1. When the application instantiates, a controlling view named `mainView` is created and its `initWithFrame` method is called.

2. This initializes the angle and X-Y-Z axes, and loads the desktop wallpaper into a `UIAutocorrectImageView` where it is scaled down to half its size. The image is displayed in the middle of the screen.

3. A timer is started to call the `handleTimer` method every 0.01 seconds. With each timer heartbeat, the angle is increased and wraps around after reaching 360 degrees (6.283 radians).

4. The transformation is modified using the `LKTransformRotate` method and applied to the layer. This gives the appearance of the image rotating in the middle of the screen.

5. Every time the angle wraps, different axes are set, effectively changing the direction in which the object is rotating.

Further Study

Explore transformations a little more and try these exercises:

1. Check out the *LKTransform.h* and *LKLayer.h* prototypes in your tool chain's *include* directory. These can be found in */usr/local/arm-apple-darwin/include/ LayerKit/*.

2. Check out *http://en.wikipedia.org/wiki/Axis_angle*, which explains how axis angles work. This might come in handy at designing custom rotation transformations.

3. Check out Apple's Core Animation guide on the Apple Developer Connection web site. The Core Animation functions mirror the iPhone's LayerKit functions. It can be found at: *http://developer.apple.com/documentation/Cocoa/Conceptual/ CoreAnimation_guide/*.

## CHAPTER 6

Making Some Noise

If there was ever any doubt whether the iPhone was intended to be a music device, the presence of three different frameworks on the iPhone just for sound should be all the answer you need. The Core Audio, Celestial, and Audio Toolbox frameworks all provide different levels of sound functionality. In addition to this, the iPhone runs an audio daemon called mediaserverd that aggregates the sound output of all applications and governs events such as volume and ringer switch changes. There are a lot of moving pieces involved in the iPhone's sound framework, but Apple has provided some great interfaces that make the task painless.

Core Audio: It's Great, but You Can't Use It

Of the three frameworks available, Core Audio is the most low-level, and least accessible. Core Audio provides a direct interface to the iPhone's sound device. There is only one sound device, so only one process can be talking to it at any time. Unlike the Mac OS X desktop, which allows developers to share Core Audio resources, the iPhone has an audio daemon that binds to the device as the iPhone is booted, setting what is called hog mode. *Hog mode* is a flag hardcoded into the Core Audio framework that prevents any other application from being able to say, "Hey, I'd like to make some sound, can you give up control of the sound card for a minute?" In other words, the audio daemon hogs the sound card all to itself, requiring all sounds to be played through the daemon instead of directly.

The Core Audio framework was the first framework figured out by developers, and some very early iPhone applications attempted to use it to deliver a digital sound stream. This required a terrible and ugly hack requiring the user to kill the mediaserverd process. The program could then be heard, but this hack killed the rest of the sound on the entire iPhone. Many people were so desperate to play video games on the iPhone that they actually did this. Now that the Celestial and Audio Toolbox frameworks have been figured out, there's no longer any need to use Core Audio, and all of the applications that formerly used it have been updated.

If you'd still like to learn about the Core Audio framework, the good news is that it's nearly identical to the desktop version. The Apple Developer Connection web site provides many resources for the Core Audio framework at *http://developer.apple.com/ audio/*.

Celestial

Celestial is the preferred iPhone framework for playing sound and music files and recording sound from the built-in microphone. Celestial uses an AVController class to play sound samples, which are represented as AVItem objects. The framework also supports an optional AVQueue class to arrange playback of different samples.

What Celestial is not useful for is playing a digital stream; that is, a raw output channel of sound. That will be covered in the next section on the Audio Toolbox. Celestial works only with audio files.

To tap into Celestial, your application must be linked to the Celestial framework. Using the tool chain, link Celestial to your application by adding the following arguments to the compiler arguments described in Chapter 2:

```
$ arm-apple-darwin-gcc -o MyApp MyApp.m -lobjc \
    -framework CoreFoundation \
    -framework Foundation \
    -framework Celestial
```

To add this option to the sample makefile from Chapter 2, add the Celestial framework to the linker flags section so that the library is linked in:

```
LDFLAGS =    -lobjc \
         -framework CoreFoundation \
         -framework Foundation \
         -framework Celestial
```

ringerState

Playing sounds can be very useful for many types of applications, but it's up to the developer to ensure that the user's desire to silence her phone is respected. Before a sound is played, you should first check the ringer state—the mute switch on the side of the phone. To check this, UIKit provides a method named ringerState within the UIHardware class.

```
int ringerState = [ UIHardware ringerState ];
```

When the mute toggle is switched to "sound" mode, a value of 1 is returned. When it is in "mute" mode, a value of 0 is returned. If the ringer is muted, it's common practice to use the phone's built-in vibrator in lieu of an audible notification. An example of this can be found in the appendix. Muting is voluntary—that is, the operating system does not enforce this because some applications were meant to generate sound regardless of the ringer switch. For example, the iPod application plays music even if the ringer is turned off, allowing the user to listen to a song without being interrupted by incoming phone calls (if she's on the treadmill, for example).

The Audio Controller

The AVController class establishes a connection to the iPhone's audio daemon. It's also responsible for controlling all sound that is played through it. Think of the AVController as the scrubber at the bottom of your iPod application (the bar containing your play, pause, navigation, and volume control). The class handles all of these functions, as well as setting the equalizer, sound frequency, and even repeat mode.

```
AVController * av = [ [ AVController alloc ] init ];
```

Volume

The volume can be set for either individual sound samples or the entire controller. To set it within the scope of the controller, call the AVController's setVolume method.

```
[ av setVolume: 1.0 ]
```

The volume is a floating-point number from 0.0 to 1.0. Adjusting the volume on the controller level will cause a volume window to appear to the user. This is useful for handling mute requests and the like.

Setting the volume for an individual sound sample will be shown in the upcoming section "Audio Samples."

Repeat mode

To tell the controller to repeat a sound after it has finished playing, call setRepeatMode, passing an integer value as an argument.

```
[ av setRepeatMode: 1 ];
```

The repeat mode must be set after an item has begun playing. The valid repeat modes are as follows.

Mode	Description
0	Repeat Off
1	Repeat On

Although set on a controller level, only the current sample will be repeated—even if more than one sound sample is queued up to play.

Sample rate

The sample rate is the playback frequency sounds should be played at. This should match the frequency at which samples were originally recorded, and can be set either

---

manually, using the setRate method shown here, or automatically by leaving the option alone.

```
NSError *err;
[ av setRate: 44100.0 error: &err ];
if (err != nil) {
    NSLog(@"The following error has occured: %@", err);
}
```

Many Celestial methods need to be able to report an error. The NSError class is used for this. NSError is similar to an NSString object, which is standard across both the iPhone and Mac OS X desktop operating systems. This class builds on the NSString base class and encapsulates additional information pertaining to error codes. More information about NSError and NSString can be found in the Cocoa reference available on the Apple Developer Connection web site.

Equalizer preset

An equalizer adjusts the relative volume of different frequencies to produce a clearer sound. Different equalizers improve the user's experience for different types of recordings and music, and Apple uses a preset collection of equalizers heavily in iTunes and follow-up products. The iPhone supports 22 different equalizer presets that can be set using the setEQPreset method.

```
[ av setEQPreset: 0 ];
```

The default setting is to use no EQ, and if you're only playing event sounds, there's little reason to change this. If you're playing a radio broadcast or writing a third-party player, however, the following table can be used to set the desired preset.

Preset	Description
0	Off
1	Acoustic
2	Bass Booster
3	Bass Reducer
4	Classical
5	Dance
6	Deep
7	Electronic
8	Flat
9	Hip Hop
10	Jazz
11	Latin
12	Loudness
13	Lounge

Preset	Description
14	Piano
15	Pop
16	R&B
17	Rock
18	Small Speakers
19	Spoken Word
20	Treble Booster
21	Treble Reducer
22	Vocal Booster

Mute

Muting the audio channel is as easy as sending a message to `setMuted`. This method applies not only to the sound currently playing, but also to every sound subsequently played through the controller object.

```
[ av setMuted: NO ];
```

Audio Samples

So far, you've instantiated an `AVController` object that builds an audio channel, but nothing has been provided to play samples yet. Create each sample to be played as an `AVItem` object. The following code snip creates an `AVItem` to reference an existing sound file on the iPhone. The `NSError` class introduced in the last section is also used here also to capture errors.

```
NSError *err;
AVItem *item = [ [ AVItem alloc ]
    initWithPath: @"/Library/Ringtones/Pinball.m4r" error: &err
];
if (err != nil) {
    NSLog(@"The following error has occured: %@", err);
}
```

Playing URLs

URLs can also be played using the same `AVItem` class by specifying a URL instead of a file path.

```
AVItem *item = [ [ AVItem alloc ]
    initWithPath: @"http://path-to-sound-file" error: &err
];
```

This can be useful, but keep in mind that your application will require a network connection to play these sounds. A slow or lagged connection could also slow the application.

Sample volume

To set the volume for a specific sample, the `AVItem`'s `setVolume` method can be called. Unlike the controller's method, using `setVolume` here will not affect the rest of the audio channel, nor will it display a volume change window to the user.

```
[ item setVolume: 0.5 ];
```

Equalizer preset

An individual sample also has its own EQ property, which can be set using the same table shown earlier. This sets the EQ of the sample only, and will remain in effect for as long as the object exists.

```
[ item setEQPreset: 0 ];
```

Duration

Once the object has been created, you can find the sample's duration in seconds.

```
float duration = [ item duration ];
```

Playing an item

Once the desired audio object properties have been set, the object can now be attached to the audio controller for playing.

```
BOOL ok;
[ av setCurrentItem: item preservingRate:NO ];
ok = [ av play:nil ];
```

The Boolean return value from the `play` method will be true if the audio controller accepted your request to play the item. If another item is currently playing, it will reject your request and return `NO`.

Pausing

To pause playing, call the controller's pause method.

```
[ av pause ];
```

Example: Hello, Sound!

This example creates an audio controller and audio sample using an existing ring tone on the iPhone, then plays the sound. If any errors occur, it will be displayed in the text view. Otherwise, the text "Hello, Sound!" will be displayed and you should hear some noise.

To compile this example, you'll need to include the Celestial framework in your build statement:

```
$ arm-apple-darwin-gcc -o MyExample MyExample.m -lobjc \
    -framework Foundation \
```

```
    -framework CoreFoundation \
    -framework UIKit \
    -framework Celestial
```

Examples 6-1 and 6-2 contain the code.

Example 6-1. Audio controller example (MyExample.h)

```
#import <CoreFoundation/CoreFoundation.h>
#import <UIKit/UIKit.h>
#import <UIKit/UITextView.h>
#import <Celestial/AVController.h>
#import <Celestial/AVItem.h>

@interface MainView : UIView
{
    UITextView   *textView;
    AVController *av;
    AVItem       *item;
}

- (id)initWithFrame:(CGRect)frame;
- (void)dealloc;

@end

@interface MyApp : UIApplication
{
    UIWindow *window;
    MainView *mainView;
}

- (void)applicationDidFinishLaunching:(NSNotification *)aNotification;
@end
```

Example 6-2. Audio controller example (MyExample.m)

```
#import "MyExample.h"
int main(int argc, char **argv)
{
    NSAutoreleasePool *autoreleasePool = [
        [ NSAutoreleasePool alloc ] init
    ];
    int returnCode = UIApplicationMain(argc, argv, [ MyApp class ]);
    [ autoreleasePool release ];
    return returnCode;
}

@implementation MyApp

- (void)applicationDidFinishLaunching:(NSNotification *)aNotification {
    window = [ [ UIWindow alloc ] initWithContentRect:
        [ UIHardware fullScreenApplicationContentRect ]
    ];
```

Example 6-2. Audio controller example (MyExample.m) (continued)

```
    CGRect rect = [ UIHardware fullScreenApplicationContentRect ];
    rect.origin.x = rect.origin.y = 0.0f;

    mainView = [ [ MainView alloc ] initWithFrame: rect ];

    [ window setContentView: mainView ];
    [ window orderFront: self ];
    [ window makeKey: self ];
    [ window _setHidden: NO ];
}
@end

@implementation MainView
- (id)initWithFrame:(CGRect)rect {

    if ((self == [ super initWithFrame: rect ]) != nil) {

        NSError *err;
        textView = [ [ UITextView alloc ] initWithFrame: rect ];
        [ textView setTextSize: 18 ];
        [ textView setText: @"Hello, Sound!" ];
        [ self addSubview: textView ];

        av = [ [ AVController alloc ] init ];
        item = [ [ AVItem alloc ]
            initWithPath:@"/Library/Ringtones/Pinball.m4r" error:&err
        ];

        if (err != nil) {
            [ textView setText: err ];
        } else {
            BOOL playedOK;
            [ av setCurrentItem: item preservingRate:NO ];
            playedOK = [ av play:nil ];
            if (playedOK == NO) {
                [ textView setText: @"An error has occurred." ];
            }
        }

    }

    return self;
}

- (void)dealloc
{
    [ self dealloc ];
    [ super dealloc ];
}

@end
```

What's Going On

The audio controller example works like this:

1. The application instantiates and displays a textbox with the text, "Hello, Sound!"

2. An AVController object is instantiated followed by an AVItem object pointing to the Pinball ringtone, located at */Library/Ringtones/Pinball.m4r*.

3. If the AVItem initialized with an error, the text in the text view is replaced with the error message. Otherwise, the sample is set as the current item on the controller.

4. The controller is told to play, a call that plays the current item, and returns a Boolean identifying whether the command was successful.

5. If the Boolean value NO is returned, something went wrong and an error is displayed to the user in the text view.

Audio Queues

One limitation of the audio controller is that it can deal with only one audio sample at a time. If two sounds need to be played in succession, there's no way to tell the controller object to do this without abruptly killing the currently playing sound. Audio queues provide a solution to this problem by creating an array-like structure where samples can be queued up for ordered play.

This section discusses the audio queues available in the audio controller's AVController class, which play prerecorded audio selections from files. If an application generates its own sounds, it should use the Audio Toolbox audio queue described later in this chapter.

The queue provided by the audio controller's class is the AVQueue class:

```
AVQueue *avq = [ [ AVQueue alloc ] init ];
```

An audio queue is attached to the audio controller, at which point the controller acknowledges it as the source for all future playback.

```
[ av setQueue: avq ];
```

Sound samples, which are instantiated as AVItem objects, can then be added, removed, and rearranged on the queue using a number of available methods:

Add a sample to the end of the queue
```
[ avq appendItem: item ];
```

Insert a sample after another sample, identified by the other sample's AVItem object
```
[ avq insertItem: item afterItem: other_item error: &err ];
```

Insert a sample at a specific position in the queue
```
[ avq inertItem: item atIndex: 4 error: &err ];
```

Remove a sample, identified by the sample's AVItem *object*
> [avq removeItem: item];

Remove a sample, identified by a position in the queue
> [avq removeItemAtIndex: 3];

Remove all items within a given range by position on the queue
> [avq removeItemsInRange: NSMakeRange(3, 4)];

> The NSMakeRange function takes two arguments: the start position and the length of the range. This example removes samples 3–7.

Remove all audio samples from the queue
> [avq removeAllItems];

When the controller is instructed to play, it will step through each item in the queue.

> [av play: nil];

The play method is called in the same fashion as it is when there is no queue, but because the queue has been attached to the controller, it will use the queue as the sample source without any special instructions. During playback, items may be added, removed, or rearranged on the queue so long as the playback hasn't reached the affected items.

Example: Alternating Ringtones

In the previous example, a ringtone was played directly through the controller without a queue. Any attempts to set the current item to a new sample during playback would have been ignored. In this example, two ringtones will be played through an audio queue, one after the other.

Compile this example using the following command line:

```
$ arm-apple-darwin-gcc -o MyExample MyExample.m -lobjc \
    -framework Foundation \
    -framework CoreFoundation \
    -framework UIKit \
    -framework Celestial
```

Examples 6-3 and 6-4 contain the code.

Example 6-3. Audio queue example (MyExample.h)

```
#import <CoreFoundation/CoreFoundation.h>
#import <Foundation/Foundation.h>
#import <UIKit/UIKit.h>
#import <UIKit/UITextView.h>
#import <Celestial/AVController.h>
#import <Celestial/AVItem.h>
#import <Celestial/AVQueue.h>

@interface MainView : UIView
{
```

Example 6-3. Audio queue example (MyExample.h) (continued)

```
    UITextView    *textView;
    AVController  *av;
    AVItem        *item1, *item2;
    AVQueue       *avq;
}

- (id)initWithFrame:(CGRect)frame;
- (void)dealloc;

@end

@interface MyApp : UIApplication
{
    UIWindow *window;
    MainView *mainView;
}

- (void)applicationDidFinishLaunching:(NSNotification *)aNotification;
@end
```

Example 6-4. Audio queue example (MyExample.m)

```
#import "MyExample.h"

int main(int argc, char **argv)
{
    NSAutoreleasePool *autoreleasePool = [
        [ NSAutoreleasePool alloc ] init
    ];
    int returnCode = UIApplicationMain(argc, argv, [ MyApp class ]);
    [ autoreleasePool release ];
    return returnCode;
}

@implementation MyApp

- (void)applicationDidFinishLaunching:(NSNotification *)aNotification {
    window = [ [ UIWindow alloc ] initWithContentRect:
        [ UIHardware fullScreenApplicationContentRect ]
    ];

    CGRect rect = [ UIHardware fullScreenApplicationContentRect ];
    rect.origin.x = rect.origin.y = 0.0f;

    mainView = [ [ MainView alloc ] initWithFrame: rect ];

    [ window setContentView: mainView ];
    [ window orderFront: self ];
    [ window makeKey: self ];
    [ window _setHidden: NO ];
}
@end
```

Example 6-4. Audio queue example (MyExample.m) (continued)

```
@implementation MainView
- (id)initWithFrame:(CGRect)rect {

    if ((self == [ super initWithFrame: rect ]) != nil) {

        NSError *err;
        textView = [ [ UITextView alloc ] initWithFrame: rect ];
        [ textView setTextSize: 18 ];
        [ textView setText: @"Hello, Sound!" ];
        [ self addSubview: textView ];

        av = [ [ AVController alloc ] init ];
        avq = [ [ AVQueue alloc ] init ];

        item1 = [ [ AVItem alloc ]
            initWithPath:@"/Library/Ringtones/Pinball.m4r" error:&err
        ];
        if (err != nil)
            [ textView setText: err ];

        item2 = [ [ AVItem alloc ]
            initWithPath:@"/Library/Ringtones/Blues.m4r" error: &err
        ];
        if (err != nil)
            [ textView setText: err ];

        [ avq appendItem: item1 error: &err ];
        [ avq appendItem: item2 error: &err ];

        [ av setQueue: avq ];
        [ av play:nil ];
    }

    return self;
}

- (void)dealloc
{
    [ self dealloc ];
    [ super dealloc ];
}

@end
```

What's Going On

1. The application instantiates and displays a textbox with the default text, "Hello, Sound!".

2. An `AVController` and `AVQueue` objects are instantiated.

3. Instead of creating a single AVItem object, two are created: one for the Pinball ringtone, and another for the Blues ringtone, both located in the */Library/Ringtones* directory.

4. If either AVItem initializes with an error, the text in the text view is replaced with the error message.

5. Both samples are added to the audio queue object.

6. The audio queue object is attached to the controller, and the controller is instructed to play.

7. Both audio samples are played through the queue in the order they were added.

Recording Sound

Celestial not only plays sounds, but records them as well. Using the AVRecorder object, an application can use the iPhone's built-in microphone to record and then write an audio file out to disk.

The AVRecorder class can be spooky, in that the iPhone gives no indication that any recording is taking place. Malware could easily be written to eavesdrop on an iPhone user without their knowledge. It's up to the developer to notify the user that sound is being recorded.

A typical initialization for AVRecorder is:

```
NSURL *url = [ [ NSURL alloc ] initWithString: @"/tmp/rec.amr" ];
avr = [ [ AVRecorder alloc ] init ];
[ avr setFilePath: url ];
```

The recorder object uses a NSURL object, which is similar to an NSString. It contains the path on disk to write the recorded file to. This is the only parameter needed by the recorder object before it is ready to record. The filename in the example ends with an *.amr* extension, which reflects the default recording format: Adaptive Multi-Rate. The AMR codec is a compressed audio format developed by Ericsson. Many mobile devices use it because it provides superior compression of voice recordings.

To begin recording, the recorder first activates the microphone, and then it starts recording.

```
[ avr activate: nil ];
[ avr start ];
```

To stop recording, a message is sent to the stop method, and finally, the microphone is deactivated.

```
[ avr stop ];
[ avr deactivate ];
```

Example: Voice Recorder

In this example, the user is presented with a Record button. Touching it begins recording through the microphone and presents the user with a stop button to press when she's finished. The resulting file will be written to /tmp/rec.amr. This file can be copied over to the desktop (for instance, by using the following secure copy command on the desktop terminal window), where it can be played using QuickTime or any other media player:

```
$ scp root@iphone:/tmp/rec.amr .
```

To compile this example, remember to include the Celestial framework in your build statement:

```
$ arm-apple-darwin-gcc -o MyExample MyExample.m -lobjc \
    -framework Foundation \
    -framework CoreFoundation \
    -framework UIKit \
    -framework Celestial
```

Examples 6-5 and 6-6 contain the code.

Example 6-5. Audio recorder example (MyExample.h)

```
#import <CoreFoundation/CoreFoundation.h>
#import <UIKit/UIKit.h>
#import <UIKit/UIAlertSheet.h>
#import <UIKit/UINavigationBar.h>
#import <Celestial/AVRecorder.h>

@interface MainView : UIView
{
    UIAlertSheet    *recordSheet;
    UINavigationBar *navBar;
    AVRecorder      *avr;
}

- (id)initWithFrame:(CGRect)frame;
- (void)dealloc;
@end

@interface MyApp : UIApplication
{
    UIWindow *window;
    MainView *mainView;
}

- (void)applicationDidFinishLaunching:(NSNotification *)aNotification;
@end
```

Example 6-6. Audio recorder example (MyExample.m)

```
#import "MyExample.h"

int main(int argc, char **argv)
{
    NSAutoreleasePool *autoreleasePool = [
        [ NSAutoreleasePool alloc ] init
    ];
    int returnCode = UIApplicationMain(argc, argv, [ MyApp class ]);
    [ autoreleasePool release ];
    return returnCode;

}

@implementation MyApp

- (void)applicationDidFinishLaunching:(NSNotification *)aNotification {
    window = [ [ UIWindow alloc ] initWithContentRect:
        [ UIHardware fullScreenApplicationContentRect ]
    ];

    CGRect rect = [ UIHardware fullScreenApplicationContentRect ];
    rect.origin.x = rect.origin.y = 0.0f;

    mainView = [ [ MainView alloc ] initWithFrame: rect ];

    [ window setContentView: mainView ];
    [ window orderFront: self ];
    [ window makeKey: self ];
    [ window _setHidden: NO ];
}
@end

@implementation MainView
- (id)initWithFrame:(CGRect)rect {
    if ((self == [ super initWithFrame: rect ]) != nil) {

        navBar = [ [UINavigationBar alloc] initWithFrame:
            CGRectMake(rect.origin.x, rect.origin.y, rect.size.width, 48.0f)
        ];
        [ navBar setDelegate: self ];
        [ navBar enableAnimation ];
        [ navBar showLeftButton:nil withStyle: 0
                    rightButton:@"Record" withStyle: 1 ];

        [ self addSubview: navBar ];
    }

    return self;
}

- (void)alertSheet:(UIAlertSheet *)sheet buttonClicked:(int)button
{
```

Example 6-6. Audio recorder example (MyExample.m) (continued)

```
    [ avr stop ];
    [ avr deactivate ];
    [ sheet dismiss ];
}

- (void)navigationBar:(UINavigationBar *)navbar buttonClicked:(int)button
{
    /* Start recording on button press */

    NSURL *url = [ [ NSURL alloc ] initWithString: @"/tmp/rec.amr" ];

    avr = [ [ AVRecorder alloc ] init ];
    [ avr setFilePath: url ];
    [ avr activate: nil ];
    [ avr start ];

    recordSheet = [ [ UIAlertSheet alloc ] initWithFrame:
        CGRectMake(0, 240, 320, 240)
    ];
    [ recordSheet setTitle: @"Now Recording" ];
    [ recordSheet setBodyText:@"Sound is now being recorded. Press the button below to
stop." ];
    [ recordSheet setDestructiveButton:
        [ recordSheet addButtonWithTitle:@"Stop" ]
    ];
    [ recordSheet setDelegate: self ];
    [ recordSheet presentSheetInView: self ];
}

- (void)dealloc
{
    [ self dealloc ];
    [ super dealloc ];
}

@end
```

What's Going On

Here's how the audio recording process works:

1. The application instantiates through the main( ) function and returns an instance of the application, just like every other application.

2. The window is created with MainView as the content. The statement creating MainView also calls its initWithFrame member. This creates the view and navigation bar, and returns.

3. When the user presses the Record button, the runtime calls buttonClicked. This subroutine creates a new instance of AVRecorder and begins recording. It then creates an alert sheet called recordSheet, which prompts the user to stop the recording.

4. When the user presses the stop button on the alert sheet, the runtime automatically calls the UIAlertSheet buttonClicked method.

5. This method stops the recording and dismisses the sheet. The recorder will have written its output to */tmp/rec.amr*.

Further Study

Try some of these exercises to get more comfortable with Celestial:

• Merge the two examples in this section so that the voice recorder will automatically play back the file it has recorded when the user presses stop.

• Experiment with recording and determine just how much time can be recorded before the iPhone runs out of resources.

• Check out the *AVController.h*, *AVItem.h*, *AVQueue.h*, and *AVRecorder.h* prototypes in your tool chain. You'll find these in */usr/local/arm-apple-darwin/include/Celestial*.

Audio Toolbox

The Audio Toolbox framework is new to Leopard, and is available on the desktop and iPhone platforms. As an extension to Core Audio, Audio Toolbox provides many low-level functions for processing sound on a bit stream level. Unlike Core Audio, many of Audio Toolbox's components can be used on the iPhone. The framework includes many APIs that provide access to the raw data within audio files and many conversion tools.

Unlike many of the frameworks covered in this book so far, the Audio Toolbox framework is predominantly C-oriented. Many references for Audio Toolbox are available on the Apple Developer Connection web site. These include:

Core Audio Overview: Audio Toolbox framework
    *http://developer.apple.com/documentation/MusicAudio/Conceptual/
    CoreAudioOverview/Introduction/chapter_1_section_1.html*

Audio Toolbox Framework Reference
    *http://developer.apple.com/documentation/MusicAudio/Reference/
    CAAudioTooboxRef/index.html*

Audio File Services Reference
    *http://developer.apple.com/documentation/MusicAudio/Reference/
    AudioFileConvertRef/Reference/reference.html*

Audio File Stream Services Reference
    *http://developer.apple.com/documentation/MusicAudio/Reference/
    AudioStreamReference/AudioStreamReference.pdf*

Audio Queue Services Reference
   http://developer.apple.com/documentation/MusicAudio/Reference/
   AudioQueueReference/AudioQueueReference.pdf

Because it exists on the desktop platform, the Audio Toolbox framework is documented fairly well. We won't cover it in its entirety here, but only the pieces specific to the iPhone. Many pieces of the framework, such as MIDI controllers and Music Player APIs, aren't relevant to or even available on the iPhone.

The "Other" Audio Queue: For Application-Generated Sound

The Celestial AVQueue class explained in the last section is appropriate for queuing self-contained, prerecorded audio samples. But there has been much demand in the iPhone development community for a facility that can play audio streams generated on the fly by applications such as games.

Such applications can use the Audio Toolbox, which has its own implementation of an audio queue, designed for raw sound data. This is useful for applications that generate their own continuous digital sound stream. The Audio Toolbox queue is entirely independent of Celestial's controller framework, and works with streams of raw audio data rather than complete files.

Think of the audio queue as a conveyor belt full of boxes. On one end of the conveyor belt, boxes are filled with chunks of sound, and on the other end, they are dumped into the iPhone's speakers. These boxes represent sound buffers that carry bits around, and the conveyor belt is the audio queue. The conveyor belt dumps your sound into the speakers and then circles back around to have the boxes refilled. It's your job as the programmer to define the size, type, and number of boxes, and write the software to fill the boxes with sound when needed.

Unlike the Celestial queue, the Audio Toolbox queue is strictly first-in-first-out. While the Celestial queue lets you rearrange audio samples sitting in the queue, the Audio Toolbox conveyor belt plays the samples in the order they are added.

Audio Toolbox's audio queue works like this:

1. An audio queue is created and assigned properties that identify the type of sound that will be played (format, sample rate, etc.).
2. Sound buffers are attached to the queue, which will contain the actual sound frames to be played. Think of a sound frame as a single box full of sound, whereas a sample is a single piece of digital sound within the frame.
3. The developer supplies a callback function, which the audio queue calls every time a sound buffer has been exhausted. This refills the buffer with the latest sound frames from your application.

Audio queue structure

Because the Audio Toolbox framework uses low-level C interfaces, it has no concept of a class. There are many moving parts involved in setting up an audio queue, and to make our examples more understandable, all of the different variables used will be encapsulated into a single user-defined structure we call `AQCallbackStruct`.

```
typedef struct AQCallbackStruct {
    AudioQueueRef queue;
    UInt32 frameCount;
    AudioQueueBufferRef mBuffers[AUDIO_BUFFERS];
    AudioStreamBasicDescription mDataFormat;
} AQCallbackStruct;
```

The following components are grouped into this structure to service the audio framework:

`AudioQueueRef queue`

> A pointer to the audio queue object your program will create.

`UInt32 frameCount`

> The total number of samples to be copied per audio sync. This is largely up to the implementer.

`AudioQueueBufferRef mBuffers`

> An array containing the total number of sound buffers that will be used. The proper number of elements will be discussed later in the section "Sound buffers."

`AudioStreamBasicDescription mDataFormat`

> Information about the format of audio that will be played.

Before the audio queue can be created, you have to initialize instances of these variables.

```
AQCallbackStruct aqc;
aqc.mDataFormat.mSampleRate = 44100.0;
aqc.mDataFormat.mFormatID = kAudioFormatLinearPCM;
aqc.mDataFormat.mFormatFlags = kLinearPCMFormatFlagIsSignedInteger
    | kAudioFormatFlagIsPacked;
aqc.mDataFormat.mBytesPerPacket = 4;
aqc.mDataFormat.mFramesPerPacket = 1;
aqc.mDataFormat.mBytesPerFrame = 4;
aqc.mDataFormat.mChannelsPerFrame = 2;
aqc.mDataFormat.mBitsPerChannel = 16;
aqc.frameCount = 735;
```

In this example, we prepare a structure for 16-bit (two bytes per sample) stereo sound (two channels) with a sample rate of 44 Khz (44,100). Our output sample will be provided in the form of two two-byte *short* integers, hence four total bytes per frame (two bytes for the left and right channel, each).

The sample rate and frame size dictate how often the iPhone will ask for more sound. With a frequency of 44,100 samples per second, we can make our application sync the sound every 60th of a second by defining a frame size of 735 samples (44,100/60 = 735).

The format we'll be providing in this example is PCM (raw data), but 27 different formats are available.

kAudioFormatLinearPCM	kAudioFormatMACE6	kAudioFormatTimeCode
kAudioFormatAC3	kAudioFormatULaw	kAudioFormatMIDIStream
kAudioFormat60958AC3	kAudioFormatALaw	kAudioFormatParameterValueStream
kAudioFormatAppleIMA4	kAudioFormatQDesign	kAudioFormatAppleLossless
kAudioFormatMPEG4AAC	kAudioFormatQDesign2	kAudioFormatMPEG4AAC_HE
kAudioFormatMPEG4CELP	kAudioFormatQUALCOMM	kAudioFormatMPEG4AAC_LD
kAudioFormatMPEG4HVXC	kAudioFormatMPEGLayer1	kAudioFormatMPEG4AAC_HE_V2
kAudioFormatMPEG4TwinVQ	kAudioFormatMPEGLayer2	kAudioFormatMPEG4AAC_Spatial
kAudioFormatMACE3	kAudioFormatMPEGLayer3	kAudioFormatAMR

 Not all of these formats may be supported, depending on the software version of your iPhone.

Provisioning audio output

Once the audio queue's properties have been defined, a new audio queue object can be provisioned. The AudioQueueNewOutput function is responsible for provisioning an output channel and attaching it to the queue. The prototype function looks like this:

```
AudioQueueNewOutput(
    const AudioStreamBasicDescription *inFormat,
    AudioQueueOutputCallback           inCallbackProc,
    void *                             inUserData,
    CFRunLoopRef                       inCallbackRunLoop,
    CFStringRef                        inCallbackRunLoopMode,
    UInt32                             inFlags,
    AudioQueueRef *                    outAQ);
```

and can be broken down as follows:

inFormat

The pointer to a structure describing the audio format that will be played. We defined this structure earlier as a member of data type AudioStreamBasicDescription within our AQCallbackStruct structure.

inCallbackProc

The name of a callback function that will be called when the audio queue has an empty buffer that needs data.

inUserData

A pointer to data the developer can optionally pass to the callback function. It will contain a pointer to the instance of the user-defined `AQCallbackStruct` structure, which should contain information about the audio queue as well as any information relevant to the application about the samples being played.

inCallbackRunLoopMode

Tells the audio queue how it should expect to loop the audio. When `NULL` is specified, the callback function runs whenever a sound buffer becomes exhausted. Additional modes are available to run the callback under other conditions.

inFlags

Not used; reserved.

outAO

When the `AudioQueueNewOutput` function returns, this pointer will be set to the newly created audio queue. The presence of this argument allows an error code to be used as the return value of the function.

An actual call to this function, using the audio queue structure created earlier, looks like this:

```
AudioQueueNewOutput(&aqc.mDataFormat,
    AQBufferCallback,
    &aqc,
    NULL,
    kCFRunLoopCommonModes,
    0,
    &aqc.queue);
```

In this example, the name of the callback function was specified as `AQBufferCallback`. This function will be created in the next few sections. It is the function that will be responsible for taking sound output from your application and copying it to a sound buffer.

Sound buffers

A *sound buffer* contains sound data in transit to the output device. Going back to our box-on-a-conveyor-belt concept, the buffer is the box that carries your sound to the speakers. If you don't have enough sound to fill the box, it ends up going to the speakers incomplete, which could lead to gaps in the audio. The more boxes you have, the more sound you can queue up in advance to avoid running out (or running slow). The downside is that it also takes longer for the sound at the speaker end to catch up to the sound coming from the application. This could be problematic if the character in your game jumps, but the user doesn't hear it until after he's landed.

When the sound is ready to start, sound buffers are created and primed with the first frames of the your application's sound output. The minimum number of buffers needed to start playback on an Apple desktop is only one, but on the iPhone it is three. In applications that might cause high CPU usage, it may be appropriate to use even more buffers to prevent under-runs. To prepare the buffers with the first frames of sound data, each buffer is primed in the order it is created. This means by the time you prime the buffers, you'd better have some sound to fill them with.

```
#define AUDIO_BUFFERS 3

unsigned long bufferSize;

bufferSize = aqc.frameCount * aqc.mDataFormat.mBytesPerFrame;
for (i=0; i<AUDIO_BUFFERS; i++) {
    AudioQueueAllocateBuffer(aqc.queue,
        bufferSize, &aqc.mBuffers[i]);
    AQBufferCallback (&aqc, aqc.queue, aqc.mBuffers[i]);
}
```

When this code executes, the audio buffers are filled with the first frames of sound data from your application. The queue is now ready to be activated, which turns on the conveyor belt sending the sound buffers to the speakers. As this occurs, the buffers are emptied of their contents (no, memory isn't zeroed) and the boxes come back around the conveyor belt for a refill.

```
AudioQueueStart(aqc.queue, NULL);
```

Later on, when you're ready to turn off the sound queue, just use the AudioQueueDispose function, and everything stops:

```
AudioQueueDispose(aqc.queue, true);
```

Callback function

The audio queue is now running, and every 60th of a second, the application is asked to fill a new sound buffer with data. What hasn't been explained yet is how this happens. After a buffer is emptied and is ready to be refilled, the audio queue calls the callback function you specified as the second argument to AudioQueueNewOutput. This callback function is where the application does its work; it fills the box that carries your output sound to the speakers. You have to call it before starting the queue in order to prime the sound buffers with some initial sound. The queue then calls the function each time a buffer needs to be refilled. When called, you'll fill the audio queue buffer that is passed in by copying the latest sound frame from your application—in our example, 735 samples.

```
static void AQBufferCallback(
    void *aqc,
    AudioQueueRef inQ,
    AudioQueueBufferRef outQB)
{
```

The callback structure you created at the very beginning, aqc, is passed as a user-defined argument, followed by pointers to the audio queue itself and the audio queue buffer to be filled.

```
AQCallbackStruct *inData = (AQCallbackStruct *)aqc;
```

Because the AQCallbackStruct structure is considered user data, it's supplied to the callback function as a void pointer, and needs to be cast back to an AQCallbackStruct structure (here, named inData) before it can be accessed. This code grabs a pointer to the raw audio data inside the buffer so that the application can write its sound into it.

```
short *CoreAudioBuffer = (short *) outQB->mAudioData;
```

The CoreAudioBuffer variable represents the space inside the sound buffer where your application's raw samples will be copied at every sync. Your application will need to maintain a type of "record needle" to keep track of what sound has already been sent to the audio queue.

```
if (inData->frameCount > 0) {
```

The frameCount variable is the number of frames that the buffer is expecting to see. This should be equivalent to the frameCount that was supplied in the AQCallbackStruct structure—in our example, 735.

```
outQB->mAudioDataByteSize = 4 * inData->frameCount;
```

This is where you tell the buffer exactly how much data it's going to get: a packing list for the box. The total output buffer size should be equivalent to the size of both stereo channels (two bytes per channel = four bytes) multiplied by the number of frames sent (735).

```
for(i = 0 ; i < inData->frameCount * 2; i += 2) {
    CoreAudioBuffer[i]   = ( LEFT CHANNEL DATA );
    CoreAudioBuffer[i+1] = ( RIGHT CHANNEL DATA );
}
```

Here, the callback function steps through each output frame in the buffer and copies the data from what will be your application's outputted sound into CoreAudioBuffer. Because the left and right channels are interleaved, the loop will have to account for this by skipping in increments of two.

```
        AudioQueueEnqueueBuffer(inQ, outQB, 0, NULL);
    } /* if (inData->frameCount > 0) */
} /* AQBufferCallback */
```

Finally, once the frame has been copied into the sound buffer, it's placed back onto the play queue.

Example: PCM Player

Because the Audio Toolbox framework lives in C land, this is a good opportunity to show an example for the iPhone that doesn't use Objective-C or the UIKit framework. This example uses good old-fashioned C and is run on the command line with a filename. It loads a raw PCM file and then plays it using the Audio Toolbox's audio queue. Because your application will likely be generating data internally, and not use a file, we'll read the file into a memory buffer first and then play from the memory buffer to illustrate the practical concept. This should set the stage for most applications to hook into this same architecture.

Because a raw PCM file doesn't contain any information about its frequency or frame size, this example will have to assume its own. We'll use a format for 16-bit 44 KHz Mono uncompressed PCM data. This is defined by the three definitions made at the top of the program:

```
#define BYTES_PER_SAMPLE 2
```

16-bit = 2 bytes

```
#define SAMPLE_RATE 44100
```

44,100 samples per second = 44 KHz

```
typedef unsigned short sampleFrame;
```

An unsigned short is equivalent to two bytes (per sample).

If you can't find a raw PCM file to run this example with, you can use a .wav file so long as it's encoded in 16-bit 44 KHz raw PCM. Alternatively, you may adapt this example to use a different encoding by changing mFormatID within the audio queue structure. The example won't make any attempt to parse file headers of a .wav; it just assumes the data you're providing is raw, which is what a game or other type of application would provide. Wave file headers will get passed to the audio channel with the rest of the data, and so you might hear a slight click or two of junk before the raw sound data inside the file is played.

To compile this example with the tool chain, use the command line:

```
$ arm-apple-darwin-gcc -o playpcm playpcm.c \
  -framework AudioToolbox -framework CoreAudio -framework CoreFoundation
```

Because Leopard also includes the Audio Toolbox framework, this example can be compiled on the desktop as well.

```
$ gcc -o playpcm playpcm.c \
  -framework AudioToolbox -framework CoreAudio -framework CoreFoundation
```

Example 6-7 contains the code.

Example 6-7. Audio Toolbox example (playpcm.c)

```c
#include <stdio.h>
#include <stdlib.h>
#include <errno.h>
#include <sys/stat.h>
#include <AudioToolbox/AudioQueue.h>

#define BYTES_PER_SAMPLE 2
#define SAMPLE_RATE 44100
typedef unsigned short sampleFrame;

#define FRAME_COUNT 735
#define AUDIO_BUFFERS 3

typedef struct AQCallbackStruct {
    AudioQueueRef queue;
    UInt32 frameCount;
    AudioQueueBufferRef mBuffers[AUDIO_BUFFERS];
    AudioStreamBasicDescription mDataFormat;
    UInt32 playPtr;
    UInt32 sampleLen;
    sampleFrame *pcmBuffer;
} AQCallbackStruct;

void *loadpcm(const char *filename, unsigned long *len);
int playbuffer(void *pcm, unsigned long len);
void AQBufferCallback(void *in, AudioQueueRef inQ, AudioQueueBufferRef outQB);

int main(int argc, char *argv[]) {
    char *filename;
    unsigned long len;
    void *pcmbuffer;
    int ret;

    if (argc < 2) {
        fprintf(stderr, "Syntax: %s [filename]\n", argv[0]);
        exit(EXIT_FAILURE);
    }

    filename = argv[1];
    pcmbuffer = loadpcm(filename, &len);
    if (!pcmbuffer) {
        fprintf(stderr, "%s: %s\n", filename, strerror(errno));
        exit(EXIT_FAILURE);
    }

    ret = playbuffer(pcmbuffer, len);
    free(pcmbuffer);
    return ret;
}

void *loadpcm(const char *filename, unsigned long *len) {
    FILE *file;
```

Example 6-7. Audio Toolbox example (playpcm.c) (continued)

```
    struct stat s;
    void *pcm;

    if (stat(filename, &s))
        return NULL;
    *len = s.st_size;
    pcm = (void *) malloc(s.st_size);
    if (!pcm)
        return NULL;
    file = fopen(filename, "rb");
    if (!file) {
        free(pcm);
        return NULL;
    }
    fread(pcm, s.st_size, 1, file);
    fclose(file);
    return pcm;
}

int playbuffer(void *pcmbuffer, unsigned long len) {
    AQCallbackStruct aqc;
    UInt32 err, bufferSize;
    int i;

    aqc.mDataFormat.mSampleRate = SAMPLE_RATE;
    aqc.mDataFormat.mFormatID = kAudioFormatLinearPCM;
    aqc.mDataFormat.mFormatFlags =
        kLinearPCMFormatFlagIsSignedInteger
        | kAudioFormatFlagIsPacked;
    aqc.mDataFormat.mBytesPerPacket = 4;
    aqc.mDataFormat.mFramesPerPacket = 1;
    aqc.mDataFormat.mBytesPerFrame = 4;
    aqc.mDataFormat.mChannelsPerFrame = 2;
    aqc.mDataFormat.mBitsPerChannel = 16;
    aqc.frameCount = FRAME_COUNT;
    aqc.sampleLen = len / BYTES_PER_SAMPLE;
    aqc.playPtr = 0;
    aqc.pcmBuffer = pcmbuffer;

    err = AudioQueueNewOutput(&aqc.mDataFormat,
        AQBufferCallback,
        &aqc,
        NULL,
        kCFRunLoopCommonModes,
        0,
        &aqc.queue);
    if (err)
        return err;

    aqc.frameCount = FRAME_COUNT;
    bufferSize = aqc.frameCount * aqc.mDataFormat.mBytesPerFrame;
```

Example 6-7. Audio Toolbox example (playpcm.c) (continued)

```c
    for (i=0; i<AUDIO_BUFFERS; i++) {
        err = AudioQueueAllocateBuffer(aqc.queue, bufferSize,
            &aqc.mBuffers[i]);
        if (err)
            return err;
        AQBufferCallback(&aqc, aqc.queue, aqc.mBuffers[i]);
    }

    err = AudioQueueStart(aqc.queue, NULL);
    if (err)
        return err;

    while(aqc.playPtr < aqc.sampleLen) { select(NULL, NULL, NULL, NULL, 1.0); }
    sleep(1);
    return 0;
}

void AQBufferCallback(
    void *in,
    AudioQueueRef inQ,
    AudioQueueBufferRef outQB)
{
    AQCallbackStruct *aqc;
    short *coreAudioBuffer;
    short sample;
    int i;

    aqc = (AQCallbackStruct *) in;
    coreAudioBuffer = (short*) outQB->mAudioData;

    printf("Sync: %ld / %ld\n", aqc->playPtr, aqc->sampleLen);
    if (aqc->playPtr >= aqc->sampleLen) {
        AudioQueueDispose(aqc->queue, true);
        return;
    }

    if (aqc->frameCount > 0) {
        outQB->mAudioDataByteSize = 4 * aqc->frameCount;
        for(i=0; i<aqc->frameCount*2; i+=2) {
            if (aqc->playPtr > aqc->sampleLen || aqc->playPtr < 0)
                sample = 0;
            else
                sample = (aqc->pcmBuffer[aqc->playPtr]);
            coreAudioBuffer[i]   =    sample;
            coreAudioBuffer[i+1] = sample;
            aqc->playPtr++;
        }
        AudioQueueEnqueueBuffer(inQ, outQB, 0, NULL);
    }
}
```

What's Going On

Here's how the playpcm program works:

1. The application's main( ) function is called on program start, which extracts the filename from the argument list (as supplied on the command line).

2. The main( ) function calls loadpcm( ), which determines the length of the audio file and loads it into memory, returning this buffer to main( ).

3. The playbuffer( ) function is called with the contents of this memory and its length. This function builds our user-defined AQCallbackStruct structure, whose construction is declared at the beginning of the program. This structure holds pointers to the audio queue, sound buffers, and the memory containing the contents of the file that was loaded. It also contains the sample's length and an integer called playPtr, which acts as record needle, identifying the last sample that was copied into the sound buffer.

4. A new sound queue is initialized and started. The callback function is called once for each sound buffer used, to sync the first samples into memory. The audio queue is then started. The program then sits and sleeps until the sample is finished playing.

5. As audio is played, the sound buffers become exhausted one by one. Whenever a buffer needs more sound data, the AQBufferCallback function is called.

6. The AQBufferCallback function increments playPtr and copies the next sound frames from memory to be played into the sound buffer. Because raw PCM samples are mono, the same data is copied into the left and right output channels.

7. When playPtr exceeds the length of the sound sample, this breaks the wait loop set up in playpcm( ), causing the function to return back to main( ) for cleanup and exit.

Further Study

- Modify this example to play 8-bit PCM sound by changing the data type for sampleFrame and BYTES_PER_SAMPLE. You'll also need to amplify the volume as the sound sample is now one byte large, but the audio queue channel is two bytes large.

- Check out *AudioQueue.h* in Mac OS X Leopard on the desktop. This can be found in */System/Library/Frameworks/AudioToolbox.framework/Headers/*.

Volume Control

Samples played through the Celestial framework are played at a high enough level to automatically track with the system volume. The low level that the Audio Toolbox framework function on is, however, oblivious to system volume. So the output volume is static regardless of what the iPhone's volume is set to. Controlling the volume of an audio queue requires that the developer use higher-level functions to read the volume and scale the sound stream to track with it.

Audio Toolbox and Celestial meet when you manage high-level settings such as sound volume. Sound volume is a function of mediaserverd—the audio daemon you were introduced to earlier that is hogging the Core Audio. This daemon is largely married to the Celestial framework. Thus, the Celestial framework can be used to read the volume and intercept volume button presses.

Before covering the volume, it's important to discuss what to do with it when playing through Audio Toolbox. The volume is reported as a value between 0.0 and 1.0 (e.g., 0% and 100%). In the callback function used in the previous section, sound frames were copied from the application's output into sound buffers whenever a sync occurred. If we assume that the application has retrieved the current volume and stored it in a variable named _volume, the bold text in the following code shows the changes to this routine to incorporate the user's volume preference.

```
for(i=0; i<aqc->frameCount*2; i+=2) {
    if (aqc->playPtr > aqc->sampleLen || aqc->playPtr < 0)
        sample = 0;
    else
        sample = (aqc->pcmBuffer[aqc->playPtr]);
    coreAudioBuffer[i]   = sample * _volume;
    coreAudioBuffer[i+1] = sample * _volume;
    aqc->playPtr++;
}
```

In other words, when the volume is at its maximum, the actual sample data is being played (e.g., sample * 1.0). When the volume is at any other setting, the sample value is multiplied by the volume setting's value so that it is decreased by the factor of the volume. If you wanted the maximum volume to be louder, you could just multiply _volume by a factor of two or three, although this would run the risk of overdriving your audio.

Reading the volume

Audio Toolbox lives in C land, while Celestial requires an Objective-C context. To merge the two worlds, a global variable is the easiest way to allow the two to communicate data. In this example, this global variable is called _volume.

Celestial delegates volume and ringer control to the AVSystemController class. To read the volume from Celestial, create an instance of this:

```
NSString *audioDeviceName;
float _volume;
```

```
AVSystemController *avs =
    [ AVSystemController sharedAVSystemController ];
[ avs getActiveCategoryVolume: &_volume andName: &audioDeviceName ];
```

When the getActiveCategoryVolume method is notified, it sets the value of _volume to the current volume in the range 0.0 through 1.0. This will be seen automatically by the Audio Toolbox code, provided _volume is a global variable, and cause future sample frames to be multiplied by the new value.

Volume change notifications

Using the getActiveCategoryVolume method as a one-time read is useful for setting the output volume when the program starts, but won't change anything if the volume is adjusted while using the application. To accomplish this, add an *observer* to the application. The observer monitors specific system events and notifies the given method when the event occurs.

```
[ [ NSNotificationCenter defaultCenter ] addObserver: self
    selector:@selector(volumeChange:)
    name: @"AVSystemController_SystemVolumeDidChangeNotification"
    object: avs ];
```

This code sets a method named volumeChange as the observer for system volume changes. The volumeChange method is then defined in the calling class:

```
- (void)volumeChange:(NSNotification *)notification {
    AVSystemController *avsc = [ notification object ];
    NSString *audioDeviceName;
    [ avsc getActiveCategoryVolume:&_volume
        andName:&audioDeviceName ];
}
```

When the volumeChange method is notified, an AVSystemController object is passed in with the notification. This object is then used to reread the volume into _volume, where it will be picked up by the AQBufferCallback function feeding the audio queue.

Example: What's My Volume?

This example builds off of the "Hello, World!" example from Chapter 3, except that the volume is printed instead of a hokey greeting message. When one of the volume buttons is pressed, the observer we set up notifies volumeChanged, which rechecks the volume and updates the text.

This example can be compiled using the following command line. You'll need to link in the Celestial, Core Audio, and Audio Toolbox frameworks.

```
$ arm-apple-darwin-gcc -o MyExample MyExample.m -lobjc \
    -framework CoreFoundation -framework Foundation -framework UIKit \
    -framework Celestial -framework AudioToolbox -framework CoreAudio
```

Examples 6-8 and 6-9 show the code.

Example 6-8. Volume example (MyExample.h)

```
#import <CoreFoundation/CoreFoundation.h>
#import <UIKit/UIKit.h>
#import <UIKit/UITextView.h>
#import <Celestial/AVSystemController.h>

@interface MainView : UIView
{
    UITextView         *textView;
    AVSystemController *avs;
}

- (id)initWithFrame:(CGRect)frame;
- (void)dealloc;
- (void)displayVolume;

@end

@interface MyApp : UIApplication
{
    UIWindow *window;
    MainView *mainView;
}

- (void)applicationDidFinishLaunching:(NSNotification *)aNotification;
@end
```

Example 6-9. Volume example (MyExample.m)

```
#import "MyExample.h"

float _volume;

int main(int argc, char **argv)
{
    NSAutoreleasePool *autoreleasePool = [
        [ NSAutoreleasePool alloc ] init
    ];
    int returnCode = UIApplicationMain(argc, argv, [ MyApp class ]);
    [ autoreleasePool release ];
    return returnCode;
}

@implementation MyApp

- (void)applicationDidFinishLaunching:(NSNotification *)aNotification {
    window = [ [ UIWindow alloc ] initWithContentRect:
        [ UIHardware fullScreenApplicationContentRect ]
    ];

    CGRect rect = [ UIHardware fullScreenApplicationContentRect ];
    rect.origin.x = rect.origin.y = 0.0f;
```

Example 6-9. Volume example (MyExample.m) (continued)

```objc
    mainView = [ [ MainView alloc ] initWithFrame: rect ];

    [ window setContentView: mainView ];
    [ window orderFront: self ];
    [ window makeKey: self ];
    [ window _setHidden: NO ];
}
@end

@implementation MainView
- (id)initWithFrame:(CGRect)rect {

    if ((self == [ super initWithFrame: rect ]) != nil) {
        NSString *audioDeviceName;

        avs = [ AVSystemController sharedAVSystemController ];
        [ avs getActiveCategoryVolume:&_volume andName:
          &audioDeviceName ];

        textView = [ [ UITextView alloc ] initWithFrame: rect ];
        [ textView setTextSize: 18 ];
        [ self displayVolume ];
        [ self addSubview: textView ];

        [ [ NSNotificationCenter defaultCenter ] addObserver: self
            selector:@selector(volumeChange:)
            name:
              @"AVSystemController_SystemVolumeDidChangeNotification"
            object: avs ];
    }

    return self;
}

- (void)displayVolume
{
    NSString *text;

    text = [ [ NSString alloc ] initWithFormat: @"Volume is set to %f", _volume ];
    [ textView setText: text ];
}

- (void)volumeChange:(NSNotification *)notification {
    AVSystemController *avsc = [ notification object ];
    NSString *audioDeviceName;

    [ avsc getActiveCategoryVolume:&_volume
          andName:&audioDeviceName ];
    [ self displayVolume ];
}

- (void)dealloc
```

Example 6-9. Volume example (MyExample.m) (continued)

```
{
    [ self dealloc ];
    [ super dealloc ];
}
```

@end

What's Going On

The volume example's process flow is as follows:

1. When the application instantiates, a MainView object gets created and its initWithFrame method is called.

2. The initWithFrame method creates an instance of AVSystemController and delegates an observer to notify the volumeChange method of notifications for system volume changes.

3. The volume is initially read once, and the text view is displayed.

4. When the user presses one of the volume buttons on the side of the phone, the observer notifies the volumeChange method.

5. The volumeChange method reads the new system volume and calls a method named displayVolume to update the output text.

Further Study

Check out the *AVSystemController.h* prototype in your tool chain's *include* directory. This can be found in */usr/local/arm-apple-darwin/include/Celestial*.

## CHAPTER 7

Advanced UIKit Design

Chapter 3 introduced the UIKit framework, which is the heart of all GUI applications on the iPhone. This chapter covers the most aesthetically rich components of the iPhone's UIKit framework and shows you how to make your own software look as spectacular as Apple's own preloaded applications.

Remember that to tap into the UIKit, your application must be linked to it. Just like any other framework, UIKit is a shared object. Using the tool chain, UIKit can be linked in by adding the following arguments to your command-line arguments:

```
$ arm-apple-darwin-gcc -o MyApp MyApp.m -lobjc \
    -framework CoreFoundation \
    -framework Foundation \
    -framework UIKit
```

If you're using a makefile, as illustrated in Chapter 2, add the UIKit framework to the linker flags section:

```
LDFLAGS = lobjc \
          -framework CoreFoundation \
          -framework Foundation \
          -framework UIKit
```

The following advanced components of UIKit will be covered in this chapter:

Controls

UIKit provides a set of controls that include switches, segmented controls, and sliders. Controls are used in preference tables, navigation bars, and other visual elements. The UIControl class is designed to be a versatile widget-type class capable of connecting to many different types of objects.

Preferences tables

A special type of view class has been designed specifically for managing program settings. Preferences tables provide hooks for wiring up controls and allow logical groupings of similar options. The preferences table view is a table-like class that ties many different types of individual cells and controls together into a polished window.

Progress indicators

Progress indicators notify the user that an operation is in progress and convey status in the form of spinning icons and thermometers. The application can tell the indicator when to start and stop, and can control the progress bar's completion.

Image handling

UIKit provides many classes for the manipulation and display of images. These classes can load most popular types of images and display, transform, layer, and clip them anywhere on the screen. Image classes are intended for static images that don't require much animation. For high-performance graphics in games, read up on the Core Surface framework in Chapter 5.

Section lists

When working with large, grouped lists of data, you may find it necessary to order information by category. Section lists are used in the mobile phone application to sort contacts and songs, and can be used to group any type of items into categories with custom headings. An alphabetical Rolodex-type scroll bar can also be used to quickly flip to the first letter of a section heading.

Keyboards

The iPhone supports 10 different keyboard styles, which are used widely by applications for various kinds of input. Apple's Mail application uses one type of keyboard containing special characters for email address entry, whereas Safari uses a keyboard suitable for URL input sporting a .COM button.

Pickers

While not technically a control, Pickers provide a unified method of input for selecting options from a list. Pickers present lists in the form of spinning dials, which can be tailored to behave in different ways. Date and time pickers are more specialized versions of this class, allowing the selection of custom dates, times, and time periods.

Button bars

Button bars are icon and text bars appearing at the bottom of an application. They are the preferred method of logically separating similar views of different data or providing different modes of functionality within an application. The iPod application uses button bars to separate playlists, artists, songs, and videos from each other, while the phone application uses a button bar to separate different functions of the phone (keypad, contacts, etc.).

Orientation changes

UIKit's UIHardware class provides access to the iPhone's orientation sensor. This allows the developer to know when the iPhone switches between portrait and landscape modes, and at what angle the handset is being held. You can read the iPhone's accelerometer directly to detect minor variations of angle, or use a simpler API to obtain the general orientation of the handset.

Web views and scrollers

A web view class is built-in to the UIKit framework, allowing applications to display a web page or a local file within a window. This is powerful for network-based tools that might choose to use web pages to refresh "latest news" windows or display other information. Web views can also display small PDFs and other files locally and remotely.

Web views, like many other objects with a lot of content, are heavily dependent on scrollers. Scrollers provide a potentially large field on which to place a view, and allow portions of that view to be scrolled across a smaller window region. You've been using them indirectly with tables and lists, and here you'll see just how they work.

Controls

Controls are diverse, widget-like utility classes designed to augment an application's user interface. UIKit supports many different types of controls. Some are very specific to certain applications (such as UIScrubberControl), while others are buried deep enough within higher-level classes that most developers won't need to use them directly (such as UIRemoveControl).

The controls used on the iPhone are noticeably different from those used in desktop applications. Desktop controls such as checkboxes and radio buttons simply won't cut it on a high-resolution device with limited touch screen precision (e.g., no stylus). For each desktop control used, a special control has been designed specifically for the iPhone.

Controls are practical enhancements to classes derived from UITableCell, specifically table cells, preferences table cells, and other similar classes. Some can also be used with navigation bars and other types of view objects. There are three compact, general-purpose controls appropriate for most applications, which will be covered in this section. Other control-like objects, such as progress indicators and pickers, are given entire sections in this chapter.

Controls are derived from the UIControl base class, which is derived from the UIView class. This means it has many of the same properties as the other view classes you've looked at so far. Controls initialize with a view region and behave largely in the same manner as UIView objects.

Segmented Control

The segmented control replaces the radio button used on desktop operating systems and instead provides an interface similar to the front of a dishwasher. The user sees a pushbutton bar where pushing one button causes all others to pop out. Segmented controls are useful where a limited number of related selections are available for one option.

Creating the control

A segmented control is initialized with a view region. The frame's coordinates are offset to the view hosting the control, which is usually the cell of a preferences table or a navigation bar.

```
UISegmentedControl *segCtl = [ [UISegmentedControl alloc]
    initWithFrame:CGRectMake(70.0, 8.0, 180.0, 30.0)
    withStyle: 0
    withItems: NULL ];
```

One of three different styles for segmented controls can be chosen depending on where the control is being used.

Style	Description
0	Large white buttons with gray border, appropriate for preference cells
1	Large white buttons with black border, appropriate for table cells
2	Small gray buttons, appropriate for navigation bars

Each segment within a segmented view is represented by a button containing a label or image. A segment must be created for each available option. You can have as many segments as will fit on the screen, but only one segment can be selected by the user at any time. Options for a "mood" control might look like the snippet below.

```
[ segCtl insertSegment:0 withTitle:@"Happy" animated: YES ];
[ segCtl insertSegment:1 withTitle:@"Sad" animated: YES ];
[ segCtl insertSegment:2 withTitle:@"Mad" animated: YES ];
```

This code adds three buttons to a segment control: Happy, Sad, and Mad. Each button is assigned its own segment number: 0, 1, 2, and so on.

Segments can also be removed.

To remove an individual segment, use the removeSegment method:

```
[ segCtl removeSegment: 0 animated: YES ];
```

To remove all segments at once, invoke removeAllSegments. This causes the control to shed it buttons visibly.

```
[ segCtl removeAllSegments ];
```

If, at any time, it's necessary to change the title of a button, use the setTitle method:

```
[ segCtl setTitle:@"Glad" forSegment: 0 ];
```

Images

In addition to text, segmented controls can also display images inside a button. Any images used should be included in the application's program folder as discussed in Chapter 2. An image can be added to an existing segment using the setImage method:

```
[ segCtl setImage: [ UIImage applicationImageNamed:@"happy.png" ]
      forSegment: 0
];
```

Or, if the segment hasn't been added yet, a different version of the insertSegment method will allow an image to be specified as the segment is added:

```
[ segCtl insertSegment: 0
            withImage: [ UIImage applicationNames:@"happy.png" ]
            animated: YES
];
```

The control itself doesn't do any image scaling, so it will try to display your image on the button even if the image is too large. This requires care in designing button images to ensure they fit into the button space.

Momentary clicks

The default behavior of the segmented control is to let the user select one option at a time and hold that button in until another is selected. This behavior can be changed slightly to automatically release the button shortly after it is pressed. Use the setMomentaryClick method to enable this behavior.

```
[ segCtl setMomentaryClick: YES ];
```

Displaying the control

Once the control has been configured, it can be displayed by adding it as a subview to any type of object that can host it. These include table cells, navigation bars, and other view objects:

```
[ parentView addSubview: segCtl ];
```

Reading the control

To read the current value of a segmented control, use the selectedSegment method. This returns an integer corresponding to the segment number that is currently selected. The value is set based on the number assigned to it when it was first inserted into the control.

```
int x = [ segCtl selectedSegment ];
```

Simply reading the value of the control will suffice for most needs, such as in the case of preferences tables, which need to read it only when the user exits the page. In some cases, however, a notification needs to be sent at the time the button is pressed.

For this extra functionality, create a subclass of UISegmentedControl and override the control's mouseDown or mouseUp methods (depending on when you want to receive the notification). These events can be used to trigger a read and any necessary action at the time the button is pressed. The template for this follows.

```
@interface MySegmentedControl : UISegmentedControl
{

}
- (void)mouseDown:(struct __GSEvent *)event;
- (void)mouseUp:(struct __GSEvent *)event;
@end
```

Now, override the mouseDown or mouseUp method so that the value can be read when a button in this class is pressed or released.

```
@implementation MySegmentedControl
- (void)mouseDown:(struct __GSEvent *)event {

    int x = [ self selectedSegment ];

    /* Do something here */
}
@end
```

Switch Control

In the same way that the segmented control replaced the radio button, the switch control replaced the checkbox. Switch controls are used in preference panes to turn features on and off.

The switch control is by far the simplest control to use, but can still be customized to a degree.

Creating the control

A switch control is initialized using the standard initWithFrame method. This method defines its size and coordinates relative to the class hosting it, such as a table cell or navigation bar.

```
UISwitchControl *switchControl = [ [ UISwitchControl alloc ]
    initWithFrame: CGRectMake(170.0f, 5.0f, 120.0f, 30.0f)
];
```

If the switch is a dangerous one that could result in a performance impact or have other consequences, it's best to label it with warning colors. A UISwitchControl object can be made to use an alternate set of colors, appearing bright orange when activated. Use the setAlternateColors method to set this when the control is created.

```
[ switchControl setAlternateColors: YES ];
```

Displaying the control

Once the control is created and initialized, it can be displayed by adding it to a compatible view object, such as a table cell or navigation bar.

```
[ tableCell addSubview: switchCtl ];
```

Reading the control

The switch control returns a floating-point value of 0.0 when off, or nonzero when on. This can be obtained by calling the object's value method.

```
float switchValue = [ switchControl value ];
```

Most applications need only read the switch value when the page is exited, such as in a preferences table. To read the value of the control at the moment it's switched, its mouseDown or mouseUp event can be intercepted. Sublcass the UISwitchControl to override these methods. For example:

```
@interface MySwitchControl : UISwitchControl
{

}
- (void)mouseUp:(struct __GSEvent *)event;
@end
```

When the switch is toggled, the mouseUp method will be notified, allowing instant action to be taken.

```
@implementation UIMySwitchControl
- (void)mouseUp:(struct __GSEvent *)event {
[ super mouseUp: event];
    float switchValue = [ self value ];

    /* Do something here */
}
@end
```

Slider Controls

Slider controls provide a range that the user can select from using a visual slide bar, and are configurable to meet a wide range of needs. You can set ranges for the slider values, add images at the ends, and make various other aesthetic tweaks. The slider is ideal for presenting options with wide ranges of numeric values, such as a volume setting, sensitivity controls, and even controls requiring precision adjustment. Apple must have determined sliders to be good enough to port to the iPhone, as they're commonly seen on the desktop, too.

Creating the control

The slider control is a standard UIControl object and is created in the same way as the segmented control or switch control. In fact, the switch control discussed in the last section is derived from the slider control, even though the slider control is more complex.

```
UISliderControl *sliderControl = [ [ UISliderControl alloc ]
    initWithFrame:CGRectMake(170.0f, 5.0f, 120.0f, 30.0f)];
```

The value range for the control should be set on creation so you know what data to expect in return. If you provide no default range, values between 0.0 and 1.0 are used.

```
[ sliderControl setMinValue: 0.0 ];
[ sliderControl setMaxValue: 100.0 ];
```

A default value for the slider can also be set at this time.

```
[ sliderControl setValue: 50.0 ];
```

The slider can display images at either end of the control. These can be set in a similar fashion to images in a segmented control. The images should be copied into the application's program directory, as explained in Chapter 2. Setting images causes the control's slider bar length to be decreased, so be sure to increase the size of the control when calling initWithFrame to accommodate the images.

```
[ sliderControl setMinValueImage:
    [ UIImage applicationImageNamed:@"min.png" ]
];

[ sliderControl setMaxValueImage:
    [ UIImage applicationImageNamed: @"max.png" ]
];
```

For precision controls, it may be important to show the user what the current numeric value is. The setShowValue method can be invoked to display this next to the slider.

```
[ sliderControl setShowValue: YES ];
```

Displaying the control

As is standard for UIView objects, the control can be displayed by adding it as a subview to a table cell, navigation bar, or other compatible object.

```
[ tableCell addSubview: sliderControl ];
```

Reading the control

The slider control reads as a floating-point value within the range you specified at the control's creation. The value can be queried using its value method.

```
float sliderValue = [ sliderControl value ];
```

Most applications need to read the value of the slider only when the user exits the page, such as with a preferences table. To read the value as the slider is changed, you must intercept the mouseDown or mouseUp event. The UISliderControl can be subclassed and its event methods overridden, using the following template.

```
@interface MySliderControl : UISliderControl
{

}
```

```
- (void)mouseUp:(struct __GSEvent *)event;
@end
[ super mouseUp: event ];
@implementation MySliderControl
- (void)mouseUp:(struct __GSEvent *)event {

    float x = [ self value ];

    /* Do something here */
}
@end
```

Further Study

- Read how controls are used in preferences tables in the next section of this book.
- Try to think of the different types of view classes where attaching controls might be useful, and what you can do with them.
- Check out *UISegmentedControl.h*, *UISwitchControl.h*, and *UISliderControl.h* in your tool chain's *include* directory. You'll find it in */usr/local/arm-apple-darwin/include/UIKit*.

Preferences Tables

Preferences tables provide an aesthetically rich interface for displaying and changing program settings. These tables can be seen in the iPhone's Settings application, but most third-party applications provide a settings interface of their own to avoid making changes to the preloaded environment. Preferences tables provide resizable cells capable of hosting controls, text boxes, and informational text. They also provide a mechanism for logically grouping similar preferences together.

Creating a Preferences Table

Some forethought must be put into implementing a UIPreferencesTable class, as a callback-oriented *data binding* is used to query for the information used to fill the table. This is done in a similar fashion to the UITable objects you learned about in Chapter 3, but with a higher level of complexity. The runtime class invokes a set of methods in the data source to return information about the preferences table—the number and size of each cell, objects within cells, and information about logical groupings. Much to the discouragement of iPhone's open source community, this is very different from an object-oriented model where each cell would have its own properties and simply be added as objects. Instead, the construction for the entire preferences table is bulky and complex in spite of Apple's traditionally elegant design style.

Just to recap, the preferences table refers to the complete settings page. A table can have many logical groupings of like settings. Within each group, a single table cell is used to display each individual setting to the user. The content for the cell includes optional title, text, and controls, if any.

The conversation between a preferences table and its data source looks (something) like Figure 7-1.

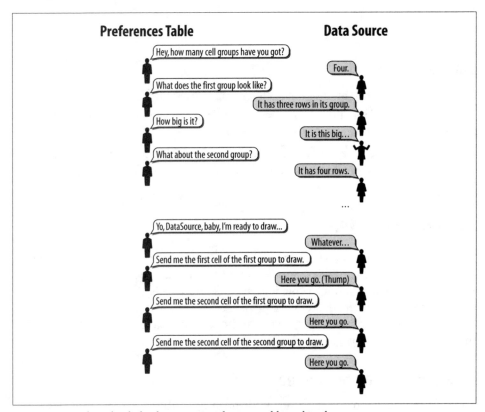

Figure 7-1. Analogy for dialog between a preferences table and its data source

Because a preferences table is assembled in two pieces (the table and the data source), the cleanest way to put one together is to create a subclass of UIPreferencesTable and have it act as its own data source. This allows your application to simply create an instance of the class and display it on the screen.

Subclassing the preferences table

To create a self-contained preferences table, create a subclass of UIPreferencesTable and include all of the methods needed to bind to itself as a data source. The following example creates a subclass named MyPreferencesTable:

```
@interface MyPreferencesTable : UIPreferencesTable
{

}

/* Preferences table methods */

- (id)initWithFrame:(CGRect)rect;
- (void)dealloc;

/* Data source methods */

- (int)numberOfGroupsInPreferencesTable:(UIPreferencesTable *)aTable;
- (UIPreferencesTableCell *)preferencesTable:
    (UIPreferencesTable *)aTable cellForGroup:(int)group;
- (float)preferencesTable:(UIPreferencesTable *)aTable
    heightForRow:(int)row
    inGroup:(int)group
    withProposedHeight:(float)proposed;
- (BOOL)preferencesTable:(UIPreferencesTable *)aTable
    isLabelGroup:(int)group;
- (UIPreferencesTableCell *)preferencesTable:
    (UIPreferencesTable *)aTable
    cellForRow:(int)row
    inGroup:(int)group;
```

The methods used for the data source break down like this:

numberOfGroupsInPreferencesTable

> Returns the number of logical groups in the table. This also includes text label groups, which are groups used to add small, embossed text to a cell. Group labels should not be included in the group count.

cellForGroup

> Returns a UIPreferencesTableCell object to act as the group heading for a given group. These cells are created as UIPreferencesTextTableCell objects, and are assigned a group title using the cell's setTitle method.

heightForRow

> Returns the height for a given row. This method is provided with a proposed height that can be returned as a default. It's ultimately up to the developer what height any given cell should be; you can return the proposed height or a custom height, depending on the type of object being created. This method is also called for group headings, using a row number of -1.

isLabelGroup

> Returns a Boolean value specifying whether the cells in a given group should be treated as text labels. Text labels are smaller than group labels, and are used to provide informational text. When YES is returned, the group will be displayed as small, embossed text rather than a white cell.

cellFowRow

> Returns the preference cell object for whatever row and group is specified. Whenever a preference is brought into view, this method is called to obtain the UIPreferencesTableCell object representing the row. This method is called multiple times for the same cell, and so cell objects must be cached in memory.

Caching preference cells

Each preference cell in a preferences table is "forgotten" by the table after it scrolls off the screen. When it scrolls back into view, the cellFowRow method is called again for that row. This can present a problem if you're creating a new row every time the method is called, and can also slow scrolling down considerably.

In a nutshell, the cellForRow method should be written so that repeated queries for the same preferences cell will return a pointer to an existing cell, rather than recreate it each time. By creating a matrix, you can store pointers for each cell and return to them later to satisfy subsequent queries. Create a matrix of cell pointers in your preferences table subclass. This will hold all of the pointers to cells you create later.

```
#define NUM_GROUPS 3
#define CELLS_PER_GROUP 4

UIPreferencesTableCell *cells[NUM_GROUPS][CELLS_PER_GROUP];
UIPreferencesTableCell *groupcell[NUM_GROUPS];
```

Here, NUM_GROUPS and CELLS_PER_GROUP represent the number of logical groups in the preferences table and the highest number of cells in any given group. These values will be used to initialize the matrix when the preferences table's initWithFrame method is called, so they're created here as constants.

Initialization

After you create a preferences table object, you display it either by attaching it to an existing view or transitioning to it from a controlling view. This can be done when the user presses a settings button, or automatically the first time the program runs. The following code instantiates the MyPreferencesTable subclass you've created:

```
MyPreferencesTable *preferencesTable = [ [ MyPreferencesTable alloc ]
    initWithFrame: viewRect ];
```

After the object has been created, its reloadData method must be called to load all the elements in the preference table. This causes the table to invoke its data source and begin loading information about cell groupings and geometry.

```
[ preferencesTable reloadData ];
```

Preferences table cells

Each cell in a preferences table gets created as a UIPreferencesTableCell object, or a subclass of it. Cells are returned through the cellForRow callback method, which you

---

must write and which is called by the preferences table class automatically as new rows are being drawn on the screen. For example, if the cellForRow method is called specifying row 0 group 0, the method might return a cell using code like the following:

```
UIPreferencesTableCell *cell = [ [ UIPreferencesTableCell alloc ]
    init ];
[ cell setTitle:@"Music Volume" ];
[ cell setShowSelection: NO ];
return cell;
```

Text cells

A text cell is a subclass of UIPreferencesTableCell, but is designed to display (and optionally allow editing of) text. The following snippet is an example of how to create one.

```
UIPreferencesTextTableCell *cell = [
    [ UIPreferencesTextTableCell alloc ] init ];
[ cell setTitle: @"Version" ];
[ cell setEnabled: NO ];
[ cell setValue: @"1.0.0" ];
return cell;
```

Use the setEnabled method to enable editing:

```
[ cell setEnabled: YES ];
```

The value can be read using the value method:

```
NSString *text = [ cell value ];
```

Controls

The UIPreferencesControlTableCell object is derived from the base UIPreferencesTableCell class and can accommodate a control. Controls can be added to regular UIPreferencesTableCell objects as subviews, but the UIPreferencesControlTableCell class can completely encapsulate a control.

```
UIPreferencesControlTableCell *cell =
    [ [ UIPreferencesControlTableCell alloc ] init ];
UISliderControl *musicVolumeControl = [ [ UISliderControl alloc ]
    initWithFrame:CGRectMake(170.0f, 5.0f, 120.0f, 55.0f) ];
[ musicVolumeControl setMinValue: 0.0 ];
[ musicVolumeControl setMaxValue: 10.0 ];
[ musicVolumeControl setValue: 3.5 ];

[ cell setControl: musicVolumeControl ];
```

The control can then be referenced from the object, relieving you of the need to keep a pointer to the control in your class:

```
UISliderControl *musicVolumeControl = [ cell control ];
```

This example creates a slider control with a frame in the right portion of the preferences cell. It then sets the slider as the control for the cell. All of this takes place in the cellForRow method before returning the newly created cell.

Displaying the Preferences Table

The preferences table can be displayed by adding it as a subview to an existing view or transitioning to it with a UITransitionView.

Add a preference table as a subview as follows:

```
[ self addSubview: preferencesTable ];
```

whereas a transition might look like this:

```
[ transitionView transition: 1 toView: preferencesTable ];
```

Example: Shoot-'Em-Up Game Settings

A spaceship shoot-'em-up game is being written and needs a set of preferences to control everything from sound volume to debugging messages. In this example, the UIPreferencesTable class is subclassed to create our own MyPreferencesTable object. This object serves as a preferences table and its own data source. It creates each cell and assigns some of the controls you learned about in the previous section. A MyPreferencesTable object is built as a self-contained preferences table that can be used by the MainView class.

This example can be built with the tool chain from the command line as follows:

```
$ arm-apple-darwin-gcc -o MyExample MyExample.m MyPreferencesTable.m\
    -lobjc -framework CoreFoundation -framework UIKit
```

Examples 7-1 and 7-2 contain the code for the application and main view, while Examples 7-3 and 7-4 create the preferences table itself.

Example 7-1. Preferences table example (MyExample.h)

```
#import <CoreFoundation/CoreFoundation.h>
#import <UIKit/UIKit.h>
#import "MyPreferencesTable.h"

@interface MainView : UIView
{
    MyPreferencesTable *preferencesTable;
}
- (id)initWithFrame:(CGRect)rect;
- (void)dealloc;
@end

@interface MyApp : UIApplication
{
    UIWindow *window;
```

Example 7-1. Preferences table example (MyExample.h) (continued)

```
    MainView *mainView;
}
- (void)applicationDidFinishLaunching:(NSNotification *)aNotification;
@end
```

Example 7-2. Preferences table example (MyExample.m)

```
#import "MyExample.h"

int main(int argc, char **argv)
{
    return UIApplicationMain(argc, argv, [ MyApp class ]);
}


@implementation MyApp
- (void)applicationDidFinishLaunching:(NSNotification *)aNotification {
    window = [ [ UIWindow alloc ] initWithContentRect:
        [ UIHardware fullScreenApplicationContentRect ]
    ];

    CGRect rect = [ UIHardware fullScreenApplicationContentRect ];
    rect.origin.x = rect.origin.y = 0.0f;

    mainView = [ [ MainView alloc ] initWithFrame: rect ];

    [ window setContentView: mainView ];
    [ window orderFront: self ];
    [ window makeKey: self ];
    [ window _setHidden: NO ];
}
@end


@implementation MainView
- (id)initWithFrame:(CGRect)rect {
    if ((self == [ super initWithFrame: rect ]) != nil) {

        preferencesTable = [ [ MyPreferencesTable alloc ] initWithFrame: rect ];
        [ preferencesTable reloadData ];
        [ self addSubview: preferencesTable ];
    }

    return self;
}

- (void)dealloc
{
    [ self dealloc ];
    [ super dealloc ];
}
@end
```

Example 7-3. Preferences table example (MyPreferencesTable.h)

```
#import <UIKit/UIKit.h>
#import <UIKit/UIPreferencesTable.h>
#import <UIKit/UIPreferencesTextTableCell.h>
#import <UIKit/UISwitchControl.h>
#import <UIKit/UISegmentedControl.h>
#import <UIKit/UISliderControl.h>

#define NUM_GROUPS 3
#define CELLS_PER_GROUP 4

@interface MyPreferencesTable : UIPreferencesTable
{
    UIPreferencesTableCell *cells[NUM_GROUPS][CELLS_PER_GROUP];
    UIPreferencesTableCell *groupcell[NUM_GROUPS];

    UISliderControl     *musicVolumeControl;
    UISliderControl     *gameVolumeControl;
    UISegmentedControl *difficultyControl;

    UISliderControl     *shipStabilityControl;
    UISwitchControl     *badGuyControl;
    UISwitchControl     *debugControl;
}

- (id)initWithFrame:(CGRect)rect;
- (int)numberOfGroupsInPreferencesTable:(UIPreferencesTable *)aTable;
- (UIPreferencesTableCell *)preferencesTable:
    (UIPreferencesTable *)aTable
    cellForGroup:(int)group;
- (float)preferencesTable:(UIPreferencesTable *)aTable
    heightForRow:(int)row
    inGroup:(int)group
    withProposedHeight:(float)proposed;
- (BOOL)preferencesTable:(UIPreferencesTable *)aTable
    isLabelGroup:(int)group;
- (UIPreferencesTableCell *)preferencesTable:
    (UIPreferencesTable *)aTable
    cellForRow:(int)row
    inGroup:(int)group;
@end
```

Example 7-4. Preferences table example (MyPreferencesTable.m)

```
#import "MyPreferencesTable.h"

@implementation MyPreferencesTable
- (id)initWithFrame:(CGRect)rect {
    if ((self == [ super initWithFrame: rect ]) != nil) {
        int i, j;

        for(i=0;i<NUM_GROUPS;i++) {
            groupcell[i] = NULL;
```

Example 7-4. Preferences table example (MyPreferencesTable.m) (continued)

```
            for(j=0;j<CELLS_PER_GROUP;j++)
                cells[i][j] = NULL;
        }

        [ self setDataSource: self ];
        [ self setDelegate: self ];
    }

    return self;
}

- (int)numberOfGroupsInPreferencesTable:(UIPreferencesTable *)aTable {

    /* Number of logical groups, including labels */
    return NUM_GROUPS;
}

 - (int)preferencesTable:(UIPreferencesTable *)aTable
    numberOfRowsInGroup:(int)group
{
    switch (group) {
        case(0):
            return 4;
            break;
        case(1):
            return 4;
            break;
        case(2):
            return 1; /* Text label group */
            break;
    }
}

- (UIPreferencesTableCell *)preferencesTable:
    (UIPreferencesTable *)aTable
    cellForGroup:(int)group
{
    if (groupcell[group] != NULL)
        return groupcell[group];

    groupcell[group] = [ [ UIPreferencesTableCell alloc ] init ];
    switch (group) {
        case (0):
            [ groupcell[group] setTitle: @"General Settings" ];
            break;
        case (1):
            [ groupcell[group] setTitle: @"Advanced Settings" ];
            break;
    }
    return groupcell[group];
}
```

Example 7-4. Preferences table example (MyPreferencesTable.m) (continued)

```
- (float)preferencesTable:(UIPreferencesTable *)aTable
    heightForRow:(int)row
    inGroup:(int)group
    withProposedHeight:(float)proposed
{
    /* Return height for group titles */
    if (row == -1) {
        if (group < 2)
            return 40;
    }

    /* Segmented controls are larger than the others */
    if (group == 0 && row == 2)
        return 55.0;

    return proposed;
}

- (BOOL)preferencesTable:(UIPreferencesTable *)aTable
    isLabelGroup:(int)group
{
    if (group == 2)
        return YES;
    return NO;
}

- (UIPreferencesTableCell *)preferencesTable:
    (UIPreferencesTable *)aTable
    cellForRow:(int)row
    inGroup:(int)group
{
    UIPreferencesTableCell *cell;

    if (cells[group][row] != NULL)
        return cells[group][row];

    cell = [ [ UIPreferencesTableCell alloc ] init ];
    [ cell setEnabled: YES ];

    switch (group) {
        case (0):
            switch (row) {
                case (0):
                    [ cell setTitle:@"Music Volume" ];
                    musicVolumeControl = [ [ UISliderControl alloc ]
                        initWithFrame: CGRectMake(170, 5, 120, 55)
                    ];
                    [ musicVolumeControl setMinValue: 0.0 ];
                    [ musicVolumeControl setMaxValue: 10.0 ];
                    [ musicVolumeControl setValue: 3.5 ];
                    [ cell addSubview: musicVolumeControl ];
                    break;
```

Example 7-4. Preferences table example (MyPreferencesTable.m) (continued)

```
        case (1):
            [ cell setTitle:@"Game Sounds" ];
            gameVolumeControl = [ [ UISliderControl alloc ]
                initWithFrame: CGRectMake(170, 5, 120, 55)
            ];
            [ gameVolumeControl setMinValue: 0.0 ];
            [ gameVolumeControl setMaxValue: 10.0 ];
            [ gameVolumeControl setValue: 5.0 ];
            [ cell addSubview: gameVolumeControl ];
            break;
        case (2):
            [ cell setTitle:@"Difficulty" ];
            difficultyControl = [[ UISegmentedControl alloc ]
                initWithFrame: CGRectMake(170, 5, 120, 55) ];
            [ difficultyControl insertSegment:0
                withTitle:@"Easy" animated: NO ];
            [ difficultyControl insertSegment:1
                withTitle:@"Hard" animated: NO ];
            [ difficultyControl selectSegment: 0 ];

            [ cell addSubview: difficultyControl ];
            break;
        case (3):
            [ cell release ];
            cell = [ [ UIPreferencesTextTableCell alloc ]
                init ];
            [ cell setTitle: @"Cheat Code" ];
            [ cell setEnabled: YES ];
            [ cell setValue: @"None" ];
            break;
    }
    break;
case (1):
    switch (row) {
        case (0):
            [ cell setTitle:@"Ship Stability" ];
            shipStabilityControl = [
                [ UISliderControl alloc ]
                initWithFrame: CGRectMake(170f, 5, 120, 55)
            ];
            [ shipStabilityControl setMinValue: 0.0 ];
            [ shipStabilityControl setMaxValue: 100.0 ];
            [ shipStabilityControl setValue: 45.0 ];
            [ shipStabilityControl setShowValue: YES ];
            [ cell addSubview: shipStabilityControl ];
            break;
        case (1):
            [ cell setTitle:@"Extra Bad Guys" ];
            badGuyControl = [ [ UISwitchControl alloc ]
                initWithFrame:CGRectMake(170, 5, 120, 30)
            ];
            [ badGuyControl setValue: 0.0 ];
```

Example 7-4. Preferences table example (MyPreferencesTable.m) (continued)

```
                        [ cell addSubview: badGuyControl ];
                        break;
                    case (2):
                        [ cell setTitle:@"Debugging" ];
                        debugControl = [ [ UISwitchControl alloc ]
                            initWithFrame:CGRectMake(170, 5, 120, 30)
                        ];
                        [ debugControl setValue: 0.0 ];
                        [ debugControl setAlternateColors: YES ];
                        [ cell addSubview: debugControl ];
                        break;
                    case (3):
                        [ cell release ];
                        cell = [ [ UIPreferencesTextTableCell alloc ]
                            init ];
                        [ cell setTitle: @"Version" ];
                        [ cell setEnabled: NO ];
                        [ cell setValue: @"1.0.0" ];
                        break;

                }
                break;
            case (2):
                [ cell setTitle:
                  @"Settings will take effect on the next restart"
                ];
                break;
        }

        [ cell setShowSelection: NO ];
        cells[group][row] = cell;
        return cell;
}
@end
```

What's Going On

You've just read through a full-blown application that displays a preferences table. Here's how it works:

1. When the application instantiates, a MainView object is created that serves as the controlling view for the application.

2. The mainView object's initWithFrame method is called by the application class. This instantiates a MyPreferencesTable object named preferencesTable and calls its initWithFrame method.

3. The preferences table's own initWithFrame method initializes the table's internal cache and configures itself as its own data source for the table.

4. The `mainView` object calls `preferenceTable`'s `reloadData` method. Because we haven't overridden `reloadData`, the parent `UIPreferencesTable` class's method is invoked. This begins the communication to the data source by calling the various data source methods. The preferences table talks to the data source to establish the basic construction and geometry of the table.

5. The `preferenceTable` object is added as a subview of `mainView`, where the underlying windowing framework calls its drawing routines.

6. For all rows that are visible on the screen, the preference table's `cellForRow` method is called.

7. The `cellForRow` method first checks to see whether a pointer already exists for the preference cell being referenced, and if not, creates a new `UIPreferencesTableCell` object. The title and options are set based on the row and group number, and any controls are created and added as subviews of the preference cell.

8. If a new cell was created, its object is returned. Otherwise, the cached pointer to the existing object is returned. In either case, the object's low-level draw routines are called internally and it is drawn on the screen.

Further Study

Now that you've had a taste of how preferences tables work, try these exercises to better acquaint yourself:

- Change the example to add real variables for each of the controls, having their own setters and getters so that their values can be exchanged with the `MainView` object.

- Use examples from Chapter 3 to build an application with two views—one table or text view and a preferences table. Assign a navigation bar button to transition users to the preferences table when they click a `Settings` button, and back to the text view when they press a `Back` button.

- See *UIPreferencesTable.h*, *UIPreferencesTextTableCell.h*, *UIPreferencesControlTableCell.h*, and *UIPreferencesTableCell.h* in your tool chain's *include* directory. You'll find it in */usr/local/arm-apple-darwin/include/UIKit*.

Progress Indicators

Progress indicators notify the user that an operation is in progress. There are two types of indicators supported in UIKit:

`UIProgressIndicator`
> This class presents a spinning clock-like animation—the kind seen when turning on the iPhone's WiFi or Bluetooth support, or when your Mac desktop boots up.

UIProgressBar

This class provides a thermometer-like readout, allowing the application to express how far along an operation is before completion.

Both types of indicators are derived from the UIView base class, meaning they can be layered on top of text views, alert sheets, most types of table cells, and any other object that derives from UIView.

UIProgressIndicator: Things That Spin

The UIProgressIndicator class is a simple animation class small enough to attach to nearly any UIView object, including table cells and alert sheets. The indicator displays a clock-like animation of tick marks making revolutions around a circle.

The indicator is created with a frame identifying the indicator's size and the coordinates relative to the view to which it is attached.

```
UIProgressIndicator *progressView = [ UIProgressIndicator alloc ]
    initWithFrame: CGRectMake(0, 0, 32, 32) ];
```

The indicator supports two styles, white (0) and dark gray (1), which are useful depending on the type of object they are being attached to. The style is set by invoking the object's setStyle method:

```
[ progressView setStyle: 0 ];
```

Use the setAnimationDuration method to adjust the amount of time it takes for one full revolution of tick marks around the circle. This value is set in seconds, and should be set according to the anticipated length of the operation. Faster operations can use faster revolutions, while operations that can take a minute or more should hint at this by using a slower rotation.

```
[ progressView setAnimationDuration: 1.0 ];
```

The progress indicator object can be added to any existing view object. Code to add it to an alert sheet might look like:

```
[ alertSheet addSubview: progressView ];
```

To start and stop the animation, use the startAnimation and stopAnimation methods:

```
[ progressView startAnimation ];
```

```
[ progressView stopAnimation ];
```

Example: A Simple Spinny Thingy

This example illustrates the construction and display of a UIProgressIndicator view. The example creates an indicator object and attaches it to the main view. An NSTimer object is then created to disable its animation after five seconds. The NSTimer object is part of the Foundation framework, and can be found in Apple's Cocoa documentation on the Apple Developer Connection web site.

To compile this example, use the tool chain on the command line as follows:

```
$ arm-apple-darwin-gcc -o MyExample MyExample.m -lobjc \
    -framework UIKit -framework Foundation
```

Examples 7-5 and 7-6 contain the code.

Example 7-5. Progress indicator example (MyExample.h)

```
#import <UIKit/UIKit.h>
#import <UIKit/UIProgressIndicator.h>

UIProgressIndicator *progressView;

@interface MainView : UIView
{

}
- (id)initWithFrame:(CGRect)frame;
- (void)dealloc;
@end

@interface MyApp : UIApplication
{
    UIWindow *window;
    MainView *mainView;
}
- (void)applicationDidFinishLaunching:(NSNotification *)aNotification;
@end
```

Example 7-6. Progress indicator example (MyExample.m)

```
#import "MyExample.h"

int main(int argc, char **argv)
{
    return UIApplicationMain(argc, argv, [ MyApp class ]);
}

@implementation MyApp

- (void)applicationDidFinishLaunching:(NSNotification *)aNotification {
    window = [ [ UIWindow alloc ] initWithContentRect:
        [ UIHardware fullScreenApplicationContentRect ]
    ];

    CGRect rect = [ UIHardware fullScreenApplicationContentRect ];
    rect.origin.x = rect.origin.y = 0.0f;

    mainView = [ [ MainView alloc ] initWithFrame: rect ];
    [ window setContentView: mainView ];
    [ window orderFront: self ];
    [ window makeKey: self ];
    [ window _setHidden: NO ];
```

Example 7-6. Progress indicator example (MyExample.m) (continued)

```
    NSTimer *timer = [ NSTimer scheduledTimerWithTimeInterval: 5.0
        target: self
        selector: @selector(handleTimer:)
        userInfo: nil
        repeats: NO ];
}

- (void) handleTimer: (NSTimer *) timer
{
    [ progressView stopAnimation ];
}
@end

@implementation MainView
- (id)initWithFrame:(CGRect)rect {

    if ((self == [ super initWithFrame: rect ]) != nil) {
        CGRect progressRect = rect;
        progressRect.size.width = 32;
        progressRect.size.height = 32;

        progressView = [ [ UIProgressIndicator alloc ]
            initWithFrame: progressRect ];
        [ self  addSubview: progressView ];
        [ progressView setAnimationDuration: 1.0 ];
        [ progressView startAnimation ];

    }

    return self;
}

- (void)dealloc
{
    [ self dealloc ];
    [ super dealloc ];
}

@end
```

What's Going On

Here's how the progress indicator example works:

1. When the application instantiates, it creates a `MainView` object and calls its `initWithFrame` method.

2. The `initWithFrame` method creates a `UIProgressIndicator` object and attaches it to the main view. The animation is set to use one-second revolutions and the animation is then started.

3. An `NSTimer` object is created with a trigger of 5.0 seconds. After this period expires, the `handleTimer` method is notified, which shuts down the animation, causing the indicator to disappear.

UIProgressBar: When Spinny Things Are Tacky

The `UIProgressBar` object is a close cousin to the `UIProgressIndicator`. Instead of displaying a drool-inciting animation, the progress bar class draws a thermometer-like indicator and provides an interface to set its fill level as your application crunches on its operation. The advantage of using a progress bar is that it can reflect more or less accurately how much work the application has actually done.

To create a progress bar, the class's initialization method includes a frame identifying the bar's size and display origin:

```
UIProgressBar progressView = [ [ UIProgressBar alloc ]
    initWithFrame: CGRectMake(0, 0, 320, 32) ];
```

The indicator supports one of two styles, white (0) and dark gray (1), which can be assigned using the `setStyle` method, according to the color of the object it's being attached to.

```
[ progressView setStyle: 0 ];
```

To display the progress bar, add it to an existing `UIView` object. Code to attach it to an alert sheet might look like:

```
[ alertSheet addSubview: progressView ];
```

Once the progress bar has been displayed, its progress can be set by the application to indicate how far along it is in its operation. After the level is set, a call to the bar's `updateIfNecessary` method is made to ensure it is propagated out to the display. The progress value is a `double` (a floating point with double precision) between 0.0 and 1.0.

```
[ progressView setProgress: 0.5 ];
```

```
[ progressView updateIfNecessary ];
```

Example: A Better Built Bar

In this example, a progress bar is created and added to the main view. An `NSTimer` object is used to trigger an update method every tenth of a second, which increases the progress bar by 1% (0.01).

While the example stops with a level of 1.0, progress bars don't make any attempt to ensure the value passed to it is valid. Passing a value greater than 1.0 will cause the progress bar to fill beyond the edge of the bar's border. Of course, this could be a useful effect in some special cases.

To compile this example, use the tool chain on the command line as follows:

```
$ arm-apple-darwin-gcc -o MyExample MyExample.m -lobjc \
    -framework UIKit -framework Foundation
```

Examples 7-7 and 7-8 contain the code.

Example 7-7. Progress bar example (MyExample.h)

```
#import <UIKit/UIKit.h>
#import <UIKit/UIProgressBar.h>

UIProgressBar *progressView;

@interface MainView : UIView
{

}
- (id)initWithFrame:(CGRect)frame;
- (void)dealloc;
@end

@interface MyApp : UIApplication
{
    UIWindow *window;
    MainView *mainView;
}
- (void)applicationDidFinishLaunching:(NSNotification *)aNotification;
@end
```

Example 7-8. Progress bar example (MyExample.m)

```
#import "MyExample.h"

int main(int argc, char **argv)
{
    return UIApplicationMain(argc, argv, [ MyApp class ]);
}

double progress = 0.0;

@implementation MyApp

- (void)applicationDidFinishLaunching:(NSNotification *)aNotification {
    window = [ [ UIWindow alloc ] initWithContentRect:
        [ UIHardware fullScreenApplicationContentRect ]
    ];

    CGRect rect = [ UIHardware fullScreenApplicationContentRect ];
    rect.origin.x = rect.origin.y = 0.0f;

    mainView = [ [ MainView alloc ] initWithFrame: rect ];

    [ window setContentView: mainView ];
    [ window orderFront: self ];
```

Example 7-8. Progress bar example (MyExample.m) (continued)

```
    [ window makeKey: self ];
    [ window _setHidden: NO ];

    NSTimer *timer = [ NSTimer scheduledTimerWithTimeInterval: 0.10
    target: self
    selector: @selector(handleTimer:)
    userInfo: nil
    repeats: YES ];
}

- (void) handleTimer: (NSTimer *) timer
{
    progress += 0.01;
    if (progress <= 1.0)
    {
        [ progressView setProgress: progress ];
        [ progressView updateIfNecessary ];
    }
}
@end

@implementation MainView
- (id)initWithFrame:(CGRect)rect {

    if ((self == [ super initWithFrame: rect ]) != nil) {

        progressView = [ [ UIProgressBar alloc ] initWithFrame: rect ];
[ progressView setStyle: 0 ];
        [ self addSubview: progressView ];
    }

    return self;
}

- (void)dealloc
{
    [ self dealloc ];
    [ super dealloc ];
}

@end
```

What's Going On

The progress bar example works just like the progress indicator example:

1. When the application instantiates, a `MainView` object is created and its `initWithFrame` method is called.

2. The `initWithFrame` method creates a `UIProgressBar` object and attaches it to the main view.

3. An NSTimer object is created with a trigger of 0.1 seconds, repeating indefinitely. Each time it triggers, the handleTimer method is notified, which increments the progress bar's value by 1% (0.01).

Progress HUDs: When It's Important Enough to Block Stuff

One other progress object exists, but is not an indicator itself. The UIProgressHUD class displays a UIProgressIndicator object and any accompanying text in a semi-transparent window. When you want to get the message across to the user that she really shouldn't be doing anything in a certain window until the operation is completed, the UIProgressHUD class is the class for you. The window is superimposed over the entire view window, dimming out and effectively blocking access to any other components on the view. This can be seen on the iPhone when certain carrier-level features are changed, and when sending SMS messages by blocking access to the keyboard.

To create a UIProgressHUD object, initialize it along with the display region of the parent object:

```
UIProgressHUD *hud = [ [ UIProgressHUD alloc ] initWithFrame: viewRect ];
```

The text of the HUD is set using the object's setText method.

```
[ hud setText: @"Please Wait. I'm doing something REALLY important." ];
```

Then, attach the HUD to a large view or window.

```
[ mainView addSubview: hud ];
```

Even though the object encapsulates a UIProgressIndicator, no startAnimation or stopAnimation methods are directly accessible. The HUD's indicator is activated and deactivated by invoking a show method.

```
[ hud show: YES ];
```

When told to show, the HUD will gray out the parent view. It will then activate the spinning indicator and display the text it was configured with. When your application has finished processing, hide the HUD:

```
[ hud show: NO ];
```

Example: Hello, HUD!

This example takes the "Hello, World" application from Chapter 3 and applies a five-second UIProgressHUD. The HUD will appear over the UITextView object and then be removed once the timer expires.

To compile this example, use the tool chain on the command line as follows:

```
$ arm-apple-darwin-gcc -o MyExample MyExample.m -lobjc \
    -framework UIKit -framework Foundation -framework CoreFoundation
```

Examples 7-9 and 7-10 contain the code.

Example 7-9. Progress HUD example (MyExample.h)

```
#import <UIKit/UIKit.h>
#import <UIKit/UITextView.h>
#import <UIKit/UIProgressHUD.h>

@interface MainView : UIView
{
    UITextView      *textView;
}

- (id)initWithFrame:(CGRect)frame;
- (void)dealloc;

@end

@interface MyApp : UIApplication
{
    UIWindow *window;
    MainView *mainView;
}

- (void)applicationDidFinishLaunching:(NSNotification *)aNotification;
@end
```

Example 7-10. Progress HUD example (MyExample.m)

```
#import "MyExample.h"

int main(int argc, char **argv)
{
    return UIApplicationMain(argc, argv, [ MyApp class ]);
}

UIProgressHUD *hud;

@implementation MyApp

- (void)applicationDidFinishLaunching:(NSNotification *)aNotification {
    window = [ [ UIWindow alloc ] initWithContentRect:
        [ UIHardware fullScreenApplicationContentRect ]
    ];

    CGRect rect = [ UIHardware fullScreenApplicationContentRect ];
    rect.origin.x = rect.origin.y = 0.0f;

    mainView = [ [ MainView alloc ] initWithFrame: rect ];

    [ window setContentView: mainView ];
```

Example 7-10. Progress HUD example (MyExample.m) (continued)

```
    [ window orderFront: self ];
    [ window makeKey: self ];
    [ window _setHidden: NO ];

    hud = [ [ UIProgressHUD alloc ] initWithFrame: rect ];
    [ hud setText: @"Please Wait" ];
    [ mainView addSubview: hud ];
    [ hud show: YES ];

    NSTimer *timer = [ NSTimer scheduledTimerWithTimeInterval: 5.0
    target: self
    selector: @selector(handleTimer:)
    userInfo: nil
    repeats: NO ];
}

- (void) handleTimer: (NSTimer *) timer
{
    [ hud show: NO ];
}
@end

@implementation MainView
- (id)initWithFrame:(CGRect)rect {

    if ((self == [ super initWithFrame: rect ]) != nil) {

        textView = [ [ UITextView alloc ] initWithFrame: rect ];
        [ textView setTextSize: 18 ];
        [ textView setText: @"Hello, World!" ];
        [ self addSubview: textView ];
    }

    return self;
}

- (void)dealloc
{
    [ self dealloc ];
    [ super dealloc ];
}

@end
```

What's Going On

The progress HUD operates in much the same way as the indicators shown earlier in the chapter:

1. When the application instantiates, a MainView object is created and its initWithFrame method is called.

---

2. The `initWithFrame` method creates a `UITextView` object and attaches it to the main view.

3. After the main view is added to the window, a `UIProgressHUD` is created and attached to it, then activated.

4. An `NSTimer` object is created with a trigger of 5.0 seconds. When the timer triggers, the `UIProgressHUD` is instructed to hide, revealing the original `UITextView` underneath.

Further Study

- Use your knowledge of alert sheets from Chapter 3 to create a "progress sheet" with no buttons. Use the `NSTimer` object to fill the bar. When it has reached its full capacity, dismiss the alert sheet automatically. This is an ideal use when your application needs to check online for updates or product announcements.

- Check out *UIProgressBar.h*, *UIProgressHUD.h*, and *UIProgressIndicator.h* prototypes in the tool chain's directory. This can be found in */usr/local/arm-apple-darwin/UIKit*.

Image Handling

The UIKit framework makes working with images a painless endeavor. With its repertoire of image handling classes, you'll be able to display, scale, clip, and layer images to deliver just the right effects for your application. Rather than bloating out a single image class with obfuscated routines, Apple's developers took the smarter path and subclassed each type of image transformation, with each offering at most a few different methods to be concerned about.

The Image Object

The `UIImage` class encapsulates the actual image. It can be used to draw directly inside a view or act as a container object in more powerful image view classes. The class provides methods to load an image from various sources, set the image's orientation on the screen, and provide information about the image. For simple graphics, `UIImage` can be used in a view's drawing routines to render images and patterns. It's an intermediary between the larger, complete image view classes and working with low-level graphics routines, such as raw Core Surface buffers.

A `UIImage` object can be created from a file, taken from a snapshot of a core surface buffer, or even imported from the desktop wallpaper. Both static and instance methods exist; these can either reference and cache images or instantiate new image objects, depending on the needs of your application.

Static methods

The easiest way to reference an image is through `UIImage`'s static methods. Rather than managing instances of images, the static methods provide a direct interface to shared objects residing in the framework's internal memory cache. This helps declutter your application and eliminates the need to clean up. Static methods exist to access images directly from your program folder, using a pathname, or from the desktop wallpaper.

`applicationImageNamed`

> The `applicationImageNamed` method is the preferred method for using application-based images, as the possibility always exists that the user will rename your application or possibly install it in a different folder, breaking direct paths. To use this method, reference the filename only. The framework will figure out where your application is installed and load the image for you.
>
> ```
> UIImage *image = [ UIImage applicationImageNamed: @"image.png" ];
> ```

`imageAtPath`

> If the image is located outside of your application folder (for example, images taken with the camera), it can be referenced using a direct path:
>
> ```
> UIImage *image = [ UIImage imageAtPath: @"/path/to/image.png" ];
> ```

`defaultDesktopImage`

> Another static method exists to return a reference to the desktop wallpaper, which is applied in the Settings application. We use it extensively throughout our examples because it relieves you from the need to upload images to use examples.
>
> ```
> UIImage *image = [ UIImage defaultDesktopImage ];
> ```

Instance methods

In addition to static references, images can also be instantiated as objects allocated by your application.

`initWithContentsOfFile`

> The most common approach is to supply the direct path to an image file:
>
> ```
> UIImage *image = [ [ UIImage alloc ] initWithContentsOfFile:
>     @"/path/to/image.png"
> ];
> ```
>
> The method can also be called with a cache argument, instructing the framework to cache the image upon loading it so that it doesn't need to be read from disk multiple times.
>
> ```
> UIImage *image = [ [ UIImage alloc ]
>     initWithContentsOfFile: @"/path/to/image.png"
>     cache: YES
> ];
> ```

```
initWithCoreSurfaceBuffer
```

If your application uses the Core Surfaces framework to create a `CoreSurfaceBuffer` video buffer (explained in Chapter 5), a `UIImage` object can be created as a snapshot of the current buffer.

```
UIImage *image = [ [ UIImage alloc ]
    initWithCoreSurfaceBuffer: screenSurface
];
```

Displaying an image

View objects have internal drawing routines that are called when their `drawRect` methods are invoked. Unlike other image classes, the `UIImage` cannot be attached directly to a view object as a subview. Instead, classes derived from `UIView` can override their `drawRect` method to include calling the drawing methods of an image object.

A view object's `drawRect` method is called whenever a portion of its window needs to be rendered. To render the contents of a `UIImage` inside the window, invoke the object's `draw1PartImageInRect` method.

```
- (void)drawRect:(CGRect)rect {
    CGRect myRect;
    CGSize imageSize = [ image size ];

    myRect.origin.x = 0;
    myRect.origin.y = 0;
    myRect.size.width = imageSize.width;
    myRect.size.height = imageSize.height;
    [ image draw1PartImageInRect: myRect ];
}
```

Be careful not to allocate any new objects inside the `drawRect` method because it's called every time the window needs to be redrawn.

Drawing patterns

If the image is a pattern, it can be repeated throughout the entire view region by using another method provided in the `UIImage` class, `drawAsPatternInRect`.

```
[ image drawAsPatternInRect: rect ];
```

This method causes the image to be tiled within the frame being drawn.

Orientation

An image's orientation determines how it's rotated in the display. Because the iPhone can be held one of six different ways, it may be necessary to rotate all of your images if the orientation changes.

```
[ image setOrientation: 1 ];
```

The following orientations can be set.

Orientation	Description
0	Default orientation
1	Image rotated 180 degrees
2	Image rotated 90 degrees counterclockwise
3	Image rotates 90 degrees clockwise

Example: Fun with Icons

This example illustrates the rendering of images and patterns within a view class's drawRect method. We create an empty view class and then override drawRect to include rendering routines, drawing up some application icons in the main window.

To compile this example, use the tool chain on the command line as follows:

```
$ arm-apple-darwin-gcc -o MyExample MyExample.m -lobjc \
    -framework CoreFoundation -framework Foundation -framework UIKit
```

Examples 7-11 and 7-12 contain the code.

Example 7-11. UIImage drawing example (MyExample.h)

```
#import <CoreFoundation/CoreFoundation.h>
#import <UIKit/UIKit.h>

@interface MainView : UIView
{

}
- (void)drawRect:(CGRect)rect;
@end

@interface MyApp : UIApplication
{
    UIWindow *window;
    MainView *mainView;
}
- (void)applicationDidFinishLaunching:(NSNotification *)aNotification;
@end
```

Example 7-12. UIImage drawing example (MyExample.m)

```
#import <Foundation/Foundation.h>
#import <CoreFoundation/CoreFoundation.h>
#import "MyExample.h"

int main(int argc, char **argv)
{
    return UIApplicationMain(argc, argv, [ MyApp class ]);
}
```

Example 7-12. UIImage drawing example (MyExample.m) (continued)

```
@implementation MyApp
- (void)applicationDidFinishLaunching:(NSNotification *)aNotification {
    window = [ [ UIWindow alloc ] initWithContentRect:
        [ UIHardware fullScreenApplicationContentRect ]
    ];

    CGRect rect = [ UIHardware fullScreenApplicationContentRect ];
    rect.origin.x = rect.origin.y = 0.0f;

    mainView = [ [ MainView alloc ] initWithFrame: rect ];
    [ window setContentView: mainView ];
    [ window orderFront: self ];
    [ window makeKey: self ];
    [ window _setHidden: NO ];

}
@end

@implementation MainView
- (void)drawRect:(CGRect)rect {
    CGRect drawRect;
    CGSize size;

    UIImage *pattern = [ UIImage imageAtPath:
        @"/Applications/MobilePhone.app/icon.png" ];
    [ pattern drawAsPatternInRect: rect ];

    UIImage *image = [ UIImage imageAtPath:
        @"/Applications/MobileSafari.app/icon.png" ];
    size = [ image size ];
    drawRect.origin.x = (320 - (size.width)) / 2;
    drawRect.origin.y = (480 - (size.height)) / 2;
    drawRect.size.width = size.width;
    drawRect.size.height = size.height;
    [ image draw1PartImageInRect: drawRect ];
}
@end
```

UIImageView: A View with a View

The UIImageView class provides a way to treat an image as a control. This is useful when an image needs to be connected to view objects, button bars, or table cells, or for applications such as slide shows, where an entire view region might contain an image.

A UIImageView object acts as a view wrapper for UIImage; that is, the UIImage object is created first, and then attached to the UIImageView object using the class's initWithImage or setImage methods.

```
UIImage *image = [ UIImage imageAtPath: @"/path/to/image.png" ];
UIImageView *imageView = [ [ UIImageView alloc ]
    initWithImage: image
];
```

The coordinates initialize as the view's frame determines the offset within the parent view where the image will be drawn.

```
CGRect rect = CGRectMake(0, 0, 320, 200);
UIImageView *imageView = [ [ UIImageView alloc ]
    initWithRect: rect ];
[ imageView setImage: [ UIImage imageAtPath:
    @"/path/to/image.png" ] ];
```

Once created, the image can then be attached to any type of view object, table cell, or other similar object.

```
[ preferencesCell addSubview: imageView ];
```

It could also be transitioned to using a `UITransitionView`:

```
[ transitionView transition: 0 toView: imageview ];
```

To scale the image, the frame's size need only be adjusted. The new size can then be applied using the class's `setFrame` method:

```
rect.size.width = 160;
rect.size.height = 240;
[ imageView setFrame: rect ];
```

UIAutocorrectImageView: Sizing It Up (or Down)

The `UIAutocorrectImageView` class is similar to the `UIImageView` class, except that the image is automatically scaled to the size specified in its frame:

```
CGRect rect;
rect.origin.x = 80;
rect.origin.y = 120;
rect.size.width = 160;
rect.size.height = 240;

UIAutocorrectImageView *imageView = [
    [ UIAutocorrectImageView alloc ]
    initWithFrame: rect
    image: [ UIImage defaultDesktopImage ]
];
```

This example creates an image view using the desktop wallpaper image. It is scaled down to 160×240 and displayed at offset 80×120 within whatever view class it's attached to.

Once the image has been created, it can be attached to any type of view object, just like a `UIImageView`.

```
[ mainView addSubview: imageView ];
```

The image is scaled to match the width and height specified in the frame, just like in a `UIImageView` class. The aspect ratio can be changed, so be careful to preserve it by properly scaling the size of the frame.

UIClippedImageView: Crop Circles—Er, Squares

Like the `UIAutocorrectImageView` class, the `UIClippedImageView` class allows a smaller display region to be defined. Instead of scaling the image to fit the frame, this class will crop the image to fit, displaying only the portion of the image in the view region.

```
CGRect rect;
rect.size.width = 160;
rect.size.height = 240;
rect.origin.x = 80;
rect.origin.y = 120;

UIClippedImageView *imageView = [ [ UIClippedImageView alloc ]
    initWithFrame: rect
    image: [ UIImage defaultDesktopImage ]
];
```

This example creates a clipped image using a 160×240 view frame, positioned in the middle of the screen. This means that only 160×240 of the entire image will be displayed, and the rest clipped.

```
CGPoint origin;

origin.x = 0;
origin.y = 0;
[ self setImageOrigin: origin ];
```

The image's origin can be changed to clip a different portion of the image. In this example, the origin is set to 0×0, which causes the 160×240 window to instantly move to the top left corner of the image. Because this can be changed while the image is being displayed, some neat tricks can be done with this class, as will be illustrated in an upcoming example.

When the image is ready to display, it can be added to an existing view object.

```
[ mainView addSubview: imageView ];
```

UICompositeImageView: Layered Transparencies

Apple is well known for their beautiful overlays and transparencies. One of the ways the iPhone makes this possible is through the use of the `UICompositeImageView` class. This class allows multiple images to be superimposed on top of one another applying differing levels of transparency and letting each image bleed through. These are great for designing custom user interfaces such as video game screens having control overlays.

The class uses a simple interface allowing images to be added one by one. Images can be superimposed on top of one another or added to different positions in the window.

```
UICompositeImageView *compositeView = [
    [ UICompositeImageView alloc ] initWithFrame: rect
];
```

Once created, images are added individually by invoking the `addImage` method.

```
[ compositeView addImage: [ UIImage defaultDesktopImage ] ];
```

Transparency

The opacity of each image can be set when the image is created (in a paint program) or when it is added to the composite view at runtime. The composite view itself can perform limited operations on the new image layer as it's added. These include the following.

Operation	Description
1	Set intensity
2	Set opacity

To make an image semitransparent, use the opacity (2) operation. An argument named `fraction` specifies the level of opacity for the image—in this example, 50%.

```
[ compositeView addImage:
    [ UIImage applicationImageNamed: @"overlay.png" ]
    operation: 2
    fraction: 0.5
];
```

Scaling and positioning

When an image is added to the composite view, it can be scaled and/or positioned on top of the other layers in various ways. `UICompositeImageView` supports two additional versions of the `addImage` method, with both accepting source and destination frames for scaling and positioning. The image object compares the two frames and carries out the changes implied by their differences.

```
CGRect src, dest;
src.origin.x = 100;
src.origin.y = 50;
src.size.width = 320;
src.size.height = 480;
dest.origin.x = 80;
dest.origin.y = 120;
dest.size.width = 160;
dest.size.height = 120;
```

```
[ compositeView addImage:
    [ UIImage applicationImageNamed: @"overlay.png" ]
    toRect: dest
    fromRect: src
];
```

This example creates two frames, src and dest. The src structure contains the original size of the image (320×480) and the coordinates to use within the source image (100×50). Anything to the left or top of the coordinates will be cropped out. The coordinates provided in the dest structure mark the upper-left corner of the composite view where the new image will be pasted.

By providing different frame sizes between the src and dest structures, you can cause the image to automatically be resized.

To do the operation described in the previous section along with scaling and positioning all in one method, another version of addImage is available. This combines all four of the input arguments to allow you to scale and position a new image while simultaneously changing its opacity or intensity:

```
[ compositeView addImage:
    [ UIImage applicationImageNamed: @"overlay.png" ]
    toRect: dest
    fromRect: src
    operation: 2
    fraction: 0.35
];
```

The example above loads an image from the application's program directory named *overlay.png*. The CGRect structures provided tell the composite view to paste the image, beginning from coordinates 100×50, into the composite view at coordinates 80×20. It also instructs the composite view to make the new layer 35% opaque.

Any number of layers can be added to a composite image. Once the composite has been completed, it can be added to an existing UIView object:

```
[ mainView addSubview: compositeView ];
```

Example: Cool Clipping Animation

The UIClippedImageView class is a fun class to work with because it allows you to perform a few effects with its clipping mechanism. In this example, we'll create a UIClippedImageView and use a timer to continually scroll the clipping region. This will create what appears to be a moving window revealing different portions of the image.

To compile this example, use the tool chain on the command line as follows:

```
$ arm-apple-darwin-gcc -o MyExample MyExample.m -lobjc \
framework UIKit -framework CoreFoundation -framework Foundation
```

Examples 7-13 and 7-14 contain the code.

Example 7-13. Clipping example (MyExample.h)

```
#import <CoreFoundation/CoreFoundation.h>
#import <UIKit/UIKit.h>

@interface MainView : UIView
{

}
- (id)initWithFrame:(CGRect)rect;
- (void)dealloc;

@end

@interface MyApp : UIApplication
{
    UIWindow *window;
    MainView *mainView;
}

- (void)applicationDidFinishLaunching:(NSNotification *)aNotification;
@end
```

Example 7-14. Clipping example (MyExample.m)

```
#import <Foundation/Foundation.h>
#import <CoreFoundation/CoreFoundation.h>
#import <GraphicsServices/GraphicsServices.h>
#import <UIKit/CDStructures.h>
#import <UIKit/UIKit.h>
#import <UIKit/UIClippedImageView.h>
#import "MyExample.h"

CGPoint origin;
UIClippedImageView *imageView;

int main(int argc, char **argv)
{
    return UIApplicationMain(argc, argv, [ MyApp class ]);
}

@implementation MyApp

- (void)applicationDidFinishLaunching:(NSNotification *)aNotification {
    window = [ [ UIWindow alloc ] initWithContentRect:
        [ UIHardware fullScreenApplicationContentRect ]
    ];

    CGRect rect = [ UIHardware fullScreenApplicationContentRect ];
    rect.origin.x = rect.origin.y = 0.0f;
```

Example 7-14. Clipping example (MyExample.m) (continued)

```
    mainView = [ [ MainView alloc ] initWithFrame: rect ];
    [ window setContentView: mainView ];
    [ window orderFront: self ];
    [ window makeKey: self ];
    [ window _setHidden: NO ];

    NSTimer *timer = [ NSTimer scheduledTimerWithTimeInterval: 0.10
    target: self
    selector: @selector(handleTimer:)
    userInfo: nil
    repeats: YES ];
}

- (void) handleTimer: (NSTimer *) timer
{
    if (origin.y > 0)
        origin.y --;
    else
        origin.y = 480;

    if (origin.x > 0)
        origin.x --;
    else
        origin.x = 320;

    [ imageView setOriginAdjustingImage: origin ];
}
@end


@implementation MainView
- (id)initWithFrame:(CGRect)rect {

    if ((self == [ super initWithFrame: rect ]) != nil) {

        origin.x = 80;
        origin.y = 120;

        rect.size.width = 160;
        rect.size.height = 240;
        rect.origin.x = 80;
        rect.origin.y = 120;

        imageView = [ [ UIClippedImageView alloc ]
            initWithFrame: rect
            image: [ UIImage defaultDesktopImage ]
        ];
        [ imageView setImageOrigin: origin ];
        [ self addSubview: imageView ];
    }

    return self;
```

Example 7-14. Clipping example (MyExample.m) (continued)

```
}

- (void)dealloc
{
    [ self dealloc ];
    [ super dealloc ];
}

@end
```

What's Going On

1. When the application instantiates, it creates an instance of the `MainView` class and calls its `initWithFrame` method.

2. The `initWithFrame` method creates a `UIClippedImageView` object using a view region in the middle of the screen and with a display size of 160×240.

3. An `NSTimer` object is created, which notifies the `handleTimer` method every `0.10` seconds. This subroutine shifts the image origin one pixel up and to the left, wrapping around if necessary.

4. When the origin is adjusted, the visible image window slides to the new coordinates, giving the appearance of sliding a window over the picture.

Further Study

- Modify this section's `UIImage` example to randomly display various application icons anywhere on the screen.

- Modify this section's `UIClippedImageView` example to shift the size of the display region using the `setFrame` method.

- Check out the *UIImage.h*, *UIImageView.h*, *UIAutocorrectImageView.h*, and *UIClippedImageView.h* prototypes in the tool chain's *include* directory. These can be found in */usr/local/arm-apple-darwin/include/UIKit*.

Section Lists

The `UITable` object was introduced in Chapter 3 as a means of displaying selectable lists of information. When a table gets long enough, finding an item can be like finding a needle in a haystack. The `UISectionList` class provides a structure similar to a `UITable`, only expanded to include individual row groupings and a Rolodex-like scroll bar to quickly flip to a section heading. Each grouping can be assigned a section title, such as genres in a book or the first letter of a contact. You'll find section lists in use in the iPhone's own contact and song lists.

The UISectionList class encapsulates a UISectionTable, which comprises the table portion of the list. Like other tables, the section list uses a data binding. A data binding is an interface to a data source, which is queried by the table for the contents and construction of the table. The data source for a section list provides the callback methods needed to build the section list's groupings, section titles, and individual row cells.

As with other table classes covered in this book, the examples provided here create a subclass of the UISectionList object that can act as the section list and its own data source. This architecture is the easiest to illustrate and ideal for creating specialized reusable classes.

Creating a Section List

To create a section list that can also act as its own data source, subclass UISectionList. The following code creates a class named MySectionList containing the methods for both a section list and its data source.

```
@interface MySectionList : UISectionList
{
        UISectionTable *table;
}

/* Section list methods */
- (id)initWithFrame:(CGRect)rect;
- (void)dealloc;

/* Data source methods */
- (int)numberOfSectionsInSectionList:(UISectionList *)aSectionList;
- (NSString *)sectionList:
    (UISectionList *)aSectionList
    titleForSection:(int)section;
- (int)sectionList:
    (UISectionList *)aSectionList
    rowForSection:(int)section;
- (int) numberOfRowsInTable: (UITable *)table;
- (UITableCell *) table: (UITable *)table
    cellForRow: (int)row
    column: (int)col;
@end
```

The following data source methods are employed by the UISectionList object:

numberOfSectionsInSectionList
    This method returns the number of sections—that is, the number of different category headings—in the section list. For example, if your application were a contact list manager, you might define up to 26 sections (one for each letter). Empty sections should be discarded from the section list, dwindling this count.

titleForSection

Each section has a title, even if it's only a single letter. If your application were a bookstore, your section headers might include "Computer Science" and "Reference." The titleForSection method is called when the title for a given section is needed. It is provided the index number of the section as an argument and returns an NSString object containing the respective name.

rowForSection

Each row in a section list is referenced by a row number. A row must be associated with the section it belongs to, so that it can appear underneath the proper section heading. The section list assumes that each section has a series or rows in sequence within your application's array of rows.

The rowForSection method asks for the starting row number of your row list corresponding to the given section. For example, if you have 10 rows in the entire table, the first section might begin at row 0, while the second section might begin at row 7. The section list would interpret this to mean that rows 0 through 6 correspond to the first section and rows 7 through 10 correspond to the second.

numberOfRowsInTable

This method returns the total number of rows in the section list across all sections.

cellForRow

Individual rows are encapsulated by UITableCell objects. This object was already covered in the section "Tables" in Chapter 3. As the rows in a section list fall within the viewable frame of the display, this method requests the cell for a given row to be returned.

Initialization

To build a fully functional section list, all of the methods described in the previous section need to be coded. We'll illustrate one way to write them in our example at the end of the section.

Creating the section list itself is done by the calling view or the application class. The list can be set as the contents of the entire window, or created as a view that is later transitioned to by a controlling view. The following code allocates a new MySectionList object and initializes it.

```
UISectionList *sectionList = [ [ MySectionList alloc ]
    initWithFrame: windowRect ];
```

Like the UITable class, the section list's reloadData method must be called to initialize the data source. This method can be overridden by your subclass to load information to display for the rows, sections, and section headings of the list.

```
[ sectionList reloadData ];
```

Accessing the table object

The section list presents its data by encapsulating a UISectionTable object. This class is derived from the base UITable class and behaves in a similar fashion. The table itself must also be initialized to set up at least one table column to display information. The section list contains a method named table that returns a pointer to a UISectionTable object. This object was created internally along with the section list object.

The following code belongs in the MySectionList object's initWithFrame method to initialize the table portion of the list.

```
UISectionTable *table = [ self table ];
UITableColumn * column = [ [ UITableColumn alloc ]
    initWithTitle:@"Column Name"
    identifier:@"column"
    width: 320.0 ];
[ table addTableColumn: column ];
[ table setSeparatorStyle: 1 ];
[ table setRowHeight: 48.0 ];
[ table setDelegate: self ];
```

The methods used for configuring the table portion of the section list are identical to the UITable object covered in Chapter 3. At least one column must be created and various table attributes can be set here.

Displaying the Section List

The section list can be displayed by setting it as a window's contents, adding it as a subview to an existing view, or transitioning it to using the UITransitionView described in Chapter 3.

To set a section list as the window contents, use setContentView:

```
[ window setContentView: sectionList ];
```

To add a section list as a subview, call addSubview:

```
[ self addSubview: sectionList ];
```

To use a transition view to transition to the section list, use code such as this:

```
[ transitionView transition: 1 toView: sectionList ];
```

As the section list is displayed, the rows coming into visibility will cause the list to query the cellForRow method. This method returns a UITableCell object for the requested row. See Chapter 3's section about UITable objects for more information about the UITableCell class.

Selection Events

When the user selects an item from the section list, a method named `tableRowSelected` is called. This method then performs whatever operations are needed by the application.

The table's built-in `selectedRow` method returns the row number selected by the user.

```
- (void)tableRowSelected:(NSNotification *)notification {
    int rowSelected = [ table selectedRow ] ];

    /* Do something here */
}
```

Example: File Selector

One valuable use for a section list is to offer a file selector to open documents, applications, or files belonging to an application. This example defines a `FileSelector` class derived from `UISectionTable` that displays a list of files matching a given extension within a given directory. The section headings for the section list are the first letters of the filenames.

To use this class, create a `FileSelector` object. Then, provide the path and extension you'd like it to use. The `reloadData` method is then called, which causes the directory to be scanned and the section list built.

```
fileSelector = [ [ FileSelector alloc ]
    initWithFrame: rect ];
[ fileSelector setPath: @"/Applications" ];
[ fileSelector setExtension: @".app" ];
[ fileSelector reloadData ];
```

Once the section list has been built, it can be added to an existing view or set as the contents of a window. For example:

```
[ mainView addSubview: fileSelector ];
```

The data source maintains several different arrays:

`files`
> Contains a list of `UITableCell` objects corresponding to each row in the section list.

`filenames`
> Contains the actual filenames of each row.

`sections`
> Contains a list of section names, which is built by the directory enumerator loop as it scans for files. The first letters of filenames are used as section titles.

`offsets`
> Contains a list of row offsets associated with section groupings across all four arrays. For example, section one might begin at row five.

To compile this example, use the tool chain's command line as follows:

```
$ arm-apple-darwin-gcc -o MyExample MyExample.m -lobjc \
    -framework UIKit -framework CoreFoundation -framework Foundation
```

Examples 7-15 and 7-16 contain the code for the file selector table, while Examples 7-17 and 7-18 show the main application.

Example 7-15. Section list example (FileSelector.h)

```
#import <CoreFoundation/CoreFoundation.h>
#import <Foundation/Foundation.h>
#import <UIKit/UIKit.h>
#import <UIKit/UISectionList.h>
#import <UIKit/UISectionTable.h>
#import <UIKit/UIImageAndTextTableCell.h>

@interface FileSelector : UISectionList
{
        UISectionTable *table;
        NSMutableArray *files;
        NSMutableArray *filenames;
        NSMutableArray *sections;
        NSMutableArray *offsets;
        NSString *path;
        NSString *extension;
}
/* FileSelector methods */
- (id)initWithFrame:(CGRect)rect;
- (void)reloadData;
- (void)setPath:(NSString *)_path;
- (void)setExtension:(NSString *)_extension;
- (void)dealloc;

/* Data source methods */
- (int)numberOfSectionsInSectionList:(UISectionList *)aSectionList;
- (NSString *)sectionList:(UISectionList *)aSectionList
    titleForSection:(int)section;
- (int)sectionList:(UISectionList *)aSectionList
    rowForSection:(int)section;
- (int) numberOfRowsInTable: (UITable *)table;
- (UITableCell *) table: (UITable *)table cellForRow:
    (int)row column:
    (int)col;
@end
```

Example 7-16. Section list example (FileSelector.m)

```
#import "FileSelector.h"

@implementation FileSelector
- (id)initWithFrame:(CGRect)rect {
    if ((self == [ super initWithFrame: rect ]) != nil) {
        path = nil;
```

Example 7-16. Section list example (FileSelector.m) (continued)

```
        extension = nil;
        files =      [ [ NSMutableArray alloc ] init ];
        sections =   [ [ NSMutableArray alloc ] init ];
        offsets =    [ [ NSMutableArray alloc ] init ];
        filenames =  [ [ NSMutableArray alloc ] init ];

        [ self setShouldHideHeaderInShortLists: NO ];
        [ self setDataSource: self ];
    }

    return self;
}

- (void)reloadData {
    NSString *file;
    NSDirectoryEnumerator *dirEnum;
    char cFileName[256], lastSection[2], mySection[2];

    if (path == nil || extension == nil) {
        return;
    }

    [ files removeAllObjects ];
    [ sections removeAllObjects ];
    [ offsets removeAllObjects ];
    [ filenames removeAllObjects ];

    dirEnum = [ [ NSFileManager defaultManager ]
        enumeratorAtPath: path ];
    while ((file = [ dirEnum nextObject ])) {
        if ([ file hasSuffix: extension ] == YES) {
        UIImageAndTextTableCell *cell = [
            [ UIImageAndTextTableCell alloc ] init
        ];

        [ cell setTitle: [ file
            substringToIndex: [ file length ] - 4 ]
        ];

        strlcpy(cFileName,
            [ file cStringUsingEncoding: NSASCIIStringEncoding ],
            sizeof(cFileName));
        mySection[0] = toupper(cFileName[0]);
        mySection[1] = 0;
        if (mySection[0] >= '0' && mySection[0] <= '9') {
            mySection[0] = '0';
        }

        if ([ sections count ] > 0) {
            NSString *lastSectionName = [ sections objectAtIndex:
```

Example 7-16. Section list example (FileSelector.m) (continued)

```
                    [ sections count ] - 1
                ];

            strlcpy(lastSection,
                [ lastSectionName
                    cStringUsingEncoding: NSASCIIStringEncoding ],
                    sizeof(lastSection));

            if (mySection[0] != lastSection[0]) {
                [ sections addObject: [
                    [ NSString alloc ] initWithCString: mySection ]
                ];
                [ offsets addObject:
                    [ NSNumber numberWithInt: [ files count ] + 1 ]
                ];
            }

        } else {
            [ sections addObject: [
                [ NSString alloc ] initWithCString: mySection ]
            ];
            [ offsets addObject: [ NSNumber numberWithInt:
                [ files count ] + 1 ]
            ];
        }

        [ files addObject: cell ];
        [ filenames addObject: file ];
        }
    }

    table = [ self table ];
    UITableColumn * column = [ [ UITableColumn alloc ]
        initWithTitle:@"Filename"
        identifier:@"filename"
        width: 320.0 ];
    [ table addTableColumn: column ];
    [ table setSeparatorStyle: 1 ];
    [ table setRowHeight: 48.0 ];
    [ table setDelegate: self ];

    [ super reloadData ];
}

- (void)setPath:(NSString *)_path {
    path = _path;
}

- (void)setExtension:(NSString *)_extension {
    extension = _extension;
}
```

Example 7-16. Section list example (FileSelector.m) (continued)

```objc
- (void)dealloc
{
    [ self dealloc ];
    [ files dealloc ];
    [ filenames dealloc ];
    [ sections dealloc ];
    [ offsets dealloc ];
    [ super dealloc ];
}

- (int)numberOfSectionsInSectionList:(UISectionList *)aSectionList {
    return [ sections count ];
}

- (NSString *)sectionList:(UISectionList *)aSectionList
    titleForSection:(int)section
{
    return [ sections objectAtIndex: section ];
}

- (int)sectionList:(UISectionList *)aSectionList rowForSection:(int)section {
        return ([ [ offsets objectAtIndex: section ] intValue ] - 1);
}

- (int) numberOfRowsInTable: (UITable *)table
{
    return [ files count ];
}

- (UITableCell *) table: (UITable *)table cellForRow: (int)row column: (int)col
{
    return [ files objectAtIndex: row ];
}

- (UITableCell *) table: (UITable *)table cellForRow:
    (int)row column:
    (int)col
    reusing: (BOOL) reusing
{
    return [ files objectAtIndex: row ];
}

- (void)tableRowSelected:(NSNotification *)notification {
    NSString *file = [ filenames objectAtIndex:
        [ table selectedRow ]
    ];
    printf("Selected: %s\n", [ file
        cStringUsingEncoding: NSASCIIStringEncoding ]);
}

@end
```

Example 7-17. Section list example (MyExample.h)

```
#import <CoreFoundation/CoreFoundation.h>
#import <Foundation/Foundation.h>
#import <UIKit/UIKit.h>
#import "FileSelector.h"

@interface MyApp : UIApplication
{
    UIWindow *window;
}


- (void)applicationDidFinishLaunching:(NSNotification *)aNotification;
@end
```

Example 7-18. Section list example (MyExample.m)

```
#import "MyExample.h"

int main(int argc, char **argv)
{
    return UIApplicationMain(argc, argv, [ MyApp class ]);
}

@implementation MyApp

- (void)applicationDidFinishLaunching:(NSNotification *)aNotification {
    window = [ [ UIWindow alloc ] initWithContentRect:
        [ UIHardware fullScreenApplicationContentRect ]
    ];

    CGRect rect = [ UIHardware fullScreenApplicationContentRect ];
    rect.origin.x = rect.origin.y = 0.0f;


    FileSelector *fileSelector = [ [ FileSelector alloc ]
        initWithFrame: rect
    ];
    [ fileSelector setPath: @"/Applications" ];
    [ fileSelector setExtension: @".app" ];
    [ fileSelector reloadData ];

    [ window setContentView: fileSelector ];
    [ window orderFront: self ];
    [ window makeKey: self ];
    [ window _setHidden: NO ];
}
@end
```

What's Going On?

1. When the application instantiates, it creates a new FileSelector object and calls its initWithFrame method. This creates necessary objects to hold rows of the section list.

2. The setPath and setExtension methods are called to assign the directory and file extension the caller would like to use. The reloadData method is then called, which causes the directory to be scanned and the file list, section headers, and cells for each row in the section list to be built. Finally, the section list is set as the window's contents.

3. The data source, which is self-contained inside the file selector class, is called to return information about the number of sections and rows in the table. The section titles are queried, and the number of rows in each section is calculated.

4. After the section list is displayed, rows coming into visibility cause the data source's cellForRow method to be called. This method returns the cell corresponding to the row requested.

5. When the user selects an item, the tableRowSelected method is called. It looks up the filename in a local index. At this point, the implementer's code is responsible for performing the appropriate action.

Further Study

- Modify the example to use a UISectionTable class exclusively, instead of the more extravagant UISectionList class.
- Check out the *UISectionList.h* and *UISectionTable.h* prototypes in the tool chain's directory. These can be found in */usr/local/arm-apple-darwin/UIKit*.

Keyboards

When Steve Jobs introduced the iPhone in one of his most anticipated keynote speeches, he expressed a vision for a device that could successfully redefine the user's experience as she saw fit—not just the buttons on an application, but the ability to create an entirely new interface based on the specific needs of an application. Jobs's hatred for physical buttons must have included physical keyboards because Apple has found a use for 10 different "virtual" keyboard styles on the iPhone, and has provided an elegant interface to define them based on what kind of input is needed.

The keyboard object is derived from the UIView class, so it can be attached to just about any view object. An application can take full advantage of the different keyboards and keyboard styles available, change options such as autocorrection, and even customize the kind of buttons used.

Creating the Keyboard

The UIKeyboard class provides an easy interface to the keyboard without needing to worry about intercepting mouse events or dealing with any of the low-level details that plague other development platforms.

The UIKeyboard object has an understandably significant pixel size, and needs to be displayed in a large controlling view, such as a main view or preferences screen. The keyboard itself is 320×235 pixels.

The following example creates a 320×235 frame. The frame's origin begins at y-axis value 245 to fill the bottom portion of the screen.

```
CGRect kbRect;
kbRect.origin.x = 0;
kbRect.origin.y = 245;
kbRect.size.width = 320;
kbRect.size.height = 235;

UIKeyboard *kb = [ [ UIKeyboard alloc ] initWithFrame: kbRect ];
```

Keyboard Properties

Apple has elegantly designed its framework so that the keyboard's behavior is defined by the text being edited rather than the keyboard itself. This causes the keyboard to automatically adapt to a new behavior when the user selects a different text field. For preferences tables and other such views consisting of many different text fields, various keyboard behaviors can be defined so that each cell will have its own style. All of the properties described in this section are set within text objects, such as UITextView, UITextTableCell, etc., and not the keyboard object.

The various keyboard properties available are explained in the following sections. They can also be found in the tool chain's *UITextTraits.h* prototype.

Keyboard style

UIKit supports 10 different keyboard styles. A keyboard style can be assigned for each text field to automatically switch it out when the user taps the cell to enter text.

The style is set using the text object's setPreferredKeyboardType method.

```
[ textView setPreferredKeyboardType: 2 ];
```

The following keyboard styles are supported.

Style	Description
0	Default keyboard: all characters available
1	Default keyboard: defaults to numbers and symbols page
2	Standard phone pad, supporting + * # symbols

Style	Description
3	URL keyboard with .COM button: supports only URI characters
4	Alphabetic keyboard with alternate phone pad
5	Default keyboard: transparent black background
6	Standard phone pad, numeric only
7	Standard phone pad, numeric only; transparent black background
8	Email address keyboard: RFC822 address characters + space
9	Email address keyboard: .COM button, no space

The keyboard and phone pad layouts are the same size, so no additional window changes are need to switch between the two.

Return key

For keyboards with a Return key, you can assign the key various styles. The key style is set using the text object's setReturnKeyType method.

```
[ textView setReturnKeyType: 4 ];
```

The following styles are supported.

Style	Description
0	Default: gray button labeled return
1	Blue button labeled Go
2	Blue button labeled Google, used for searches
3	Blue button labeled Join
4	Gray button labeled Next
5	Blue button labeled Route
6	Blue button labeled Search
7	Blue button labeled Send
8	Blue button labeled Yahoo!, used for searches

Autocapitalization

The keyboard can autocapitalize the first letter of a new line or sentence. To toggle this, use the text object's setAutoCapsType method:

```
[ textView setAutoCapsType: YES ];
```

When off, no autocapitalization is performed.

Autocorrection

When entering text, the text view and keyboard objects work together to present possible corrections to mistakes. This is based on an internal dictionary of commonly mistyped words and a typing cache that tracks and learns previously unknown words entered by the user. The dictionary is generated by the iPhone in */private/var/root/Library/Keyboard/dynamic-text.dat*.

 Apple's autocorrection logic is quite impressive in that the corrections it suggests aren't based solely on the spelling of a word, but also on what adjacent keys are in proximity of each character.

Autocorrection is enabled by default, but can be toggled using the text view's setAutoCorrectionType method:

```
[ textView setAutoCorrectionType: 1 ];
```

Apple used an integer here instead of a Boolean value, suggesting that other autocorrection techniques may be introduced at a later time.

Option	Description
0	Autocorrection enabled
1	Autocorrection disabled

Secure text entry

When typing passwords or other private data into a text window, the information shouldn't be cached in the iPhone. Turning on secure text entry disables autocorrection and word caching features for the text field. To activate secure text mode, use the setSecureTextEntry method:

```
[ textView setSecureTextEntry: YES ];
```

Single entry completion

In small input windows containing only one or two words (such as a username), you may want the autocompletion mechanism to work only once and then disengage. Use the text object's setSingleCompletionEntry to turn on this behavior:

```
[ textView setSingleCompletionEntry: YES ];
```

Displaying the Keyboard

A keyboard is added to a parent view hosting the text objects to be edited. If the keyboard is to be permanently attached, the controlling view need only create a 235-pixel high frame to house it in.

```
CGRect kbRect = CGRectMake(0, 245, 320, 235);
[ self addSubview: kb ];
```

Focusing the text object

No text objects are selected on the screen by default. The user has to tap a text box to make it active. This has the annoying side effect of leaving the keyboard in a default state until the user clicks on a text field. The keyboard is changed only when the text field becomes active. To do this, use the becomeFirstResponder method:

```
[ textView becomeFirstResponder ];
```

With this, the first keyboard that the user will see will include the properties you set in the text field.

Showing and hiding the keyboard

Instead of displaying the keyboard all the time, some applications may want to toggle it on and off. To do this, create the keyboard object, but don't add it as a subview until it is needed. When the screen is pressed, the controlling view must resize the rest of the windows to make room for the keyboard.

To detect a screen press, you could override the mouseDown and mouseUp methods, but there's a better technique for this purpose. A method named contentMouseUpInView sends a notification only when the user has tapped within the view's text entry space.

The following example toggles activation of the keyboard using a Boolean named keyboardShown. When the keyboard needs to be shown, it resizes the other window on the screen (in this case, a text view), and adds the keyboard as a subview. When it's removed, it sets the text view back to its full size and removes the keyboard from view without destroying it.

```
- (void)contentMouseUpInView:(id)_id
    withEvent:(struct __GSEvent *)_event
{
    CGRect kbRect = CGRectMake(0, 245, 320, 235);

    if (keyboardShown == NO) {
        textFrame.size.height -= 235;
        [ textView setFrame: textFrame ];
        [ self addSubview: kb ];
        keyboardShown = YES;
    } else {
        textFrame.size.height += 235;
        [ kb removeFromSuperview ];
        [ textView setFrame: textFrame ];
        keyboardShown = NO;
    }
}
```

Example: A Simple Text Editor

In Chapter 3, you built your first "Hello, World" application for the iPhone. This created a text window with some text in it, but the user couldn't edit anything. Here, we keep the examples simple, but add a custom keyboard for editing. When the user taps the text window, the keyboard will toggle, allowing her to view the text window in full frame or pop up a keyboard for editing. As she edits text, it is automatically updated in the text view. To capture the mouse events of the text view (the UITextView object), this view is subclassed to create a new class named MyTextView. The purpose of this is to override one method—contentMouseUpInView—so that we can capture mouse presses inside the view. The notifications get passed to the main view, which is set as the text view's delegate.

To compile this example, use the tool chain's command line as follows:

```
$ arm-apple-darwin-gcc -o MyExample MyExample.m -lobjc \
    -framework UIKit -framework CoreFoundation -framework Foundation
```

Examples 7-19 and 7-20 contain the code.

Example 7-19. Keyboard example (MyExample.h)

```
#import <CoreFoundation/CoreFoundation.h>
#import <GraphicsServices/GraphicsServices.h>
#import <UIKit/UIKit.h>
#import <UIKit/UITextView.h>
#import <UIKit/UIKeyboard.h>

@interface MyTextView : UITextView
{

}
- (void)contentMouseUpInView:(id)fp8 withEvent:(struct __GSEvent *)fp12;
@end

@interface MainView : UIView
{
    CGRect rect;
    MyTextView *textView;
    UIKeyboard *kb;
    BOOL keyboardShown;
}

- (id)initWithFrame:(CGRect)_rect;
- (void)contentMouseUpInView:(id)_id withEvent:(struct __GSEvent *)_event;
- (void)dealloc;

@end

@interface MyApp : UIApplication
{
    UIWindow *window;
    MainView *mainView;
}

- (void)applicationDidFinishLaunching:(NSNotification *)aNotification;
@end
```

Example 7-20. Keyboard example (MyExample.m)

```objectivec
#import "MyExample.h"

int main(int argc, char **argv)
{
    return UIApplicationMain(argc, argv, [ MyApp class ]);
}

@implementation MyTextView
- (void)contentMouseUpInView:(id)_id withEvent:(struct __GSEvent *)_event {
    [ _delegate contentMouseUpInView:(id)_id withEvent:_event ];
}

@end

@implementation MyApp

- (void)applicationDidFinishLaunching:(NSNotification *)aNotification {
    window = [ [ UIWindow alloc ] initWithContentRect:
        [ UIHardware fullScreenApplicationContentRect ]
    ];

    CGRect rect = [ UIHardware fullScreenApplicationContentRect ];
    rect.origin.x = rect.origin.y = 0.0f;

    mainView = [ [ MainView alloc ] initWithFrame: rect ];

    [ window setContentView: mainView ];
    [ window orderFront: self ];
    [ window makeKey: self ];
    [ window _setHidden: NO ];
}
@end

@implementation MainView
- (id)initWithFrame:(CGRect)_rect {
    rect = _rect;

    if ((self == [ super initWithFrame: rect ]) != nil) {
        CGRect textFrame = rect;
        CGRect kbFrame = rect;
        textFrame.size.height -= 235;
        kbFrame.origin.y = 245;
        kbFrame.size.height = 235;

        textView = [ [ MyTextView alloc ] initWithFrame: rect ];
        [ textView setTextSize: 18 ];
        [ textView setAutoCapsType: 1 ];
        [ textView setAutoCorrectionType: 0 ];
        [ textView setPreferredKeyboardType: 0 ];
        [ textView setDelegate: self ];
        [ textView becomeFirstResponder ];
        [ self addSubview: textView ];
```

Example 7-20. Keyboard example (MyExample.m) (continued)

```
        kb = [ [ UIKeyboard alloc ] initWithFrame: kbFrame ];
    }

    return self;
}

- (void)contentMouseUpInView:(id)_id withEvent:(struct __GSEvent *)_event {
    CGRect kbRect = CGRectMake(0, 245, 320, 235);
    CGRect textFrame = [ textView frame ];

    /* Toggle the keyboard */
    if (keyboardShown == NO) {
        textFrame.size.height = 245;
        [ textView setFrame: textFrame ];
        [ self addSubview: kb ];
        keyboardShown = YES;
    } else {
        textFrame.size.height = 480;
        [ kb removeFromSuperview ];
        [ textView setFrame: textFrame ];
        keyboardShown = NO;
    }
}

- (void)dealloc
{
    [ self dealloc ];
    [ super dealloc ];
}

@end
```

What's Going On

1. When the application instantiates, it creates a main controlling view named mainView and calls its initWithFrame method.

2. An instance of MyTextView, which is a subclass of UITextView, is created with a full screen frame. Many editing properties are set to define the behavior of the keyboard, including the style, autocorrection, and autocaps lock options. The text view is added to the main view and then focused using the becomeFirstResponder method.

3. A keyboard view is created using the bottom portion of the screen as a frame, but is not added to the controlling view just yet. This keeps it hidden until the user needs it.

4. When the text portion of the screen is tapped by the user, its contentMouseUpInView method is notified of this event. This method is overridden in MyTextView, and so the object sees it and passes the notification to the main view, which was assigned as its delegate.

5. The main view receives the event in its own `contentMouseUpInView` method. To display the keyboard, it adds the keyboard as a subview to the main view and shrinks the text view's frame size to accommodate.

6. When the text window is tapped by the user again, the main view is notified by the `MyTextView` object and the frame of the text view is restored to its full size. The keyboard is also removed from view, but not destroyed.

Further Study

- Using your experience with preferences tables from earlier in this chapter, create a preferences table with various text input cells and assign each cell different keyboard properties. Watch how the keyboard changes as you move from cell to cell.

- Check out the *UIKeyboard.h*, *UIKeyboardImpl.h*, and *UITextTraits.h* prototypes in your tool chain's *include* directory. These can be found in */usr/local/arm-apple-darwin/include/UIKit*.

Pickers

Pickers are click wheels for the iPhone: large, spinning dials that can host any number of different options. Pickers are used in place of drop-down menus to provide a graphically rich selection interface for the user. Close cousin to a control, the `UIPickerView` class was designed as a full-blown view class due to its sheer size on the screen. This allows it to be used almost anywhere, including a main view or in conjunction with a preferences table.

Creating a Picker

The `UIPickerView` class contains a `UIPickerTable` object, which is derived from the `UITable` object. Like other tables, the `UIPickerTable` uses a data binding. Unlike other table classes, the picker's data source isn't specified with the `dataSource` method. Instead, a delegate is used for receiving data binding requests in addition to picker events. This was likely done to give the `UIPickerView` class the simplicity of a control. The `UIPickerView` data binding is small enough that it can be tucked nicely into controlling views, although the picker itself can also be subclassed to create a self-contained picker.

When creating the picker view, use a 200-pixel-high window. Initializing the picker with any other frame sizes will cause the custom size to be ignored. The picker can be placed anywhere on another view, but is generally located at the bottom.

```
UIPickerView *pickerView = [ [ UIPickerView alloc ]
    initWithFrame: CGRectMake(0, 280, 320, 200)];
[ pickerView setDelegate: self ];
```

Picking picker properties

To toggle the output of click sounds normally heard as the picker is scrolled, use the setSoundsEnabled method:

```
[ pickerView setSoundsEnabled: YES ];
```

If the picker should allow multiple items to be selected, use the setAllowsMultipleSelection method:

```
[ pickerView setAllowsMultipleSelection: YES ];
```

The picker table

After creating the picker view, you must instruct it to create an underlying UIPickerTable object. This object holds the different items and the table construction used in the picker.

```
UIPickerTable *pickerTable = [ pickerView
    createTableWithFrame:
    CGRectMake(0, 0, 320, 200)
];
```

Just like a UITable, a picker table must have at least one column. This is created as a UITableColumn object and assigned to the picker view using a method named columnForTable:

```
column = [ [ UITableColumn alloc ]
    initWithTitle: @"Column title"
    identifier:@"mycolumn"
    width: 320
];

[ pickerView columnForTable: column ];
```

Once the view, table, and column have been created, three methods must be created in the data source class:

numberOfColumnsInPickerView

This method should return a value of 1 unless you're creating a multicolumn picker view.

numberOfRowsInColumn

In a picker view, each column can have a different number of rows. This method should return the total number of rows for the column number specified.

tableCellForRow

This method returns the actual UITableCell objects for each row in the table. Generally, these are just empty cell objects with a title. However, more complex table cell classes can be used, such as the UIImageAndTextTableCell class discussed in Chapter 3.

The prototypes and function for these methods will be illustrated in the example later in this section.

Displaying the Picker

Once you have created and configured the picker view and written a data binding, you're ready to attach the picker to your controlling view.

```
[ mainView addSubview: pickerView ];
```

Reading the Picker

To obtain the index of the selected column in the picker view, use the view's selectedRowForColumn method:

```
int selectedRow = [ pickerView selectedRowForColumn: 0 ];
```

Because the picker table is created by the picker view itself, it's difficult to subclass the table to use a tableRowSelected method. A more convenient way to read the value in real time is to create a subclass of the UIPickerView class, and then override its mouseDown method:

```
- (void)mouseDown:(struct __GSEvent *)event {
    int selectedRow = [ self selectedRowForColumn: 0 ];
    [ super mouseDown: event ];
}
```

Example: Picking Your Nose

In this example, a list of different nose styles is created and presented to the user. A controller view is first created, which then hosts the picker view as a subview. You'll be able to scroll a list of noses and choose one.

To compile this example, use the tool chain on the command line as follows:

```
$ arm-apple-darwin-gcc -o MyExample MyExample.m -lobjc \
    -framework Foundation -framework CoreFoundation -framework UIKit
```

Examples 7-21 and 7-22 contain the code.

Example 7-21. Picker example (MyExample.h)

```
#import <CoreFoundation/CoreFoundation.h>
#import <Foundation/Foundation.h>
#import <UIKit/UIKit.h>
#import <UIKit/UIPickerView.h>
#import <UIKit/UIPickerTable.h>
#import <UIKit/UITableColumn.h>

@interface MainView : UIView
{
    UIPickerView *pickerView;
    UIPickerTable *pickerTable;
    NSMutableArray *cells;
    UITableColumn *column;
}
```

Example 7-21. Picker example (MyExample.h) (continued)

```
- (id)initWithFrame:(CGRect)rect;
- (void)dealloc;

@end

@interface MyApp : UIApplication
{
    UIWindow *window;
    MainView *mainView;
}

- (void)applicationDidFinishLaunching:(NSNotification *)aNotification;
@end
```

Example 7-22. Picker example (MyExample.m)

```
#import <UIKit/UIPickerTableCell.h>
#import "MyExample.h"

int main(int argc, char **argv)
{
    return UIApplicationMain(argc, argv, [ MyApp class ]);
}

@implementation MyApp

- (void)applicationDidFinishLaunching:(NSNotification *)aNotification {
    window = [ [ UIWindow alloc ] initWithContentRect:
        [ UIHardware fullScreenApplicationContentRect ]
    ];

    CGRect rect = [ UIHardware fullScreenApplicationContentRect ];
    rect.origin.x = rect.origin.y = 0.0f;

    mainView = [ [ MainView alloc ] initWithFrame: rect ];

    [ window setContentView: mainView ];
    [ window orderFront: self ];
    [ window makeKey: self ];
    [ window _setHidden: NO ];
}
@end

@implementation MainView
- (id)initWithFrame:(CGRect)rect {
    if ((self == [ super initWithFrame: rect ]) != nil) {
        UIPickerTableCell *cell;
        NSMutableArray *noses = [ [ NSMutableArray alloc ] init ];
        int i;

        /* Create some noses */
        [ noses addObject: @"Straight" ];
```

Example 7-22. Picker example (MyExample.m) (continued)

```
        [ noses addObject: @"Aquiline" ];
        [ noses addObject: @"Retrousse" ];
        [ noses addObject: @"Busque" ];
        [ noses addObject: @"Sinuous" ];
        [ noses addObject: @"Melanesian" ];
        [ noses addObject: @"African" ];

        cells = [ [ NSMutableArray alloc ] init ];
        for(i=0;i<[ noses count ];i++) {
            cell = [ [ UIPickerTableCell alloc ]
                initWithFrame: CGRectMake(0, 0, 320, 80) ];
            [ cell setTitle: [ noses objectAtIndex: i ] ];
            [ cells addObject: cell ];
        }

        pickerView = [ [ UIPickerView alloc ]
            initWithFrame:
            CGRectMake(0, 280, 320, 200)];
        [ pickerView setDelegate: self ];
        [ pickerView setSoundsEnabled: NO ];

        pickerTable  = [ pickerView createTableWithFrame:
            CGRectMake(0, 0, 320, 200) ];

        column = [ [ UITableColumn alloc ]
            initWithTitle: @"Nose"
            identifier:@"nose"
            width: rect.size.width
        ];

        [ pickerView columnForTable: column ];
        [ self addSubview: pickerView ];
    }

printf("selected row: %d\n", [ pickerView selectedRowForColumn: 0 ]);
    return self;
}

- (int) numberOfColumnsInPickerView:(id)pickerView
{
    return 1;
}

- (int) pickerView:(id)pickerView numberOfRowsInColumn:(int)col
{
    return [ cells count ];
}

- (id) pickerView:(id)pickerView tableCellForRow:(int)row inColumn:(int)col
{
    return [ cells objectAtIndex: row ];
}
```

Example 7-22. Picker example (MyExample.m) (continued)

```
- (void)dealloc
{
    [ self dealloc ];
    [ super dealloc ];
}
```

@end

What's Going On

1. When the application instantiates, a new controlling view named `mainView` is created, and its `initWithFrame` method is called.

2. This method creates an array of nose styles and creates a `UITableCell` object for each one, pushing the cell onto an array used in the data binding.

3. A `UIPickerView` is created, and its `createTableWithFrame` method is used to create a `UIPickerTable` to hold its table contents. One column is then added to the picker. The view is then attached to the main view.

4. As the picker is rendered, it queries the data source to obtain the number of columns and rows, then queries the table cells to be displayed.

Further Study

Check out the *UIPickerView.h* and *UIPickerTable.h* prototypes in the tool chain's *include* directory. These can be found in */usr/local/arm-apple-darwin/include/UIKit*.

Date/Time Pickers

The `UIDatePicker` class is a subclass of `UIPickerView`. It allows dates, times, and durations to be selected from a customizable, self-contained picker interface. The date picker automatically configures its columns to conform to the specified style, so there's no low-level work involved in creating new instances. It can also be customized for any range of dates and with any start and end dates.

The `UIDatePicker` relies heavily on the `NSCalendarDate` class, which is part of the foundation class set used in Cocoa on the desktop. More information about this class can be found in Apple's Cocoa reference on the Apple Developer Connection web site. For the purpose of the examples used here, we'll create an `NSCalendarDate` using its simplest method, `initWithString`.

```
NSCalendarDate * myDate = [ [ NSCalendarDate alloc ]
    initWithString: @"1963-11-22 12:30:00 -0500" ];
```

Creating the Date/Time Picker

The UIDatePicker is much more straightforward than the standard UIPickerView. It builds its own data source based on the date ranges you specify. To use it, just create the object:

```
UIDatePicker *datePicker = [ [ UIDatePicker alloc ]
    initWithFrame: CGRectMake(0, 280, 320, 200)];
```

By default the picker presents the current date and time, and allows the user to select any month and time. Further customizations to the picker's operation are explained in the following subsections.

DatePicker mode

The date picker supports four different selector modes. The mode is set using the setDatePickerMode method:

```
[ datePicker setDatePickerMode: 2 ];
```

The following modes are supported.

Option	Description
0	Hour, minute, and A.M./P.M. selection
1	Month, day, and year selection
2	Day of the week + month + day, time, and A.M./P.M. selection
3	General time duration selection; number of hours and number of minutes

Highlight "Today"

To highlight the current day within the picker, use the setHighlightsToday method. This causes the word Today to be displayed and highlighted in blue for the current day.

```
[ datePicker setHighlightsToday: YES ];
```

Time intervals

The minutes dial can be set to display minutes in one-minute or five-minute intervals, with a default of one-minute. To select five-minute intervals, use the setStaggerTimeIntervals method:

```
[ datePicker setStaggerTimeIntervals: YES ];
```

Date ranges

A range of allowed dates can be specified using the setMinDate and setMaxDate methods. If the user attempts to scroll to a date beyond this range, the dial will scroll back to the closest valid date. Both methods expect an NSCalendarDate object.

```
NSCalendarDate *minDate = [ [ NSCalendarDate alloc ]
    initWithString: @"1773-12-16 12:00:00 -0500" ];
NSCalendarDate *maxDate = [ [ NSCalendarDate alloc ]
    initWithString: @"1776-07-04 12:00:00 -0500" ];

[ datePicker setMinDate: minDate ];
[ datePicker setMaxDate: maxDate ];
```

If one or both of these isn't set, the default behavior will allow the user to select any past or future date.

To set the date you would like to be displayed by default, use the setDate method:

```
[ datePicker setDate: maxDate ];
```

Sound

Just like the UIPickerView class, clicking sounds can be toggled using the setSoundsEnabled method:

```
[ datePicker setSoundsEnabled: YES ];
```

Displaying the Date Picker

Once the date picker has been created, it can be attached to a view object in the same way as a UIPickerView:

```
[ mainView addSubview: datePicker ];
```

The picker defaults to 200 pixels high, regardless of the frame size passed to it. You'll need to make sure you've allocated enough screen space to host it.

Reading the Date

The date is generally read from the date picker when the user transitions to a different view, such as leaving a preferences table. Although this class can be subclassed in the same way as the UIPickerView (to override its mouseDown events), most applications will function sufficiently by reading the date after the user has pressed a back button or some other navigation bar button.

The UIDatePicker class returns a NSCalendarDate object from its date method.

```
NSCalendarDate *selectedDate = [ datePicker date ];
```

Example: Independence Day Picker

This example illustrates the use of a basic date picker object to select a date between the Boston Tea Party (December 16, 1773) and American Independence Day (July 4, 1776). The example simply creates a UIDatePicker object and displays it to the user.

To compile this example, use the tool chain on the command line as follows:

```
$ arm-apple-darwin-gcc -o MyExample MyExample.m -lobjc \
    -framework Foundation -framework CoreFoundation -framework UIKit
```

Examples 7-23 and 7-24 contain the code.

Example 7-23. Date and time picker example (MyExample.h)

```
#import <CoreFoundation/CoreFoundation.h>
#import <Foundation/Foundation.h>
#import <UIKit/UIKit.h>
#import <UIKit/UIDatePicker.h>

@interface MainView : UIView
{
    UIDatePicker *datePicker;
}

- (id)initWithFrame:(CGRect)rect;
- (void)dealloc;

@end

@interface MyApp : UIApplication
{
    UIWindow *window;
    MainView *mainView;
}

- (void)applicationDidFinishLaunching:(NSNotification *)aNotification;
@end
```

Example 7-24. Date and time picker example (MyExample.m)

```
#import <Foundation/Foundation.h>
#import <CoreFoundation/CoreFoundation.h>
#import <UIKit/UIPickerTableCell.h>
#import "MyExample.h"

int main(int argc, char **argv)
{
    return UIApplicationMain(argc, argv, [ MyApp class ]);
}

@implementation MyApp

- (void)applicationDidFinishLaunching:(NSNotification *)aNotification {
    window = [ [ UIWindow alloc ] initWithContentRect:
        [ UIHardware fullScreenApplicationContentRect ]
    ];

    CGRect rect = [ UIHardware fullScreenApplicationContentRect ];
    rect.origin.x = rect.origin.y = 0.0f;

    mainView = [ [ MainView alloc ] initWithFrame: rect ];
```

Example 7-24. Date and time picker example (MyExample.m) (continued)

```
    [ window setContentView: mainView ];
    [ window orderFront: self ];
    [ window makeKey: self ];
    [ window _setHidden: NO ];
}
@end

@implementation MainView
- (id)initWithFrame:(CGRect)rect {
    if ((self == [ super initWithFrame: rect ]) != nil) {
        datePicker = [ [ UIDatePicker alloc ]
            initWithFrame:
            CGRectMake(0, 280, 320, 200)];

        NSCalendarDate *minDate = [ [ NSCalendarDate alloc ]
            initWithString: @"1773-12-16 12:00:00 -0500" ];
        NSCalendarDate *maxDate = [ [ NSCalendarDate alloc ]
            initWithString: @"1776-07-04 12:00:00 -0500" ];

        [ datePicker setMinDate: minDate ];
        [ datePicker setMaxDate: maxDate ];

        [ datePicker setDatePickerMode: 1 ];


        [ datePicker setStaggerTimeIntervals: YES ];

        [ datePicker setDelegate: self ];
        [ datePicker setSoundsEnabled: YES ];
        [ datePicker setDate: maxDate ];

        [ self addSubview: datePicker ];
    }

    return self;
}

- (void)dealloc
{
    [ self dealloc ];
    [ super dealloc ];
}

@end
```

What's Going On

1. When the application instantiates, it creates a main controller view named
   mainView and calls its initWithFrame method.

2. A `UIDatePicker` object is created and assigned minimum and maximum dates. Various options are also set to customize its display.

3. The date picker is added to the main view, where it is displayed to the user.

Further Study

Check out the *UIDatePicker.h* prototypes in the tool chain's *include* directory. These can be found in */usr/local/arm-apple-darwin/include/UIKit*.

Button Bars

Button bars are one of Apple's solutions for a universal device with no physical buttons. With iPhone applications so rich in features, many have four or five important functions that the user may need to get to quickly. Located at the bottom of the screen, button bars provide what would traditionally be looked at as shortcuts. Going back to Apple's book metaphor, button bars are the bookmarks to different chapters.

Many of the preloaded iPhone applications use button bars, including the Mobile Phone application, YouTube, and the iTunes Wi-Fi Music Store. They are used to separate related pages of data (e.g., Featured Music, Purchased Songs, etc.) and to provide shortcuts to different functions within a single application (e.g., Contacts, Recent Calls, Voicemail, etc.).

Creating a Button Bar

Button bars are represented by the `UIButtonBar` class in UIKit. Like navigation bars, button bars are designed to be relatively autonomous in their presentation. Internally, they handle all of the mess of button selection—they just work.

```
UIButtonBar *buttonBar = [ [ UIButtonBar alloc ]
        initInView: self
        withFrame: CGRectMake(0.0, 411.0, 320.0, 49.0)
        withItemList: [ self buttonBarItemList ] ];
[ buttonBar setDelegate: self ];
[ buttonBar setBarStyle: 1 ];
[ buttonBar setButtonBarTrackingMode: 2 ];
```

This snippet creates a `UIButtonBar` object and assigns it a display region along the bottom of the window. The button bar needs an item list, which is an array of the buttons to be displayed on the bar. Instead of providing the array inline with the code, a method returning such an array is used. Create a `buttonBarItemList` method defining all of the buttons for the bar and their properties.

```
- (NSArray *)buttonBarItemList {
    return [ NSArray arrayWithObjects:
        [ NSDictionary dictionaryWithObjectsAndKeys:
```

```
            @"buttonBarClicked:", kUIButtonBarButtonAction,
            @"History.png", kUIButtonBarButtonInfo,
            @"HistorySelected.png", kUIButtonBarButtonSelectedInfo,
            [ NSNumber numberWithInt: 1], kUIButtonBarButtonTag,
              self, kUIButtonBarButtonTarget,
            @"Page 1", kUIButtonBarButtonTitle,
            @"0", kUIButtonBarButtonType,
            nil
        ],

        nil ];
}
```

This method constructs an array of dictionary classes to contain the properties for each button. The array is terminated with nil, an empty item. Each dictionary object contains the following information about the button. Your header file must declare the variables extern because they are hidden in the framework, and not declared in any prototype.

kUIButtonBarButtonAction

The name of the method to be called when this button is clicked. All buttons can call the same buttonBarClicked routine because buttons can be tagged with a unique identifier. This will be illustrated in the upcoming example.

kUIButtonBarButtonInfo

The filename of an image to be associated with the button in its normal (unpressed) state. This image must be copied into the application's program directory as explained in Chapter 2. This example specifies the *History.png* file, an image frequently used by Apple's preloaded applications.

kUIButtonBarButtonSelectedInfo

The filename of an image to be used when the button is in its pressed state. This must also reside in the application's program directory.

kUIButtonBarButtonTag

A tag is a special object that can be passed to identify the button. In this example, the tag is treated like a button number and set as an integer. When the button click is handled later on, this tag can be used to identify which button was pushed.

kUIButtonBarButtonTarget

The object that is expected to receive a notification (specified by kUIButtonBarButtonAction). In this example, self is used to allow the calling view to receive notification of button presses.

kUIButtonBarButtonTitle

The title text to display beneath the button image.

kUIButtonBarButtonType

The type of button being created. The only valid value for button bar buttons is 0.

An `NSDictionary` object must be created for each button, followed by the terminating `nil`. Each button that is defined must be included in a button group and assigned a geometry on the button bar. This example displays five buttons. The iPhone's display is exactly 320 pixels wide, so each button should be 64 pixels wide ($5 \times 64 = 320$). A loop can be used to set up the button group's geometry.

```
int buttons[5] = { 1, 2, 3, 4, 5 };
int tag;
[ buttonBar registerButtonGroup:0 withButtons:buttons withCount:5 ];
[ buttonBar showButtonGroup: 0 withDuration: 0.0 ];
for(tag = 1; tag < 5; tag++) {
    [ [ buttonBar viewWithTag: tag ]
        setFrame: CGRectMake(((tag - 1) * 64.0), 1.0, 64.0, 48.0)
    ];
}
```

Lastly, set the default button to reflect the current view being displayed:

```
[ buttonBar showSelectionForButton: 1 ];
```

Displaying the Button Bar

Once you have created a button bar, you can add it to a view. This view can also handle the transitions to new view pages when a button is pressed. This is usually the main view, but if the program is extremely complex, different parts of it may use different button bars.

```
[ self addSubview: buttonBar ];
```

Button Badges

In some cases, your application might want to alert the user to new items on a particular page of the button bar. A badge containing a number or other text can be added to a button on the button bar to get the user's attention. The following example displays a badge with the number 3 in it on the second button.

```
[ buttonBar setBadgeValue:@"3" forButton: 2 ];
```

Intercepting Button Presses

When the button bar was created, each button was described with a dictionary object. The `kUIButtonBarButtonAction` property specifies the method to call when the button is pressed. This method can be written to service all buttons, or an individual method can be defined for each one. The method is written into the button bar's target object, as described with `kUIButtonBarButtonTarget`.

```
- (void)buttonBarClicked:(id) sender {
    int button = [ sender tag ];

    /* Do something about it here */
}
```

Example: Another Textbook Approach

In the section "Example: Page Flipping" in Chapter 3, 10 text pages were created and a navigation bar was used to flip through them. This example is similar, except we'll use five pages representing five different views in an application. Each page will be controlled by a button on a button bar which, when pressed, flips to the corresponding page. A UITransitionView is employed to perform this transition.

To run this application on your iPhone, you'll need to supply two images named *Button.png* and *ButtonSelected.png*, which are to be copied into the application's program folder. Otherwise, the button will appear with text only. You can draw these graphics yourself, or swipe some of the buttons already on the iPhone for this demo, such as */Applications/YouTube.app/History.png* and */Applications/YouTube.app/HistorySelected.png*.

To compile this program, use the tool chain on the command line as follows:

```
$ arm-apple-darwin-gcc -o MyExample MyExample.m -lobjc \
    -framework CoreFoundation -framework UIKit -framework Foundation
```

Examples 7-25 and 7-26 contain the code.

Example 7-25. Button bar example (MyExample.h)

```
#import <CoreFoundation/CoreFoundation.h>
#import <UIKit/UIKit.h>
#import <UIKit/UITransitionView.h>
#import <UIKit/UITextView.h>
#import <UIKit/UIButtonBar.h>

#define MAX_PAGES 5

extern NSString *kUIButtonBarButtonAction;
extern NSString *kUIButtonBarButtonInfo;
extern NSString *kUIButtonBarButtonInfoOffset;
extern NSString *kUIButtonBarButtonSelectedInfo;
extern NSString *kUIButtonBarButtonStyle;
extern NSString *kUIButtonBarButtonTag;
extern NSString *kUIButtonBarButtonTarget;
extern NSString *kUIButtonBarButtonTitle;
extern NSString *kUIButtonBarButtonTitleVerticalHeight;
extern NSString *kUIButtonBarButtonTitleWidth;
extern NSString *kUIButtonBarButtonType;

@interface MainView : UIView
{
        UITransitionView *transView; /* Our transition */
        UIButtonBar      *buttonBar; /* Our button bar */

        /* Some pages to scroll through */
        UITextView       *textPage[MAX_PAGES];
}
```

Example 7-25. Button bar example (MyExample.h) (continued)

```
- (id)initWithFrame:(CGRect)frame;
- (void)dealloc;
- (void)flipTo:(int)page;
- (UIButtonBar *)createButtonBar;
- (void)buttonBarClicked:(id)sender;
- (NSArray *)buttonBarItemList;
@end

@interface MyApp : UIApplication
{
    UIWindow *window;
    MainView *mainView;
}

- (void)applicationDidFinishLaunching:(NSNotification *)aNotification;
@end
```

Example 7-26. Button bar example (MyExample.m)

```
#import "MyExample.h"

int main(int argc, char **argv)
{
  NSAutoreleasePool *autoreleasePool = [
        [ NSAutoreleasePool alloc ] init
    ];
    int returnCode = UIApplicationMain(argc, argv, [ MyApp class ]);
    [ autoreleasePool release ];
    return returnCode;
}

@implementation MyApp

- (void)applicationDidFinishLaunching:(NSNotification *)aNotification {
    window = [ [ UIWindow alloc ] initWithContentRect:
        [ UIHardware fullScreenApplicationContentRect ]
    ];

    CGRect rect = [ UIHardware fullScreenApplicationContentRect ];
    rect.origin.x = rect.origin.y = 0.0f;

    mainView = [ [ MainView alloc ] initWithFrame: rect ];

    [ window setContentView: mainView ];
    [ window orderFront: self ];
    [ window makeKey: self ];
    [ window _setHidden: NO ];
}
@end

@implementation MainView
- (id)initWithFrame:(CGRect)rect {
```

Example 7-26. Button bar example (MyExample.m) (continued)

```
    if ((self == [ super initWithFrame: rect ]) != nil) {
        CGRect viewRect;
        int i;

        viewRect = CGRectMake(rect.origin.x, rect.origin.y,
            rect.size.width, rect.size.height - 48.0);

        /* Create some UITextView objects as different views */
        for(i=0;i<MAX_PAGES;i++) {
            textPage[i] = [ [ UITextView alloc ] initWithFrame: viewRect ];
            [ textPage[i] setText: [ [ NSString alloc ] initWithFormat:
                @"Some text for page %d", i+1 ] ];
        }

        /* Create our UIButtonBar */
        buttonBar = [ self createButtonBar ];
        [ self addSubview: buttonBar ];

        /* Create a transition so we can switch pages out easily */
        transView = [ [ UITransitionView alloc ] initWithFrame: viewRect ];
        [ self addSubview: transView ];

        /* Transition to the first page */
        [ self flipTo: 1 ];
    }

    return self;
}

- (void)dealloc
{
    [ self dealloc ];
    [ super dealloc ];
}

- (void)flipTo:(int)page {
    [ transView transition: 0 toView: textPage[page-1] ];
}

- (UIButtonBar *)createButtonBar {
    UIButtonBar *myButtonBar;
    myButtonBar = [ [ UIButtonBar alloc ]
        initInView: self
        withFrame: CGRectMake(0.0f, 411.0f, 320.0f, 49.0f)
        withItemList: [ self buttonBarItemList ] ];
    [ myButtonBar setDelegate: self ];
    [ myButtonBar setBarStyle: 1 ];
    [ myButtonBar setButtonBarTrackingMode: 2 ];

    int buttons[5] = { 1, 2, 3, 4, 5 };
    [ myButtonBar registerButtonGroup: 0 withButtons: buttons withCount: 5 ];
    [ myButtonBar showButtonGroup: 0 withDuration: 0.0 ];
```

Example 7-26. Button bar example (MyExample.m) (continued)

```
    int tag;

    for(tag = 1; tag < 5; tag++) {
        [ [ myButtonBar viewWithTag: tag ]
            setFrame:CGRectMake(2.0f + ((tag - 1) * 63.0), 1.0, 64.0, 48.0f)
        ];
    }
    [ myButtonBar showSelectionForButton: 3 ];

    return myButtonBar;
}
- (NSArray *)buttonBarItemList {
    return [ NSArray arrayWithObjects:
        [ NSDictionary dictionaryWithObjectsAndKeys:
            @"buttonBarClicked:", kUIButtonBarButtonAction,
            @"Button.png", kUIButtonBarButtonInfo,
            @"ButtonSelected.png", kUIButtonBarButtonSelectedInfo,
            [ NSNumber numberWithInt: 1], kUIButtonBarButtonTag,
              self, kUIButtonBarButtonTarget,
            @"Page 1", kUIButtonBarButtonTitle,
            @"0", kUIButtonBarButtonType,
            nil
        ],

        [ NSDictionary dictionaryWithObjectsAndKeys:
            @"buttonBarClicked:", kUIButtonBarButtonAction,
            @"Button.png", kUIButtonBarButtonInfo,
            @"ButtonSelected.png", kUIButtonBarButtonSelectedInfo,
            [ NSNumber numberWithInt: 2], kUIButtonBarButtonTag,
              self, kUIButtonBarButtonTarget,
            @"Page 2", kUIButtonBarButtonTitle,
            @"0", kUIButtonBarButtonType,
            nil
        ],

        [ NSDictionary dictionaryWithObjectsAndKeys:
            @"buttonBarClicked:", kUIButtonBarButtonAction,
            @"Button.png", kUIButtonBarButtonInfo,
            @"ButtonSelected.png", kUIButtonBarButtonSelectedInfo,
            [ NSNumber numberWithInt: 3], kUIButtonBarButtonTag,
              self, kUIButtonBarButtonTarget,
            @"Page 3", kUIButtonBarButtonTitle,
            @"0", kUIButtonBarButtonType,
            nil
        ],

        [ NSDictionary dictionaryWithObjectsAndKeys:
            @"buttonBarClicked:", kUIButtonBarButtonAction,
            @"Button.png", kUIButtonBarButtonInfo,
            @"ButtonSelected.png", kUIButtonBarButtonSelectedInfo,
            [ NSNumber numberWithInt: 4], kUIButtonBarButtonTag,
              self, kUIButtonBarButtonTarget,
```

Example 7-26. Button bar example (MyExample.m) (continued)

```
            @"Page 4", kUIButtonBarButtonTitle,
            @"0", kUIButtonBarButtonType,
            nil
        ],

        [ NSDictionary dictionaryWithObjectsAndKeys:
            @"buttonBarClicked:", kUIButtonBarButtonAction,
            @"Button.png", kUIButtonBarButtonInfo,
            @"ButtonSelected.png", kUIButtonBarButtonSelectedInfo,
            [ NSNumber numberWithInt: 5], kUIButtonBarButtonTag,
              self, kUIButtonBarButtonTarget,
            @"Page 5", kUIButtonBarButtonTitle,
            @"0", kUIButtonBarButtonType,
            nil
        ],

        nil
    ];
}

- (void)buttonBarClicked:(id) sender {
    int button = [ sender tag ];
    [ self flipTo: button ];
}

@end
```

What's Going On

Button bars are complicated animals. Here's how they work:

1. When the application initializes, it creates a MainView and calls its initWithFrame method. The display region is used to create a smaller region named viewRect, which takes into account the button bar's height. It is used to create a text view and a transition view for the upper portion of the screen above the button bar.

2. The initWithFrame method calls the createButtonBar method. This creates a UIButtonBar object and assigns it an array of buttons via the buttonBarItemList method. This array contains a dictionary for each button to display, defining their titles, tags, images, and what methods should be called when clicked. Because our buttons do comparable actions (differing only in the page displayed), they all invoke the same method, named the buttonBarClicked.

3. The geometry of each button is laid out in a button group and registered with the button bar. The button bar is then told to display the group.

4. The button bar is added to the main view, where it is displayed.

5. Five UITextView objects are created. These serve as the five button view examples. The initWithFrame calls a method named flipTo, which is responsible for flipping to the page number passed to it.

6. When a button is pressed, the `buttonBarClicked` method is called. This grabs the id tag of the button and calls `flipTo` again to flip to the new page. The updating of the button bar is a function of the button bar and is automatic.

Further Study

- Experiment with the placement of the button bar. Can it be placed at the top of the screen? Can multiple button bars exist in one view?
- A button bar can handle any number of different buttons. Change this example to use three large buttons, then try using eight.
- What other kinds of tags can be assigned to a button? Try and attach different objects.
- Check out the *UIButtonBar.h* prototypes in your tool chain's *include* directory. You'll find it in */usr/local/arm-apple-darwin/include/UIKit*.

Orientation Changes

The iPhone is retrofitted with hardware to sense its state in the surrounding environment. One sensor in particular, the accelerometer, is able to determine the orientation that the iPhone is being held at. How to read the orientation and what to do with it when it's changed are important for applications that need to provide landscape mode support.

Reading the Orientation

The orientation of the iPhone can be read using a static method named `deviceOrientation`, found in the `UIHardware` class:

```
int orientation = [ UIHardware deviceOrientation: YES ];
```

This method returns one of six different possible orientations identifying how the iPhone is presently being held.

Orientation	Description
0	kOrientationFlatUp: Device is laying flat, as if face up on a surface
1	kOrientationVertical: Device is held vertically, rightside-up
2	kOrientationVerticalUpsideDown: Device is held vertically, upside-down
3	kOrientationHorizontalLeft: Device is tipped to the left on its side
4	kOrientationHorizontalRight: Device is tipped to the right on its side
5	kOrientationUnknown: Device state unknown; sensor failure?
6	kOrientationFlatDown: Device is laying flat, as if face down on a surface

The sensor can be read when the application first starts up, but what's more useful is to know when the orientation has been changed. A change in the orientation is reported automatically to the UIApplication class, the class your GUI application is derived from. A method named deviceOrientationChanged can be overridden to intercept this event.

```
- (void)deviceOrientationChanged:(GSEvent *)event {
    int newOrientation = [ UIHardware deviceOrientation: YES ];

    /* Orientation has changed, do something */
}
```

For example, if the value returned corresponds with a landscape mode (kOrientationHorizontalLeft or kOrientationHorizontalRight), the application can take the appropriate steps to switch to landscape. One way to do this is to create separate UIView classes to service portrait and landscape views individually. The two views could then be transitioned back and forth as the orientation is changed:

```
[ transitionView transition: 0
    fromView: portraitView toView: landscapeView
];
```

Rotating Objects

The UIView base class supports a method named setRotationBy that allows nearly any display object in UIKit be rotated to accommodate different orientations.

```
[ textView setRotationBy: 90 ];
```

The argument provided is used to specify the angle, in degrees, to rotate the object.

Not only will objects need to be rotated to match the orientation of the iPhone, but the status bar must also be rotated. Use the setStatusBarMode method, as discussed in Chapter 3.

```
[ self setStatusBarMode: 0 orientation: 90 duration: 0
    fenceID: nil animation: 0 ];
```

Depending on whether objects are being rotated to accommodate a left turn or a right turn of the iPhone, specify a value of either 90 or –90 degrees, respectively.

The object's window will be resized to accommodate the orientation of the object, so the object's origin point also shifts. For example, to display a text view in landscape mode, use a frame defining a landscape resolution.

```
CGRect textRect = CGRectMake(-90, 70, 480, 300);
textView = [ [ UITextView alloc ] initWithFrame: textRect ];
[ textView setRotationBy: 90 ];
[ self addSubview: textView ];
```

Example: Turning the World on Its Side

In Chapter 3, one of the very first examples we introduced you to was the "Hello, World" application. We'll use this basic example to illustrate a simple landscape screen rotation. The following code draws the "Hello, World" application on its side, using a landscape mode status bar and rotating the text box to match.

To compile this example, use the tool chain on the command line as follows:

```
$ arm-apple-darwin-gcc -o MyExample MyExample.m -lobjc \
    --framework CoreFoundation -framework UIKit
```

Examples 7-27 and 7-28 contain the code.

Example 7-27. Orientation example (MyExample.h)

```
#import <CoreFoundation/CoreFoundation.h>
#import <UIKit/UIKit.h>
#import <UIKit/UITextView.h>

@interface MainView : UIView
{
    UITextView *textView;
    CGRect rect;
}
- (id)initWithFrame:(CGRect)_rect;
- (void)dealloc;
@end

@interface MyApp : UIApplication
{
    UIWindow *window;
    MainView *mainView;
}
- (void)applicationDidFinishLaunching:(NSNotification *)aNotification;
@end
```

Example 7-28. Orientation example (MyExample.m)

```
#import "MyExample.h"

int main(int argc, char **argv)
{
    return UIApplicationMain(argc, argv, [ MyApp class ]);
}

@implementation MyApp

- (void)applicationDidFinishLaunching:(NSNotification *)aNotification {
    window = [ [ UIWindow alloc ] initWithContentRect:
        [ UIHardware fullScreenApplicationContentRect ]
    ];
```

Example 7-28. Orientation example (MyExample.m) (continued)

```
    CGRect rect = [ UIHardware fullScreenApplicationContentRect ];
    rect.origin.x = rect.origin.y = 0.0f;

    mainView = [ [ MainView alloc ] initWithFrame: rect ];
    [ self setStatusBarMode: 0 orientation: 90 duration: 0 ];

    [ window setContentView: mainView ];
    [ window orderFront: self ];
    [ window makeKey: self ];
    [ window _setHidden: NO ];
}
@end

@implementation MainView
- (id)initWithFrame:(CGRect)_rect {

    if ((self == [ super initWithFrame: _rect ]) != nil) {
        rect = _rect;

        CGRect textRect = CGRectMake(-90, 70, 480, 300);
        textView = [ [ UITextView alloc ] initWithFrame: textRect ];
        [ textView setRotationBy: 90 ];
        [ textView setTextSize: 18 ];
        [ textView setText: @"Hello, World!" ];
        [ self addSubview: textView ];
    }

    return self;
}

- (void)dealloc
{
    [ self dealloc ];
    [ super dealloc ];
}
@end
```

What's Going On

1. When the application instantiates, a main view object is created, and its initWithFrame method is called.

2. The main view creates a UITextView class with a resolution of 480×300, for landscape mode.

3. The text view's setRotationBy method is invoked to rotate the object 90 degrees clockwise. It is then added to the screen.

Reading the Accelerometer

The orientation API gets its information from a small accelerometer built into the iPhone. This tiny piece of hardware reports the raw X-Y-Z position of the device. The orientation API greatly simplifies its output into an easy-to-use list of hand-held positions, but for the more daring individuals, the accelerometer's raw data can be read directly.

Erling Ellingsen spent a considerable amount of time disassembling the routines that talk to the accelerometer, and surprisingly found that the main application class, UIApplication, is sent frequent notifications of the accelerometer's state. To intercept these notifications, override the acceleratedInX method:

```
- (void)acceleratedInX:(float)xAxis Y:(float)yAxis Z:(float)zAxis {

    /* Accelerometer as X-Axis, Y-Axis, and Z-Axis */
}
```

Because the iPhone's accelerometer doesn't include a gyroscope, it can't provide information about speed, or as much detail about the state of the device as, say, a Nintendo Wii controller. It has proven useful, however, for simple applications such as bobble heads and etch-a-sketch programs, which rely on sensing when the iPhone is shaken.

Further Study

Check out the *UIView-Geometry.h* prototypes in the tool chain's *include* directory. This can be found in */usr/local/arm-apple-darwin/include/UIKit*.

Web Views and Scrollers

Chapter 3 introduced the UITextView object and its setHTML method for the creation of HTML formatted windows. The UIWebView object builds a browser-like world around a UITextView, and adds many of the basic routines you'd find in a web browser: fetching pages remotely, navigating forward and backward, and perform zooming and scaling. It is one of the core components that make Safari tick, and the best part is a UIWebView can be used in your own applications. Not only can web views display HTML pages, they can also display PDFs (local and remote), images, and any other kind of file that is supported in Safari.

Sean Heber of iApp-a-Day wrote a functional wrapper for the UIWebView class called SimpleWebView. You'll see how his class works in this section, and detail some of the improvements we've made on it.

Creating the Web View

A functional web view consists of three components:

- The UIWebView object performs all fetching, zooming, and link handling for the view.
- A UIScroller object is needed to scroll the web view, especially when zoomed.
- An NSURLRequest object is provided as the class pointing to the resource to fetch.

Sean's SimpleWebView class encapsulates these objects into a controlling UIView class based on UIView:

```
@interface SimpleWebView : UIView {
    UIWebView *webView;
    UIScroller *scroller;
    NSURLRequest *urlRequest;
}
-(id)initWithFrame:(CGRect)frame;
-(void)loadURL:(NSURL *)url;
-(void)dealloc;
```

SimpleWebView overrides its base class's initWithFrame method. It also adds a new method called loadURL that's used to load a web page or file resource. When Sean's wrapper class is initialized, UIWebView and UIScroller objects are created. The web view is then added as a layer to the scroll class.

How Scrollers Work

Think of the scroller as one of those red secret decoder slides you find in cereal boxes. Placing this small red flap of plastic over part of a secret codebook reveals a small portion of the page. The rest of the page is still there, but you can't see it until you slide the lens over it. The red lens represents the iPhone's screen, which is a window, and is the only content the user is able to see. The rest of the web page is hidden from view, falling off the screen, until the user moves the window to the part he wants to see.

Creating the scroller is like creating both a red lens and blank pages in a secret codebook. The web view is the content that gets glued onto the pages to create a scrolling content window.

```
scroller = [ [ UIScroller alloc ] initWithFrame: frame ];
[ scroller setScrollingEnabled: YES ];
[ scroller setAdjustForContentSizeChange: YES ];
[ scroller setClipsSubviews: YES ];
[ scroller setAllowsRubberBanding: YES ];
[ scroller setDelegate: self ];
[ self addSubview: scroller ];
```

The `UIScroller` class can be customized in many ways. The following options are the most commonly used:

`setScrollingEnabled: (BOOL)`
Turns on the scroll bars, allowing the scroller to do its job.

`setAdjustForContentSizeChange: (BOOL)`
Automatically reprograms its own scroll bars whenever the content bounds are changed.

`setClipsSubviews: (BOOL)`
Instructs the scroller not to clip any of the data that will be contained in it.

`setAllowsRubberBanding: (BOOL)`
When the edge of the scrollable region is reached, this feature allows the user to drag slightly beyond the top and bottom boundaries. When the user lifts her finger, the region will bounce back into place like a rubber band, giving her a visual cue that she's reached the beginning or end of the document.

`setAllowsFourWayRubberBanding: (BOOL)`
Like the previous option, this method allows for rubber banding. By default, only the top and bottom of a page have this rubber banding effect. To allow the scroller to rubber-band on all four sides, set this method in addition to the previous one.

`setBottomBufferHeight: (float)`
This method buffers the content so that a certain portion of it is hidden from the end of the scrollable region. Use this if your content has a large buffer around it, e.g., an oversized gray frame or other border you'd like to bleed off the screen.

`setContentSize: (CGSize)`
This method can be used to define the size of the content pages that will be glued onto the scroller. In the `SimpleWebView` class, this method is called whenever the image is resized.

After you create the scroller, create a `UIWebView` object and add it as a subview of the scroller. This glues the web view's content to the scroller, giving the scroller control over the viewable region of the web page.

```
webView = [ [ UIWebView alloc ]
    initWithFrame: [ scroller bounds ] ];
[ webView setTilingEnabled: YES ];
[ webView setTileSize: frame.size ];
[ webView setAutoresizes: YES];
[ webView setDelegate: self];
[ webView setEnabledGestures: 0xFF ];
[ webView setSmoothsFonts: YES ];

[scroller addSubview: webView];
```

The following properties are set in the web view:

`setTilingEnabled, setTileSize`

A `UITiledView` is a special kind of view used by Google Maps, Safari, and other specialized applications. The tiled view is designed to load content into a grid, allowing the content to be displayed even if it hasn't finished loading entirely. Because tiling is required by web views, the `UIWebView` class malfunctions without it, and won't display any content.

`setAutoresize`

Instructs the web view to automatically resize itself when new pages are loaded or the page is zoomed.

`setEnabledGestures`

By enabling gestures such as pinch and stretch, the web view can be manipulated in the same way as a Safari web page. Various `UIResponder` methods, as described in Chapter 4, can then be overridden to receive notifications of these gestures.

`setSmoothFonts`

Tells the web view to smooth fonts of the content being loaded.

A web view has now been created and added to a scroller. It's time to call the `loadURL` method and load a resource. A URL request is made to load content into the web view. An `NSURL` object specifies the address to load. This object can be created using the `NSURL`'s `initWithString` method:

```
NSURL *url = [ [ NSURL alloc ]
    initWithString: @"http://www.oreilly.com"
];
```

Inside the `SimpleWebView` class, the `loadURL` method takes the `NSURL` object and builds an `NSURLRequest`. The `NSURLRequest` object is similar to an `NSURL`, but encapsulates information such as status and response codes, which are necessary to keep track of when loading a web page. This request is handed directly to the web view:

```
NSURLRequest *urlRequest = [
    [ NSURLRequest requestWithURL: url ] retain
];
[ webView loadRequest: urlRequest ];
```

Adjusting the scrollers

Because the size of the web page was unknown when the scroll view was created, you should override two methods in the `UIScrollView` class so that the `SimpleWebView` class is notified when content has actually been loaded and is drawn. These methods are `didDrawInRect` and `didSetFrame`. Whenever the content attached to the scroll class is updated, the `didDrawInRect` method is notified, allowing it to reevaluate the content. It then adjusts its scroll bars accordingly to match the content's size. This causes the `didSetFrame` method to be invoked, which sets the scroller's content boundaries.

```
-(void)view: (UIView*)v didSetFrame:(CGRect)f
{
    if (v == webView) {
        [ scroller setContentSize: f.size ];
    }
}

-(void)view:(id)v didDrawInRect:(CGRect)f duration:(float)d
{
    if (v == webView) {
        CGSize size = [ webView bounds ].size;
        if (size.height != lastSize.height
        || size.width != lastSize.width)
        {
            lastSize = size;
            [ scroller setContentSize: size ];
        }
    }
}
```

Above, a CGSize structure named lastSize is used in the SimpleWebView class to keep track of the last reported size of the document. Whenever the user zooms the document in or out or clicks on a link, the size of the document changes. When this happens, the scroller's setContentSize method must be called to readjust the scroll bars.

Auto-smoothing on resize

One of the improvements I made to this class was the ability to automatically smooth the image whenever it was zoomed in or out. This requires you to subclass the UIWebView class itself to intercept notifications when gestures and double taps are performed.

```
@interface MyWebView : UIWebView
{

}
- (void)gestureEnded:(struct __GSEvent *)event;
- (void)doubleTap:(struct __GSEvent *)event;
@end
```

These two methods then notify the class's delegate, which is the SimpleWebView object, so that it can once again update the scroll bars.

```
- (void) gestureEnded:(struct __GSEvent *)event
{
    [ super gestureEnded: event ];
    [ _delegate gestureEnded: event ];
}

- (void) doubleTap:(struct __GSEvent *)event
{
    [ super doubleTap: event ];
    [ _delegate doubleTap: event ];
}
```

When the page is zoomed in or out, the graphics appear blurry until they're smoothed over. The SimpleWebView object calls upon a method named redrawScaledDocument to do this. This method belongs to the UIWebView class, and smoothes out the page's graphics and fonts as needed.

```
- (void)gestureEnded:(struct __GSEvent *)event {
    [ webView redrawScaledDocument ];
    [ webView setNeedsDisplay ];
    [ scroller setContentSize: [ webView bounds ].size ];
}
```

When the page has been redrawn to scale, gestureEnded calls the web view's setNeedsUpdate method, which ensures that any changes are propagated out to the screen. The size of the content must also be reevaluated because it has been zoomed, and setContentSize should be called on the scroller to update the scroll bars. Both your gestureEnded and your doubleTap functions should perform this task.

Using the SimpleWebView Class

Fortunately, the SimpleWebView class is much easier to use than to understand. To create an instance of the SimpleWebView class containing all of these pieces, a main view calls the class's initWithFrame method, followed by a call to loadURL.

```
NSURL *url = [ [ NSURL alloc ]
    initWithString: @"http://www.oreilly.com"
];

SimpleWebView *webView = [ [ SimpleWebView alloc ]
    initWithFrame: rect ];
[ webView loadURL: url ];
```

To load a local file, such a a PDF, use a *file://* URI.

```
NSURL *url = [ [ NSURL alloc ]
    initWithString: @"file:///var/root/Media/PDFs/Resume.PDF" ];
```

Once the SimpleWebView object has been created, it can be added to the main view as a subview or transitioned to as its own view.

```
[ self addSubview: webView ];
```

Example: Simple Web Browser

One of the more fun examples in this chapter, this lightweight web browser uses Sean Heber's SimpleWebView class with our improvements, combined with an address bar made out of a UITextView object. A customized, popup UIKeyboard object is also used to accept input. When the user types a URL into the address bar and clicks Go, the web view loads the specified page.

This example makes use of some override methods for the UITextView object. Earlier in this chapter, we covered keyboards and discussed the value in overriding the contentMouseUpInView method. This is used to toggle the display of a keyboard when the view is tapped. A new override named shouldInsertText is introduced in this example. This method is called whenever the user presses a key on the keyboard. The example uses it to check whether the Return key (labeled Go on the keyboard) was pressed, and if so, notify the controller view to load a new page.

This example works with web objects and local files. To access local files, delete the http:// protocol prefix and use file:// followed by the pathname. As always, please allow a few moments for web pages to load. To keep this example from consuming dozens of pages in the book, many of the aesthetic features of a browser, such as page load indicators and pretty toolbars, have been omitted. Remember, it's called a simple web browser.

To compile this application, use the tool chain on the command line as follows:

```
$ arm-apple-darwin-gcc -o MyExample MyExample.m SimpleWebView.m \
    -lobjc -framework Foundation -framework CoreFoundation \
    -framework UIKit
```

Examples 7-29 and 7-30 contain the code for the web view and scroller, while Examples 7-31 and 7-32 contain the main application and main view.

Example 7-29. Web view and scroller example (SimpleWebView.h)

```
/*
        By: Sean Heber   <sean@spiffytech.com>, J. Zdziarski
        iApp-a-Day - November, 2007
        BSD License
*/
#import <UIKit/UIKit.h>
#import <UIKit/UIScroller.h>
#import <UIKit/UIWebView.h>

@interface MyWebView : UIWebView
{

}
- (void)gestureEnded:(struct __GSEvent *)event;
- (void)doubleTap:(struct __GSEvent *)event;
@end

@interface SimpleWebView : UIView {
    MyWebView *webView;
    UIScroller *scroller;
    NSURLRequest *urlRequest;
    CGSize lastSize, size;
}
-(id)initWithFrame: (CGRect)frame;
-(id)loadURL: (NSURL *)url;
-(void)dealloc;
@end
```

Example 7-30. Web view and scroller example (SimpleWebView.m)

```
*
        By: Sean Heber  <sean@spiffytech.com>, J. Zdziarski
        iApp-a-Day - November, 2007
        BSD License
*/
#import "SimpleWebView.h"
#import <UIKit/UIView-Geometry.h>
#import <UIKit/UIView-Rendering.h>

@implementation MyWebView
- (void) gestureEnded:(struct __GSEvent *)event
{
    [ super gestureEnded: event ];
    [ _delegate gestureEnded: event ];
}

- (void) doubleTap:(struct __GSEvent *)event
{
    [ super doubleTap: event ];
    [ _delegate doubleTap: event ];
}
@end

@implementation SimpleWebView

-(void)view: (UIView*)v didSetFrame:(CGRect)f
{
    if (v == webView) {
        [ scroller setContentSize: f.size ];
    }
}

-(void)view:(id)v didDrawInRect:(CGRect)f duration:(float)d
{
    if (v == webView) {
        size = [ webView bounds ].size;
        if (size.height != lastSize.height
        || size.width != lastSize.width)
        {
            lastSize = size;
            [ scroller setContentSize: size ];
        }
    }
}

- (void)gestureEnded:(struct __GSEvent *)event {
    [ webView redrawScaledDocument ];
    [ webView setNeedsDisplay ];
    [ scroller setContentSize: [ webView bounds ].size ];
}

- (void)doubleTap:(struct __GSEvent *)event {
    struct timeval tv;
```

Example 7-30. Web view and scroller example (SimpleWebView.m) (continued)

```
    tv.tv_sec = 2;
    tv.tv_usec = 0;
    select(NULL, NULL, NULL, NULL, &tv);
    [ webView redrawScaledDocument ];
    [ webView setNeedsDisplay ];
    [ scroller setContentSize: [ webView bounds ].size ];
}

-(void)dealloc
{
        [ urlRequest release ];
        [ webView release ];
        [ scroller release ];
        [ super dealloc ];
}

-(id)initWithFrame: (CGRect)frame
{
    [ super initWithFrame: frame ];

    scroller = [ [ UIScroller alloc ] initWithFrame: frame ];
    [ scroller setScrollingEnabled: YES ];
    [ scroller setAdjustForContentSizeChange: YES ];
    [ scroller setClipsSubviews: NO ];
    [ scroller setAllowsRubberBanding: YES ];
    [ scroller setDelegate: self ];
    [ self addSubview: scroller ];

    webView = [ [ MyWebView alloc ]
        initWithFrame: [ scroller bounds ] ];
    [ webView setTilingEnabled: YES ];
    [ webView setTileSize: frame.size ];
    [ webView setAutoresizes: YES];
    [ webView setDelegate: self];
    [ webView setEnabledGestures: 0xFF ];
    [ webView setSmoothsFonts: YES ];
    [ scroller addSubview: webView ];

    return self;
}

-(id)loadURL: (NSURL *)url
{
    CGPoint zero;
    zero.x = 0;
    zero.y = 0;
    [ scroller scrollPointVisibleAtTopLeft: zero ];

    urlRequest = [ [ NSURLRequest requestWithURL: url ] retain ];
    [ webView loadRequest: urlRequest ];
}

@end
```

Example 7-31. Web view and scroller example (MyExample.h)

```
#import <CoreFoundation/CoreFoundation.h>
#import <UIKit/UIKit.h>
#import <UIKit/UITextView.h>
#import <UIKit/UIKeyboard.h>
#import "SimpleWebView.h"

@interface MyTextView : UITextView
{

}
- (void)contentMouseUpInView:(id)fp8 withEvent:(struct __GSEvent *)fp12;
- (BOOL)webView:(id)fp8 shouldInsertText:(id)character replacingDOMRange:(id)fp16
givenAction:(int)fp20;
@end

@interface MainView : UIView
{
    MyTextView *textField;
    UIKeyboard *kb;
    SimpleWebView *webView;
    BOOL keyboardEnabled;
}
- (id)initWithFrame:(CGRect)frame;
- (void)contentMouseUpInView:(id)_id withEvent:(
    struct __GSEvent *)_event;
- (void)enterPressed;
- (void)dealloc;

@end

@interface MyApp : UIApplication
{
    UIWindow *window;
    MainView *mainView;
}
- (void)applicationDidFinishLaunching:
    (NSNotification *)aNotification;
@end
```

Example 7-32. Web view and scroller example (MyExample.m)

```
#import "MyExample.h"

int main(int argc, char **argv)
{
    return UIApplicationMain(argc, argv, [ MyApp class ]);
}

@implementation MyTextView
- (void)contentMouseUpInView:(id)_id
    withEvent:(struct __GSEvent *)_event
{
```

Example 7-32. Web view and scroller example (MyExample.m) (continued)

```
    [ _delegate contentMouseUpInView:(id)_id withEvent:_event ];
}

- (BOOL)webView:(id)fp8 shouldInsertText:
    (id)character
    replacingDOMRange:(id)fp16
    givenAction:(int)fp20
{
    if ( [ character characterAtIndex:0 ] == '\n')
    {
        [ _delegate enterPressed ];
        return NO;
    }

    return [ super webView:fp8 shouldInsertText:character
        replacingDOMRange:fp16
        givenAction:fp20
    ];
}
@end

@implementation MyApp
- (void)applicationDidFinishLaunching:(NSNotification *)aNotification {
    window = [ [ UIWindow alloc ] initWithContentRect:
        [ UIHardware fullScreenApplicationContentRect ]
    ];

    CGRect rect = [ UIHardware fullScreenApplicationContentRect ];
    rect.origin.x = rect.origin.y = 0.0f;

    mainView = [ [ MainView alloc ] initWithFrame: rect ];

    [ window setContentView: mainView ];
    [ window orderFront: self ];
    [ window makeKey: self ];
    [ window _setHidden: NO ];
}
@end

@implementation MainView
- (id)initWithFrame:(CGRect)rect {

    if ((self == [ super initWithFrame: rect ]) != nil) {

        textField = [ [ MyTextView alloc ]
            initWithFrame: CGRectMake(0, 0, 320, 32) ];
        [ textField setDelegate: self ];
        [ textField setPreferredKeyboardType: 3 ];
        [ textField setAutoCorrectionType: 1 ];
        [ textField setAutoCapsType: NO ];
```

Example 7-32. Web view and scroller example (MyExample.m) (continued)

```
        [ textField setTextSize: 14 ];
        [ textField setAutoEnablesReturnKey: NO ];
        [ textField setReturnKeyType: 1 ];
        [ textField scrollToMakeCaretVisible: YES ];
        [ textField setEditable: YES ];
        [ textField setText: @"http://" ];
        [ self addSubview: textField ];

        rect.origin.y = 16;
        webView = [ [ SimpleWebView alloc ] initWithFrame: rect ];
        [ self addSubview: webView ];

        CGRect kbFrame = rect;
        kbFrame.origin.y = 245;
        kbFrame.size.height = 235;

        kb = [ [ UIKeyboard alloc ] initWithFrame: kbFrame ];
        [ kb setReturnKeyEnabled: NO ];
        [ textField becomeFirstResponder ];
        [ self addSubview: kb ];
        keyboardEnabled = YES;
    }

    return self;
}

- (void)enterPressed {
    NSURL *url = [ [ NSURL alloc ] initWithString: [ textField text ] ];
    [ kb removeFromSuperview ];
    keyboardEnabled = NO;
    [ webView loadURL: url ];
}

- (void)contentMouseUpInView:(id)_id withEvent:(struct __GSEvent *)_event {
    if (keyboardEnabled == NO) {
        [ self addSubview: kb ];
        keyboardEnabled = YES;
    } else {
        [ kb removeFromSuperview ];
        keyboardEnabled = NO;
    }
}

- (void)dealloc
{
    [ self dealloc ];
    [ super dealloc ];
}

@end
```

What's Going On

1. When the application instantiates, it creates a main view and calls its initWithFrame method. This method creates a UITextView object to serve as an address box, with custom keyboard properties associated with it. A SimpleWebView class is also created, which contains the UIWebView and UIScroller objects used to build the web view. The main view creates a UIKeyboard object, but does not add it to the view yet.

2. When the user taps the address bar, its contentMouseUpInView method is notified of the event, which in turn notifies its delegate, the main view. The main view toggles the keyboard by adding it to or removing it from the main view.

3. As the user types in the address bar, the shouldInsertText method is called for each character pressed. When the user presses the Return key (labeled Go), this notifies the delegate's enterPressed method.

4. The enterPressed method hides the keyboard and calls the SimpleWebView object's loadURL method. This resets the position of the scroller to 0×0 and proceeds to load a new web page or file.

Further Study

- To view more of Sean Heber's creations, visit the iApp-a-Day web site at *http://www.iappaday.com*.

- Check out the *UIWebView.h* and *UIScroller.h* prototypes in your tool chain's *include* directory. These can be found in */usr/local/arm-apple-darwin/include/UIKit*.

- Looking at *UIScroller.h*, experiment with some of the additional setter methods that change the properties of the scroller. What other cool behavior can you squeeze out of the class?

Miscellaneous Hacks and Recipes

Only the major iPhone frameworks have been covered in this book. Dozens of smaller, proprietary frameworks exist on the iPhone waiting to be explored. Through a little bit of hacking, some of these smaller frameworks have proven themselves useful for one-off needs. A number of other interesting recipes have also been concocted for performing tasks such as initiating a phone call or setting the iPhone's vibrator. This chapter covers some of the hacks and recipes we couldn't fit anywhere else in the book.

Dumping the Screen

The `UIApplication` class sports a method named `_dumpScreenContents` that can be used to make a screenshot on the iPhone. The method causes a file named */tmp/foo_0.png* to be written to disk.

To dump the screen contents from within your application, make sure to call the `_dumpScreenContents` method from your `UIApplication` class:

```
[ self _dumpScreenContents: nil ];
```

You'll need to have at least a main window with a content view created to take a screenshot. Every call to `_dumpScreenContents` causes the file to be written to the same location, */tmp/foo_0.png*, so be sure to move it out of the way if you're taking multiple screenshots.

To take screenshots from the command line, you can create an invisible window/view pair to capture whatever else is currently on the screen.

Example: Command-Line Screen Capture Utility

This example takes a snapshot of the screen from the command line, allowing the user to log in via SSH and capture the currently running application. To accomplish this, the example creates an invisible window and view that allows the current application on the screen to show through. When run, the example immediately dumps the screen contents into a file named */tmp/foo_0.png*.

To compile this application, use the tool chain on the command line as follows:

```
$ arm-apple-darwin-gcc -o ScreenDump ScreenDump.m -lobjc \
    -framework UIKit -framework CoreFoundation -framework Foundation
```

To use this application, first copy it over to the iPhone using SCP:

```
$ scp ScreenDump root@iphone:/usr/bin
```

SSH into the iPhone and run it from the command line:

```
$ ssh -l root iphone
# /usr/bin/ScreenDump
```

Example A-1 contains the code.

Example A-1. Screen shot example (ScreenDump.m)

```
#import <UIKit/UIKit.h>

@interface ScreenDumpApp : UIApplication
{
    UIWindow *window;
}
- (void)applicationDidFinishLaunching:(NSNotification *)aNotification;
@end

@implementation ScreenDumpApp
- (void)applicationDidFinishLaunching:(NSNotification *)aNotification {
    CGRect rect = [ UIHardware fullScreenApplicationContentRect ];

    window = [ [ UIWindow alloc ] initWithContentRect: rect ];
    [ window orderFront: self ];
    [ window makeKey: self ];
    [ window _setHidden: YES ];
    [ window setContentView: [
        [ UIView alloc ] initWithFrame: rect ]
    ];

    printf("Dumping screen contents...\n");
    [ self _dumpScreenContents: nil ];
    [ self terminate ];
}

int main(int argc, char *argv[])
{
    NSAutoreleasePool *autoreleasePool = [
        [ NSAutoreleasePool alloc ] init
    ];
    int returnCode = UIApplicationMain(
        argc,
        argv,
        [ ScreenDumpApp class ]
```

```
    );
    [ autoreleasePool release ];
    return returnCode;
}

@end
```

What's Going On

Here's how the screenshot example works:

1. When the application instantiates, a `UIWindow` and `UIView` object are immediately created. The window's `_setHidden` method is used to keep the window hidden.

2. The `UIApplication` class's instance method `_dumpScreenContents` is called, which dumps the contents of the screen into a file named */tmp/foo_0.png*.

3. The application then calls its own terminate method, effectively killing itself.

Dumping the UI Hierarchy

In the absence of a fully functional debugger for the iPhone, one aid to developers is the `_dumpUIHierarchy` method provided by the `UIApplication` class. A UI dump shows the associations of all display UI objects to each other in a parent/child type of hierarchy. For example, a navigation bar may appear like this in the dump:

```
<dict>
        <key>CGRect</key>
        <data>
        AAAAAAAAoEEAAKBDAABAQg==
        </data>
        <key>Children</key>
        <array>
                <dict>
                        <key>CGRect</key>
                        <data>
                        AAAAAAAAoEEAAAAAAAAAA==
                        </data>
                        <key>Enabled</key>
                        <false/>
                        <key>ID</key>
                        <string>&lt;UINavigationItemView: 0x22fe60&gt;</string>
                </dict>
                <dict>
                        <key>CGRect</key>
                        <data>
                        AAB3QwAA+EEAAIhCAADwQQ==
                        </data>
                        <key>Enabled</key>
                        <true/>
```

```
            <key>ID</key>
            <string>BTN Settings</string>
        </dict>
    </array>
    <key>Enabled</key>
    <true/>
    <key>ID</key>
    <string>&lt;UINavigationBar: 0x22f380&gt;</string>
</dict>
```

To invoke a dump, call the UIApplication class's _dumpUIHierarchy instance method:

```
[ self _dumpUIHierarchy: nil ];
```

An XML-formatted file will be written to */tmp/UIDump*. All windowed objects are written to the dump in the hierarchy in which they are currently allocated.

Invoking Safari

Occasionally, it may be appropriate to call Safari to bring up a web page for your application; for example, when the user presses a "donate" or "home page" button in your application's credits page. The UIApplication class supports an openURL method that can be used to seamlessly launch Safari and load a web page in a new window.

To use this, your application needs to create an NSURL object. You were introduced to the NSURL in Chapter 6, when recording sound with Celestial, and again in Chapter 7 when exploring web views. The NSURL object is passed to the application's openURL method, where the application framework processes and launches the appropriate handler application.

```
NSURL *url;
url = [ [ NSURL alloc ] initWithString: @"http://www.oreilly.com" ];
[ self openURL: url ];
```

Example: LaunchURL

In this example, the user calls the LaunchURL program from the command line with a URL as a command-line argument:

```
$ LaunchURL http://www.oreilly.com
```

To compile this application, use the tool chain on the command line as follows:

```
$ arm-apple-darwin-gcc -o LaunchURL LaunchURL.m -lobjc \
  -framework UIKit -framework CoreFoundation -framework Foundation
```

Example A-2 contains the code.

Example A-2. openURL example (LaunchURL.m)

```
mport <UIKit/UIKit.h>

@interface LaunchURLApp : UIApplication
{
    NSString *inputURL;
}
- (id)_initWithArgc:(int)argc argv:(const char **)argv;
- (void)applicationDidFinishLaunching:(NSNotification *)aNotification;
@end

@implementation LaunchURLApp
- (id)_initWithArgc:(int)argc argv:(const char **)argv {
    inputURL = [ [ NSString alloc ] initWithCString: argv[1] ];
    return [ super _initWithArgc: argc argv: argv ];
}

- (void)applicationDidFinishLaunching:(NSNotification *)aNotification {
    NSURL *url = [ [ NSURL alloc ] initWithString: inputURL ];
    [ self openURL: url ];
    [ self terminate ];
}

int main(int argc, char *argv[])
{
    NSAutoreleasePool *autoreleasePool = [ [ NSAutoreleasePool alloc ] init ];
    int returnCode;
    if (argc == 2) {
        returnCode = UIApplicationMain(argc, argv, [ LaunchURLApp class ]);
    } else {
        fprintf(stderr, "Syntax: %s [url]\n", argv[0]);
    }
    [ autoreleasePool release ];
    return returnCode;
}

@end
```

What's Going On

Here's how the LaunchURL example works:

1. When the application instantiates, it does a check of the argument count to ensure that it has been called with a URL. If something's amiss, it prints a syntax line and exits.

2. The UIApplication class's _initWithArgc method is overridden and converts the command-line argument into an NSString object. It then calls its superclass's initialization method.

3. The application's `applicationDidFinishLaunching` method is called when the application object has fully initialized. This creates an `NSURL` object out of the string and hands it to the `openURL` method.

4. Once the `openURL` method returns, the program self-terminates by calling its own terminate method.

Initiating Phone Calls

As was demonstrated in the last section, the `openURL` method calls Safari to launch web site URLs. What's actually going on is this: each protocol is associated with a specific handler application. As was the case with our last demonstration, URLs beginning with `http://` and `https://` are associated with Safari and cause it to be opened whenever `openURL` is called using those protocol prefixes. Just as `openURL` can be used to open web sites in Safari, it can also be used to place phone calls. This is done by using the protocol prefix of `tel://`:

```
NSURL *url = [ [ NSURL alloc ]
    initWithString: @"tel://212-555-1234" ];
[ self openURL: url ];
```

When the `openURL` method is used on a URL beginning with `tel://`, the phone application will be launched and the call will be automatically placed. Do try and ensure that your application doesn't have any bugs and accidentally places expensive overseas calls or prank calls to the White House.

Vibrating

The iPhone includes a built-in vibrating motor for silently notifying the user of new events. This is controlled by the MeCCA framework, which is a private C++ framework used for low-level communications with various devices including audio, Bluetooth, and other hardware. Daniel Peebles has written a low-level vibration example, which can be wrapped into an application or called as a standalone binary.

To vibrate the iPhone, create an instance of the `MeCCA_Vibrator` C++ class. The prototype for this class looks like this:

```
class MeCCA_Vibrator {
public:
    int getDurationMinMax(unsigned int&, unsigned int&);
    int activate(unsigned short);
    int activate(unsigned int, unsigned short);
    int activate(unsigned int, unsigned int, unsigned short);
    int deactivate( );
};
```

To use this class, first create a new instance of `MeCCA_Vibrator`:

```
MeCCA_Vibrator *v = new MeCCA_Vibrator;
```

The vibrator object's `activate` and `deactivate` methods can then be used to control vibration:

```
v->activate(1);
usleep(DURATION);
v->deactivate( );
```

When calling the `usleep( )` function, specify the duration, in microseconds, that you would like the vibrator to run for.

To tap into the MeCCA vibrator object, your application must be linked to the MeCCA framework. Using the tool chain, MeCCA can be linked to your application by adding the `–framework MeCCA` argument to the compiler arguments we described in Chapter 2:

```
$ arm-apple-darwin-gcc -o MyApp MyApp.m –lobjc \
    –framework CoreFoundation \
    –framework Foundation \
    –framework MeCCA
```

To add this option to the sample makefile from the previous chapter, add the MeCCA framework to the linker flags section so that the library is linked in:

```
LDFLAGS =    -lobjc \
        –framework CoreFoundation \
        –framework Foundation \
        –framework MeCCA
```

Transparent Views

Chapter 7 introduced the `UICompositeImageView` class, which allowed multiple images to be layered on top of each other, adding layers of transparency to create overlays. The `UIView` class provides a similar function called `setAlpha`, allowing a view's transparency to be adjusted.

```
[ mainView setAlpha: 0.5 ];
```

This can be useful when superimposing multiple views, such as creating semi-transparent buttons and navigation bars, to allow text or images to remain visible through the object. The alpha value ranges from 0 to 1, where 0 makes a view totally invisible and 1 makes the view completely cover whatever is below.

To use this, create two views using overlapping frames. Set the alpha level of the front view using `setAlpha`. Now, add the first view followed by the second to your controlling view. The frontmost view should be semi-transparent.

Taking Camera Photos

The Photo Library framework is a proprietary framework providing common methods for the iPhone's Camera application. One useful feature buried inside this framework is the CameraController class, which is capable of snapping 16,001,200 photos in JPEG format.

This is very cool, while also very creepy at the same time. The camera controller itself makes no attempt to notify the user that a photo is being taken, nor is there any indication on the iPhone's display. This creates the possibility for real spyware (that is, voyeurware) to easily be written and installed on a user's iPhone without her knowledge.

Installing CameraController Prototypes

The Photo Library framework is not included in the prototype collection for version 0.30 of the tool chain, so you'll need to dump it directly from the iPhone to begin using the camera controller. The *CameraController.h* prototype file can be generated using Steve Nygard's class-dump tool, available at *http://www.codethecode.com/ projects/class-dump*. To dump the contents of the Photo Library framework, use the copy of the iPhone's libraries you copied over in Chapter 2:

```
$ class-dump /usr/local/share/iphone-filesystem\
/System/Library/Frameworks/PhotoLibrary.framework/PhotoLibrary
```

This will dump all of the classes in the framework, but you'll only need one: the CameraController class. Sort through the output of class-dump to find the interface declaration. Place its contents in the file */usr/local/arm-apple-darwin/include/ PhotoLibrary/CameraController.h*. The contents you'll be copying into the file will look like this:

```
@interface CameraController : NSObject
{
    LKLayer *_cameraLayer;
    struct CameraDevice *_camera;
    struct CameraImageQueueHelper *_cameraHelper;
    id _delegate;
    UIView *_previewView;
    BOOL _isPreviewing;
}
+ (id)sharedInstance;
- (id)init;
- (void)_setIsReady;
- (BOOL)isReady;
- (void)_tookPicture:(struct __CoreSurfaceBuffer *)fp8;
- (void)_tookPicture:(struct CGImage *)fp8 jpegData:(struct __CFData *)fp12
imageProperties:(st
ruct __CFDictionary *)fp16;
- (struct CameraImageQueueHelper *)_cameraHelper;
- (BOOL)_setupCamera;
- (void)_tearDownCamera;
- (void)setDelegate:(id)fp8;
```

```
- (struct CGRect)_cameraFrame;
- (id)previewView;
- (void)startPreview;
- (void)stopPreview;
- (void)capturePhoto;

@end
```

Taking Pictures

The CameraController class uses a delegate to notify the application of two kinds of events: ready state and picture taken. You must override two methods to accept these notifications.

The cameraControllerReadyStateChanged method is notified whenever the camera's state has changed (for example, when it is placed in preview mode). Your own implementation of this method won't need to perform any special function, but it must exist in your application to avoid generating an exception. This method is useful if you wish to provide some form of notification to the user that the camera is active, such as displaying a red blinking dot.

```
- (void)cameraControllerReadyStateChanged:
    (NSNotification *)aNotification
{
    /* Take any action here */
}
```

The tookPicture method is notified whenever a picture is actually taken. The runtime passes the function the raw JPEG data containing the contents of the 1,600 × 1,200 image as well as a UIImage object containing its preview. You'll need to override this method to access the photo itself.

```
-(void)cameraController:(id)sender
    tookPicture:(UIImage*)picture
    withPreview:(UIImage*)preview
    jpegData:(NSData*)rawData
    imageProperties:(struct __CFDictionary *)imageProperties
{
    /* Save or work with picture here */
}
```

To take a picture, create an instance of the CameraController class:

```
CameraController *camera = [ [ CameraController alloc ] init ];
```

State and picture notifications should then be directed to a specific object:

```
[ camera setDelegate: self ];
```

When you're ready to snap a picture, first place the camera in preview mode, then call its capturePhoto method:

```
[ camera startPreview ];
[ camera capturePhoto ];
```

After a photo has been snapped, the `tookPicture` method will be notified, allowing you to save the image or work with it in some other way. When you're finished with the camera, you should turn off the preview mode.

```
[ camera stopPreview ];
```

The image data is provided as an `NSDATA` structure. This is a foundation class present in the Cocoa framework, and is designed to encapsulate raw data into an object. More information about this structure can be found in the Cocoa Reference available on the Apple Developer Connection web site.

Example: Snap App

This example provides a command-line utility for snapping a photo. The program will output "Smile" to `stdout` and snap a photo one second later. A filename to a JPEG file is provided on the command line.

To compile this example, use the tool chain on the command line as follows:

```
$ arm-apple-darwin-gcc -o snap snap.m -lobjc \
-framework CoreFoundation -framework Foundation -framework UIKit \
-framework PhotoLibrary
```

Example A-3 contains the code.

Example A-3. Camera controller example (snap.m)

```
#import <Foundation/Foundation.h>
#import <PhotoLibrary/CameraController.h>
#import <UIKit/UIKit.h>

@interface SnapApp : UIApplication
{
    NSString *filename;
}
- (id)_initWithArgc:(int)argc argv:(const char **)argv;
- (void)applicationDidFinishLaunching:(NSNotification *)aNotification;
@end

@implementation SnapApp
- (id)_initWithArgc:(int)argc argv:(const char **)argv {
    filename = [ [ NSString alloc ] initWithCString: argv[1] ];
    return [ super _initWithArgc: argc argv: argv ];
}

- (void)cameraControllerReadyStateChanged:(NSNotification *)aNotification
{

}

-(void)cameraController:(id)sender
    tookPicture:(UIImage*)picture
    withPreview:(UIImage*)preview
```

```
        jpegData:(NSData*)rawData
        imageProperties:(struct __CFDictionary *)imageProperties
{
    [ rawData writeToFile: filename atomically: NO ];
    [ self terminate ];
}

- (void)applicationDidFinishLaunching:(NSNotification *)aNotification {
    CameraController *camera = [ [ CameraController alloc ] init ];

    [ camera setDelegate: self ];
    [ camera startPreview ];

    printf("Smile...\n");
    sleep(1);
    [ camera capturePhoto ];
    [ camera stopPreview ];
}

int main(int argc, char *argv[])
{
    NSAutoreleasePool *autoreleasePool = [
        [ NSAutoreleasePool alloc ] init ];
    int returnCode;
    if (argc == 2) {
        returnCode = UIApplicationMain(argc, argv,
        [ SnapApp class ]);
    } else {
        fprintf(stderr, "Syntax: %s [filename]\n", argv[0]);
    }
    [ autoreleasePool release ];
    return returnCode;
}
@end
```

What's Going On

1. When the application instantiates, a CameraController object is created and placed into preview mode to ready the camera. Its delegate is set to self, the application instance running.

2. This triggers a notification to cameraControllerReadyStateChanged. In our example, this performs no action.

3. One second later, the controller's capturePhoto method is called, instructing it to take a snapshot.

4. The application's tookPicture method is called, providing the pointer to an NSDATA structure containing the image's raw JPEG data.

5. The NSDATA structure's writeToFile method is called, storing the file on disk.

Cover Flow-Style Album Flipping

Chapter 5 covered Layer Kit transformations, which allow a layer to be rotates, scaled, and transformed in many other ways. Layer Kit is the foundation for Apple's Cover Flow technology, which is used in selecting albums from the iPod application while in landscape mode.

Layton Duncan of Polar Bear Farm, a software designer for the iPhone, has graciously provided code adapting Apple's CovertFlow example (from XCode tools' examples) to the iPhone. The application's source and images can be downloaded in their entirety at the Polar Bear Farm web site, *http://www.polarbearfarm.com*.

We've spiced up Layton's example a bit to use the iPhone's photo album as the album covers. So be sure to snap a few photos with your iPhone before trying this example.

To compile this example, use the tool chain on the command line as follows:

```
$ arm-apple-darwin-gcc -o CovertFlow CovertFlow.m -lobjc \
    -framework CoreFoundation -framework Foundation -framework UIKit \
    -framework LayerKit -framework CoreGraphics \
    -framework GraphicsServices
```

Examples A-4 and A-5 contain the code.

Example A-4. LayerKit album example (CovertFlow.h)

```
#import <Foundation/Foundation.h>
#import <CoreFoundation/CoreFoundation.h>
#import <UIKit/UIKit.h>
#import <UIKit/UIApplication.h>
#import <UIKit/UIScroller.h>
#import <UIKit/UIView-Hierarchy.h>
#import <LayerKit/LayerKit.h>
#import <LayerKit/LKScrollLayer.h>
#import <GraphicsServices/GraphicsServices.h>

/* Number of pixels scrolled before next cover comes front */
#define SCROLL_PIXELS 60.0

/* Size of each cover */
#define COVER_WIDTH_HEIGHT 128.0

@interface CFView : UIScroller
{
    BOOL beating;
}
- (id) initWithFrame:(struct CGRect)frame;
- (void) mouseDragged:(GSEvent*)event;
- (void) heartbeatCallback;
@end

@interface CovertFlowApplication : UIApplication
```

Example A-4. LayerKit album example (CovertFlow.h) (continued)

```
{
    UIWindow *window;
    CFView *mainView;
    LKScrollLayer *cfIntLayer;
    NSMutableArray *pictures;
    int selected;
}
+ (CovertFlowApplication *)sharedInstance;
- (void) jumpToCover:(int)index;
- (void) layoutLayer:(LKScrollLayer *)layer;
@end
```

Example A-5. LayerKit album example (CovertFlow.m)

```
#import <CoreFoundation/CoreFoundation.h>
#import <Foundation/Foundation.h>
#import <UIKit/CDStructures.h>
#import <UIKit/UIWindow.h>
#import <UIKit/UIView.h>
#import <UIKit/UIView-Hierarchy.h>
#import <UIKit/UIHardware.h>
#import <UIKit/UIResponder.h>
#import <GraphicsServices/GraphicsServices.h>
#import <UIKit/UIView-Geometry.h>
#import <CoreGraphics/CGGeometry.h>
#import <UIKit/UIKit.h>
#import <LayerKit/LayerKit.h>
#import <LayerKit/LKLayer.h>
#import <LayerKit/LKScrollLayer.h>
#import <LayerKit/LKAnimation.h>
#import <LayerKit/LKTransition.h>
#import <LayerKit/LKTransaction.h>
#import <LayerKit/LKTimingFunction.h>
#import "CovertFlow.h"
#import "math.h"

static CovertFlowApplication *sharedInstance;

int main(int argc, char **argv)
{
    NSAutoreleasePool *autoreleasePool = [
        [ NSAutoreleasePool alloc ] init
    ];
    int returnCode = UIApplicationMain(argc, argv,
        [ CovertFlowApplication class ]);
    [ autoreleasePool release ];
    return returnCode;
}

@implementation CFView
-(id)initWithFrame:(struct CGRect)frame
{
```

```
    if ((self == [super initWithFrame: frame]) != nil) {
        [self setTapDelegate:self];
        [self setDelegate:self];
        beating = NO;
        [ self startHeartbeat: @selector(heartbeatCallback) inRunLoopMode:nil ];
    }
    return self;
}

- (void) mouseDragged:(GSEvent*)event
{
    if (beating == NO) {

        /* User started flicking through covers.
         * Start a heartbeat to update the coverflow
         */

        beating = YES;
        [ self startHeartbeat: @selector(heartbeatCallback) inRunLoopMode:nil ];
    }
    [ super mouseDragged: event ];
}

- (void)heartbeatCallback
{
    [ [ CovertFlowApplication sharedInstance ]
        jumpToCover:(int) roundf(([ self offset ].y/SCROLL_PIXELS))
    ];

    if (! [self isScrolling] )
    {
        /* Stop the heartbeat when scrolling stops */
        [ self stopHeartbeat: @selector(heartbeatCallback) ];
        beating = NO;
    }
}
@end

@implementation CovertFlowApplication
+ (CovertFlowApplication *)sharedInstance
{
    if (!sharedInstance) {
        sharedInstance = [ [ CovertFlowApplication alloc ] init ];
    }
    return sharedInstance;
}

- (void)applicationDidFinishLaunching:(NSNotification *)aNotification
{
    UIImageView *background;
    CGRect rect;
    NSString *file, *path;
```

```
NSDirectoryEnumerator *dirEnum;
int i, j;

/* Read the pictures directory */
path = [ [ NSString alloc ] initWithString:
    @"/var/root/Media/DCIM/100APPLE" ];
pictures = [ [ NSMutableArray alloc] init ];
dirEnum = [ [ NSFileManager defaultManager ] enumeratorAtPath: path ];
while ((file = [ dirEnum nextObject ])) {
    if ( [ [ file pathExtension ] isEqualToString: @"THM" ])
    {
        [ pictures addObject: [ [ NSString alloc ] initWithString:
            [ path stringByAppendingPathComponent: file ] ] ];
    }
}
j = [ pictures count ];

window = [ [ UIWindow alloc ] initWithContentRect:
    [ UIHardware fullScreenApplicationContentRect ] ];

rect = [ UIHardware fullScreenApplicationContentRect ];
rect.origin.x = rect.origin.y = 0.0f;

sharedInstance = self;
mainView = [ [ CFView alloc ] initWithFrame: rect ];

/* Set the # of pixels to drag before the scroller moves */
[ mainView setScrollHysteresis: 64.0 ];

/* Disable rubber banding */
[ mainView setAllowsFourWayRubberBanding: NO ];

/* Cause the scroller to become stiffer */
[ mainView setScrollDecelerationFactor: 0.9999 ];

/* Set the scroll view to snap to pixel boundaries */
[ mainView setGridSize:CGSizeMake(SCROLL_PIXELS, SCROLL_PIXELS) ];

[ window setContentView: mainView ];
[ window orderFront: self ];
[ window makeKey: self ];
[ window _setHidden: NO ];

/* Initialize the CovertFlow layer */
cfIntLayer = [ [ LKScrollLayer alloc ] initWithBounds:
    CGRectMake(0, 0, rect.size.width, rect.size.height + 128)
];
[ cfIntLayer setDelegate:self ];

/* Position the CovertFlow layer in the middle of the scroll view */
cfIntLayer.position = CGPointMake(160, 304);
[ cfIntLayer setDelegate:self ];
```

Example A-5. LayerKit album example (CovertFlow.m) (continued)

```
    /* Load the album covers */
    for (i=0; i<j; i++) {
        NSString *filename = [ pictures objectAtIndex: i ];

        background = [ [ [ UIImageView alloc ] initWithFrame:
                CGRectMake(0, 0, COVER_WIDTH_HEIGHT, COVER_WIDTH_HEIGHT)
            ]
            autorelease
        ];
        [ background setImage: [ [ UIImage alloc ] initWithContentsOfFile: filename ] ];
        [ cfIntLayer addSublayer: [ background _layer ] ];
    }

    /* Set the size of the scroll view proportionately to the # covers */
    [ mainView setContentSize:
        CGSizeMake(320, ( (rect.size.height) + (SCROLL_PIXELS*j) ) )
    ];

    /* Add the album layer to the main layer */
    selected = 0;
    [ [ mainView _layer ] addSublayer:cfIntLayer ];
    [ self layoutLayer: cfIntLayer ];
}

- (void) jumpToCover:(int)index
{
    if (index != selected) {
        selected = index;
        [ self layoutLayer:cfIntLayer ];
    }
}

-(void) layoutLayer:(LKScrollLayer *)layer
{
    LKLayer *sublayer;
    NSArray *array;
    size_t i, count;
    CGRect rect, cfImageRect;
    NSSize cellSize, spacing, margin;
    CGSize size;
    LKTransform leftTransform, rightTransform, sublayerTransform;
    float zCenterPosition, zSidePosition;
    float sideSpacingFactor, rowScaleFactor;
    float angle = 1.39;
    int x;

    size = [ layer bounds ].size;

    zCenterPosition = 60;        /* Z-Position of selected cover */
    zSidePosition = 0;           /* Default Z-Position for other covers */
    sideSpacingFactor = .85;     /* How close should slide covers be */
    rowScaleFactor = .55;        /* Distance between main cover and side covers */
```

Example A-5. LayerKit album example (CovertFlow.m) (continued)

```
leftTransform = LKTransformMakeRotation(angle, -1, 0, 0);
rightTransform = LKTransformMakeRotation(-angle, -1, 0, 0);

margin   = NSMakeSize(5.0, 5.0);
spacing  = NSMakeSize(5.0, 5.0);
cellSize = NSMakeSize (COVER_WIDTH_HEIGHT, COVER_WIDTH_HEIGHT);

margin.width += (size.width - cellSize.width * [ pictures count ]
              - spacing.width * ([ pictures count ] - 1)) * .5;
margin.width = floor (margin.width);

/* Build an array of covers */
array = [ layer sublayers ];
count = [ array count ];

sublayerTransform = LKTransformIdentity;
/* Set perspective */
sublayerTransform.m34 = -0.006;

/* Begin an LKTransaction so that all animations happen simultaneously */
[ LKTransaction begin ];
[ LKTransaction setValue: [ NSNumber numberWithFloat:0.3f ]
    forKey:@"animationDuration" ];

for (i = 0; i < count; i++)
{
    sublayer = [ array objectAtIndex:i ];
    x = i;

    rect.size = *(CGSize *)&cellSize;
    rect.origin = CGPointZero;
    cfImageRect = rect;

    /* Base position */
    rect.origin.x = size.width / 2 - cellSize.width / 2;
    rect.origin.y = margin.height + x * (cellSize.height + spacing.height);

    [ [ sublayer superlayer ] setSublayerTransform: sublayerTransform ];

    if (x < selected)        /* Left side */
    {
        rect.origin.y += cellSize.height * sideSpacingFactor
                    * (float) (selected - x - rowScaleFactor);
        sublayer.zPosition = zSidePosition - 2.0 * (selected - x);
        sublayer.transform = leftTransform;
    }
    else if (x > selected)   /* Right side */
    {
        rect.origin.y -= cellSize.height * sideSpacingFactor
                    * (float) (x - selected - rowScaleFactor);
        sublayer.zPosition = zSidePosition - 2.0 * (x - selected);
        sublayer.transform = rightTransform;
```

```
        }
        else                    /* Selected cover */
        {
            sublayer.transform = LKTransformIdentity;
            sublayer.zPosition = zCenterPosition;

            /* Position in the middle of the scroll layer */
            [ layer scrollToPoint: CGPointMake(0, rect.origin.y
                - (([ layer bounds ].size.height - cellSize.width)/2.0))
            ];

            /* Position the scroll layer in the center of the view */
            layer.position =
                CGPointMake(160.0f, 240.0f + (selected * SCROLL_PIXELS));
        }
        [ sublayer setFrame: rect ];


    }
    [ LKTransaction commit ];
}

@end
```

What's Going On

1. When the application instantiates, its applicationDidFinishLaunching method is called by the runtime.

2. This method first walks through the iPhone's album directory and takes inventory of all thumbnail images. It then initializes a new window and subclass of the UIScroller view, named CFView, into an object named mainView. Various properties of the scroll view are defined here.

3. Each photo album thumbnail is loaded into a UIImage object and then assigned to a layer. When the application has finished initializing, the layoutLayer method is called.

4. The layoutLayer method positions every layer in the view to be oriented according to its position. The selected album is brought to the front, while others are rotated using the rightTransform and leftTransform LKTransform objects.

5. When the user drags his finger, the mouseDragged method is called. This causes a new cover to be selected and causes layoutLayers to be called again.

6. An LKTransaction is created to ensure that all objects are animated at the same time. The newly selected album is oriented to the front of the screen. When the transaction is committed, the Layer Kit framework performs all of the tweening so that it automatically occurs during the specified time interval for the animation (0.03s).

Index

We'd like to hear your suggestions for improving our indexes. Send email to *index@oreilly.com*.

UIWindow class, 28
UIWindow object, 29

V

vibrating, 248
views, 27, 28–40
    text views (see text views)
    transition views (see transition views)
voice recorder example, 129–132
_volume variable, 144
volumeChange method, 145

W

web browser example, 235–242
web views, 151, 230
    creating, 231
    simple web browser example, 235–242
    SimpleWebView class, 235
windows, 27, 28

X

XCode integration, 18
XCode tools, 12

Z

ZiPhone, 2
zoomyIn animation, 105
zoomyOut animation, 105

About the Author

Jonathan Zdziarski is better known in the hacker community as "NerveGas." He has played a key role in opening the iPhone's environment to third-party software development, and is hailed on many geek news sites for cracking this device and leading the effort to write the first open source applications. Jonathan was the first to develop an application that takes full advantage of the major iPhone APIs with NES.app, a portable Nintendo Entertainment System emulator.

Jonathan is also a full-time research scientist and longtime mobile hacker. Prior to the iPhone, Jonathan was well known for uncovering vulnerabilities in Verizon's online systems and hacking popular Verizon phones to restore functionality once crippled by the communications behemoth.

Colophon

The animal on the cover of *iPhone Open Application Development* is a Pardine lynx, an animal more commonly known today as the Iberian or Spanish lynx (*Lynx pardinus*). Once thought of as a subspecies of the Eurasian lynx, the Pardine lynx is now classified as a separate species.

In contrast to the pale Eurasian lynx, the Pardine lynx has bold, leopard-like spots that stand out against its grayish or golden coat. Its face is more cat-like as well, and its look is distinguished by a short bobtail with a black tip and a small cluster of black hair atop each of its ears.

The lynx relies upon the hair at its ears to amplify sound when hunting. Its favorite prey is the rabbit, although as the numbers of rabbits in Europe have declined, the lynx has resorted to hunting deer, birds, and rodents. Patience is a virtue of the lynx; the animal will often wait several hours behind a rock for its prey to come close enough to pounce upon.

At one time, the Pardine lynx lived all along the Iberian Peninsula, but because of recent deforestation and aggressive human hunters, it now lives and breeds in just two small areas of Andalusia. It is thought by many to be the most endangered feline species in the world. If the Pardine lynx were to become extinct, it would be the first wild cat to be so in more than 2,000 years.

The cover image is from *Lydekker's Royal History*. The cover font is Adobe ITC Garamond. The text font is Linotype Birka; the heading font is Adobe Myriad Condensed; and the code font is LucasFont's TheSans Mono Condensed.

Related Titles from O'Reilly

Database

The Art of SQL

Database in Depth

FileMaker Pro 9: The Missing Manual

Head First SQL

High Performance MySQL

Learning MySQL

Learning PHP and MySQL, *2nd Edition*

Learning SQL

Learning SQL on SQL Server 2005

Managing & Using MySQL, *2nd Edition*

MySQL Cookbook, *2nd Edition*

MySQL in a Nutshell

MySQL Pocket Reference, *2nd Edition*

MySQL Reference Manual

MySQL Stored Procedure Programming

Oracle Essentials, 4th *Edition*

Oracle PL/SQL Best Practices, *2nd Edition*

Oracle PL/SQL Language Pocket Reference, 4*th Edition*

Practical PostgreSQL

Programming SQL Server 2005

The Relational Database Dictionary

SQL Cookbook

SQL in a Nutshell, *2nd Edition*

SQL Pocket Guide, *2nd Edition*

SQL Tuning

Understanding MySQL Internals

Our books are available at most retail and online bookstores.

To order direct: 1-800-998-9938 • *order@oreilly.com* • *www.oreilly.com*

Online editions of most O'Reilly titles are available by subscription at *safari.oreilly.com*

The O'Reilly Advantage

Stay Current and Save Money

Did you know that if you register
your O'Reilly books, you'll get
automatic notification and upgrade
discounts on new editions?

**And that's not all! Once you've registered
your books you can:**

» Win free books, T-shirts and O'Reilly Gear

» Get special offers available only to registered
O'Reilly customers

» Get free catalogs announcing all our new
titles (US and UK Only)

**Registering is easy! Just go to
www.oreilly.com/go/register**